SEEKING MANDELA

In the series

Politics, History, and Social Change

edited by John C. Torpey

Brian A. Weiner, *Sins of the Parents: The Politics of National Apologies in the United States*

Marc Garcelon, *Revolutionary Passage: From Soviet to Post-Soviet Russia, 1985–2000*

Götz Aly and Karl Heinz Roth, translated by Assenka Oksiloff, *The Nazi Census: Identification and Control in the Third Reich*

Immanuel Wallerstein, *The Uncertainties of Knowledge*

Michael R. Marrus, *The Unwanted: European Refugees from the First World War Through the Cold War*

SEEKING MANDELA

PEACEMAKING BETWEEN ISRAELIS AND PALESTINIANS

Heribert Adam and
Kogila Moodley

Temple University Press
PHILADELPHIA

Temple University Press
1601 North Broad Street
Philadelphia PA 19122
www.temple.edu/tempress

Published 2005
Printed in the United States of America

⊗ The paper used in this publication meets the requirements of the American National Standard for Information Sciences—Permanence of Paper for Printed Library Materials, ANSI Z39.48-1992

Library of Congress Cataloging-in-Publication Data

Adam, Heribert.
Seeking Mandela : peacemaking between Israelis and Palestinians / Heribert Adam and Kogila Moodley.
p. cm. — (Politics, history, and social change)
Includes bibliographical references and index.
ISBN 1-59213-395-9 (cloth : alk. paper) – ISBN 1-59213-396-7 (pbk. : alk. paper)
1. Arab-Israeli conflict. 2. Apartheid. 3. Israel—Politics and government. 4. South Africa—Politics and government. 5. Reconciliation—Political aspects—Israel. 6. Reconciliation—Political aspects—South Africa. I. Moodley, Kogila. II. Title. III. Series.

DS119.7.A32 2005
956.05′3—dc22

2004062129

2 4 6 8 9 7 5 3 1

For Simon Pimstone and Lawrence Seeff,
our sons in law,
in appreciation of stimulating discussions about multiple homelands

Contents

Preface

Reflections on Moral Literacy

This study has been written within the paradigms and in support of the broad Israeli-Palestinian peace movement. These pragmatic compromisers have unfortunately been marginalized by the escalating violence and the advance of extremist policies among both Jews and Palestinians. The false notion that if you are not with *us,* you must be with *them* has gained ground on both sides in this polarized conflict. The majority of the Jewish diaspora in particular rallies behind Israeli government policy, regardless of that policy's consequences. We try to understand this uncritical ethnic solidarity that falsely equates critiquing the government with denying Israel's right to exist—or, with harboring anti-Semitic views. In the ideological battle, frequent references to the anti-apartheid struggle are made wherein Palestinians are equated with black South Africans. Shimon Peres, on the other hand, writes after meeting Mandela in 1993, "Two persecuted people, the blacks and the Jews can celebrate a new future."[1] We explore both problematic analogies at length, but above all we are interested in the lessons one can glean from South Africa's negotiated settlement that can be applied to a solution to the Israeli-Palestinian conflict.

Our metaphor, "Seeking Mandela," speculates on what would have happened in the Middle East had a Palestinian Mandela or Gandhi provided unifying moral and strategic leadership—or if one were to emerge and do so in the future. (The real Mandela visited the area only once on a private stopover in 1999.) We do not adhere to the theory that history is primarily shaped by "great men" or that the icon Mandela is infallible. Yet a social movement's policy is inevitably influenced by the moral clarity of leaders who are admired because of their principled guidance.

Ultimately, the African National Congress (ANC) emerged victorious not because it had militarily or strategically defeated its adversary, but because it had captured the moral high ground against all odds.

In venturing into this emotional minefield, we need guideposts, which can be called *moral literacy.* Like the *political literacy* of informed citizens, a moral literacy ought to underlie those citizens' daily judgments. Moral literacy denotes the ability to distinguish between legitimate and illegitimate behavior, regardless of what is legal or customary in a given situation. Despite postmodernist relativism's popularity, our goal is to highlight universally acceptable criteria by which the antagonists in a polarized conflict can be held accountable—a common ground by which their mutual atrocities can be judged and by which peace can be negotiated.

A polarized struggle inevitably produces great moral confusion among the participants and onlookers alike. In South Africa, the effort to dismantle apartheid forced the parties to clarify their positions on which methods of liberation and resistance are legitimate and which are immoral. The South African Truth Commission further pronounced what constitutes human rights violations in a just war. It concluded that even in a just war, the forces of liberation may not defend themselves "by *all* means possible." Attacking civilians or killing prisoners, for example, constitute "injustice in war" and violations of the Geneva Convention of legitimate warfare. When the partisans in the Middle East conflict refer to the anti-apartheid struggle, they often ignore these moral lessons. The British philosopher Ted Honderich, for instance, exemplifies this moral confusion by advocating "*liberation-terrorism* to get freedom and power for a people when it is clear that nothing else will get it for them."[2] Honderich blatantly appropriates the South African case and misinterprets its relationship to the Israeli-Palestinian conflict by morally justifying suicide bombing and glorifying martyrdom:

> I myself have no serious doubt, to take the outstanding case, that the Palestinians have exercised a moral right in their terrorism against the Israelis. They have had a moral right to terrorism as certain as was the moral right, say, of the African people of South Africa against their white captors and the apartheid state. Those Palestinians who have resorted to necessary killing have been right to free their people, and those who have killed themselves in the cause of their people have sanctified themselves.[3]

Despite its "armed struggle" the ANC, as the main voice of black South Africa, has never endorsed terrorism, defined as intentional harming of innocent civilians. In fact, the ANC admonished local combatants who deviated from this policy and successfully constrained its frustrated cadres to channel their anger into disciplined resistance. Not one suicide has been committed in the cause of a thirty-year-long armed struggle, although in practice the ANC drifted increasingly toward violence during the latter years of apartheid.

Our moral reasoning, hopefully without moralizing, also requires reflection on positionality when dealing with a very sensitive and controversial topic. Our Marxist friends (the few who are left) argue that, politically, "you stand where you sit." We do not believe in such determinism that denies agency. We also guard against similar ethnic homogenizing, which assumes that peoples' attitudes are primarily shaped by their ethnic background and that members of the same group view the world in more or less the same manner. Obviously vast intra-group differences characterize both Jews and Palestinians or white and black South Africans who are not monolithic entities. We also do not believe in *collective guilt*. However, there exists *collective responsibility* when crimes are committed in the name of your nation or you have unwittingly benefited from your group's actions. This should be the case even if you took no part in these crimes or may have actively opposed them. At the very least, sensitivity about ethnic positionality and the strong emotions associated with it can be expected.

In ethnic terms, we are neither Jewish nor Arab/Palestinian by birth, but we identify with each for different reasons: We identify with Jews as a long-standing persecuted minority, whose survivors had nowhere to go in the 1940s; and we identify with Palestinians as a displaced, dispossessed, and discriminated against minority as a consequence of Jewish settlements. Not being an insider to either side of the conflict may disadvantage us, but the outsider status also immunizes against too-partisan and too-emotional involvement, which flaws much of the literature on the Middle East. As comparative analysts with long involvement in other conflict resolutions, we hope to escape the ethnic bias of own group affinity. This may enhance our ability to envisage scenarios beyond wishful thinking and moral condemnation. Otherwise, we deemphasize ethnicity as a criterion that endows automatic competence to pass moral judgments. For example, we doubt the notion that ethnic origin bestows a special moral authority to pronounce unquestionable views on memorialization or reparation. The brilliant architects who designed imaginative memorials in Berlin and elsewhere never claimed that their Jewish origin inspired them or that only descendants of victims should be the arbiters of appropriate memory.

There is also the argument that only insiders should write about intra-group affairs—that is, only Jews are allowed to criticize fellow Jews. Given the all-pervasive anti-Semitism, one Jewish friend suggested, all non-Jews are potential perpetrators and only potential victims can judge fellow victims. This logic reminded us of the claim of some feminists, that all men are potential rapists and therefore too tainted for credible involvement in women affairs. In this vein, black South Africans could argue that whites as perpetrators and beneficiaries of apartheid have no right to complain about black racism. Yet, intra-group affairs are never confined in their impact. In an increasingly interconnected world, it behooves outsiders to concern themselves with their neighbors.

The logic of political Zionism falsely assumes that anti-Semitism is an irreducible part of Gentile society. One writer articulates this widespread notion: "I believe that anti-Jewish genocide cannot be laid to rest as a discrete historical episode, but remains a possibility implicit in the deep structure of Christian and Islamic cultures, East and West."[4] But anti-Semitism is a contrived, manufactured, and learned phenomenon. Therefore, it can be unlearned. If anti-Semitism were indeed "an essential aspect of non-Jewish human nature, and as a consequence, Jews can never hope to achieve equality of rights as religious and cultural minorities in Gentile societies,"[5] only an exclusive Jewish state could guarantee Jewish rights. All enlightened Gentiles would have to be supporters of political Zionism. The progress of Jewish equality and full integration into Western societies, the relics of anti-Semitism notwithstanding, would only be a delusion. These claims and assumptions are obviously historically and factually absurd; any support for Zionism can only be derived from a specific historical context—such as the Holocaust—not from innate cultural attitudes, which are constantly changing, let alone human nature. Rejecting the notion of anti-Semitism as an immutable part of "non-Jewish human nature" does not deny the possibility that anti-Semitic fascism could reappear in some parts of the world, but this is an empirical question, neither inevitable nor predictable, but dependent on historical circumstances.

Outsiders need to be careful when commenting on others' experiences of oppression and sense of vulnerability. Historically, Jews have been and continue to be victimized. If one takes the pronouncements of Islamist extremists seriously, Jews are again singled out and the margin of error in Israel is small. Writing about a deadly conflict from the privilege of living in a safe environment does not expose the commentator to the consequences of proposed "solutions." Refraining from prescriptions therefore is wise counsel for those who are not required to bear the risks. Yet there is a contribution to be made by outsider analysis. To view one's own world through the eyes of others may well offer insights about unintended consequences and alternative arrangements. Uniqueness can only be discerned through comparisons. Critical comparisons are not usually received appreciatively and reactions range from self-righteous rejection to thoughtful introspection. One friendly reader of an earlier draft chapter concluded pithily: "A mixture of sense and nonsense." We can only hope that the persuasive, sensible parts predominate.

As both insiders and outsiders, we have studied ethnic conflicts in many countries for the past thirty years. For the reasons mentioned, seldom have we felt so constrained to write as we have about our experiences in Israel. That one of us is of German origin and that the other has lived through apartheid victimization evokes special sensitivities. It is the heavy burden of an atrocious anti-Semitic history that cautions against judging the descendants of centuries-long persecution, culminating in the horrendous

Holocaust. Vulnerable, traumatized people long for security and protection at any cost, even at the price of expansionism. With Arab resistance to new Jewish settlers, the historically displaced inevitably engaged in displacement themselves. After four wars since 1948, the mythology of a promised land resulted in the Jewish domination of its Arab population. However, can the recent American settlers on the West Bank and Gaza still claim victimhood? With state subsidies and army protection, they confiscate more Arab land and use five times the scarce water per capita than the Palestinians are allocated.

We have often faced the questions: Why concern yourself with Israel at all, when there are so many more horrific human rights violations committed by Israel's Arab critics? Why else does the world pick on the Middle East's only democracy, if not for the world's latent anti-Semitism? The suspicion runs deep and may even be partly justified while it serves at the same time as a convenient armor to silence any criticism of the Jewish state. Indeed, Israel should not be held more accountable than others. Israel receives disproportionate scrutiny in global forums for a variety of reasons: First, it is precisely because Israel is a Western democracy for its Jewish majority that it is judged by these standards. Western commentators feel a greater affinity to a like-minded polity than to an autocratic Third World state. Second, the Jewish state enjoys a sophisticated diaspora for which it claims to be the spiritual home and sanctuary. Third, as a Western outpost in a strategic environment, the country is heavily bankrolled by U.S. taxpayers and donors and is therefore linked to its outside supporters. Fourth, radical Islamists use Israeli policies to mobilize anti-Western sentiment. In the streets of Iraq, for example, American troops are called "Jews." Unconditional U.S. support for Israeli expansionism potentially unites Muslim moderates with jihadists. If the silent struggle between Muslim modernizers and religious zealots ultimately decides the success of the "war on terrorism," leaving the Israel-Palestine issue unresolved ignites rage and drives the Muslim moderates into the extremist camp. In short, the Israeli domination of Palestinians not only harms Israeli society, but serves, together with Iraq, as the incubator of global anti-U.S. antagonism. The frontlines of this global contest are marked by what many consider the new "apartheid wall" in Palestine.

Above all, as former collective victims, survivors and descendants are expected to be particularly sensitive not to repeat ethnic discrimination. In short, concerns with Israeli policy for many reasons must be distinguished from anti-Semitism. Criticism of its government does not question the legitimacy of the state of Israel, neither should it be construed as an attack on Jewishness.

Thomas Friedman has written: "Criticizing Israel is not anti-Semitic, and saying so is vile. But singling out Israel for opprobrium and international sanction out of all proportion to any other party in the Middle East is anti-Semitic, and not saying so is dishonest."[6] One must agree with Friedman that

Israel's Arab antagonists warrant much more condemnation. Their oppression of women and homosexuals and their generally autocratic, corrupt, and self-serving systems highlight democratic deficits that have yet to be rectified in any Arab state. However, the strained effort at balance when comparing Israeli and Palestinian fighting also accepts the moral equivalence of the two peoples' antagonism and thereby easily dilutes the occupation as the central cause of the strife and suffering on both sides.

The occupation demeans and degrades not only the occupied but also the occupier, who has the prime moral responsibility for the enduring conflict. The media's moral accounting of the conflict remains one of the most contested issues, with both sides accusing reporters of heavy bias. For example, former long-time BBC Middle East correspondent Tim Llewellyn has criticized the BBC for its effort at "balance" in its reporting on Israel, compared with its reporting on apartheid South Africa:

> When suicide bombers attack inside Israel the shock is palpable. The BBC rarely reports the context, however. Many of these acts of killing and martyrdom are reprisals for assassinations by Israel's death squads, soldiers and agents who risk nothing as they shoot from helicopters or send death down a telephone line. I rarely see or hear any analysis of how many times the Israelis have deliberately shattered a period of Palestinian calm with an egregious attack or murder. "Quiet" periods mean no Israelis died . . . it is rarely shown that during these "quiet" times Palestinians continued to be killed by the score. In South Africa, the BBC made it clear that the platform from which it was reporting was one of abhorrence of the state crime of apartheid. No Afrikaner was ritually rushed into a studio to explain a storming of a township. There is no such platform of the BBC's in Israel/Palestine, where the situation is as bad as apartheid, discrimination, racism, ethnic cleansing as rife as ever it was in the Cape or the Orange Free State.[7]

At the same time, the Israeli government has singled out BBC correspondents, accusing them of "hostile" reporting and restricting their access to information.

Problematic ethnic solidarity may also be questioned. We know many Jewish friends who are deeply troubled about Israeli policies. Yet these highly principled colleagues remain silent and will not criticize Israeli government policy publicly, particularly abroad. Elie Wiesel, who rightly assailed the world's initial silence about the Holocaust, personifies this contradiction best: "As a Jew I see my role as a . . . defender of Israel. I defend even her mistakes. Yes, I feel that as a Jew who resides outside Israel I must identify with whatever Israel does—even with her errors. That is the least Jews in the Diaspora can do for Israel: either speak up in praise or keep silent."[8] Such uncritical solidarity elevates fallible policies into the realm of the sacred. Acquiescence in the face of injustice constitutes complicity. Learning from the Holocaust implies concern for human rights everywhere. Why should breaking ranks on Israel amount to a betrayal of identity? On the contrary, it reaffirms a cherished Jewish tradition of rational argumentation that risks being lost by an unquestioning loyalty. The several hundred conscientious objectors who refuse military service in the occupied territories (but would defend Israel proper) bravely uphold this tradition of autonomous reasoning. Yet they are ostracized as betraying fellow Jews.

We are puzzled as to why morally sensitive individuals react allergically to the slightest condemnation of Israeli behavior. People who rightly celebrate the Jewish overrepresentation in the anti-apartheid resistance react uncomfortably when the possibility of Israeli apartheid is merely queried. Amiable conversations turn sour and the non-kosher topic is dropped with consensual self-censorship. Prominent liberal defenders of human rights the world over explicitly state that they will never venture into this emotional minefield. At an international academic conference, the mere designation of an official Jewish state as an "ethnic state" drew the outraged reaction of a prominent U.S. liberal colleague: "What about Turks in Germany?"—as if two xenophobias cancel each other out. "France and Britain are ethnic states—why should Jews be forbidden to long for the same?" is another frequently heard retort. Indeed, Jews, like any other nation, have a right to live in their own state, but should not treat their citizens differentially.

What causes the extraordinary ethnic solidarity and lack of erosion of Jewish nationalism (Zionism) at the height of its success? The answer lies in moral validity. One can question whether *objectively* there is moral validity to a given national identity. *Subjectively*, however, there are degrees of moral validity to national identity. The belief in moral validity is deeply embedded and bolstered by histories of felt wrongs. In the Jewish case, moral validity is fed not by an *imagined* injustice or defeat that happened centuries ago (as in Serbian or Quebec nationalism), but by a *living* history peopled by survivors and descendants. Jewish historical suffering has evolved into a collective resolve to not let it happen again that few other national identities display. Afrikaner national identity, for example, was not imbued with the same moral validity, despite the loss of 10 percent of the Afrikaner population in the Anglo-Boer war. Afrikaner moral standing was constantly undermined by exclusion and domination of blacks, even subconsciously in the minds of its beneficiaries. In contrast, the similar Israeli dispossession of Palestinians is perceived as self-defense and therefore not immoral. Zionism has convinced its adherents as well as Western public opinion that Israel has historical right on its side, which other nationalisms lack. A "normal" nationalism aims at achieving a common desire of belonging, while Jewish nationalism goes beyond beneficial bonds in asserting a moral existentialism, regardless of its consequences.

Continuing anti-Semitism as well as Arab hostility reinforces this moral righteousness that blocks the erosion of Zionism. Afrikaner nationalism disintegrated when it had achieved its goals. Conflicting class interests destroyed the former unity of a once relatively homogeneous Afrikanerdom as different sections (civil servants, farmers, business owners, blue-collar workers) defined their interests differently. While apartheid ideologues also justified their rule by claiming self-defense against ANC-led communism, the collapse of the Soviet Union deprived Afrikaner nationalists of this rationalization. Continued Arab hostility sustains the Israeli perception of justifiable self-defense.

While a dominant U.S.–pro-Israel lobby blindly endorses or quietly tolerates any Israeli government policy, another vocal radical minority abroad—particularly in France and England—calls for apartheid-like sanctions. Other human rights liberals highlight the plight of victims, but they seldom analyze what causes the suffering. Most university administrations in North America, from Concordia to Harvard, would like to declare the controversial issue taboo and ban all discussions among agitated students and activist faculty. Such a position shirks rational, analytic debate where it should be encouraged. Do the calls to boycott Israel assist peace efforts in the Middle East? Progressive forces on both sides would be better served by concerned academics visiting and supporting them directly, if only to act in critical solidarity. Increased contact is also advocated by leading Palestinian intellectuals such as Edward Said, who writes:

> I believe it is our duty as Palestinian and yes, even Arab intellectuals to engage Israeli academic and intellectual audiences by lecturing at Israeli centers, openly, courageously, uncompromisingly. What have years of refusing to deal with Israel done for us? Nothing at all, except to weaken us and weaken our perception of our opponent.[9]

While we consider the academic isolation of Israel counterproductive, we sympathize with boycotting the products of illegal settlements (as advocated by Gush Shalom). We also endorse the shareholder actions of companies that directly assist and profit from the occupation, such as Caterpillar, if only for raising awareness.

One note on our methodological guiding thread: In analyzing emotionally charged conflicts, one ought to guard against four traps: moralizing, theologizing, medicalizing, and personalizing.

Moralizing focuses on what ought to happen rather than what is likely to occur. We all have our moral preferences, but we must avoid being blinded by them. Wishful thinking all too often overrides the need for a hard-nosed reality check. Realistic accounting turns out to be depressing and uncomfortable but is preferable to living with illusions about the inevitable triumph of good over evil. "Restoring Hope" is an inspiring theme for an academic conference on a seemingly intractable conflict, but the hope must also be grounded in realism. Self-serving moral sermons about the evils of the adversary or the need for justice only preach to the converted. Laments about broken international laws or unheeded UN resolutions obscure why the lawbreaker gets away with it.

Theologizing mystifies sociopolitical events as resulting from divine intervention or inexplicable developments. To dub the South African negotiated revolution a "miracle" sounds impressive but explains nothing. The popular concept of evil does not explain terrorism. In fact, it shuts off understanding of the phenomenon by labeling it beyond understanding. The concept of evil avoids the important questions of why and when evil expresses itself. The resurrection of the term *evil* has been mainly used for denunciation. As Robert Fine has argued, the prevailing usage of *evil* tends to exonerate us—the *good*—from any responsibility other than that of destroying evil, and forcibly divides the world between Absolute Innocence and the Unspeakable Beast. Praying for better times may comfort the soul, but resting hopes on the outcome means being paralyzed. At the same time, religious beliefs must be taken seriously because people act on the basis of their firmly held faith. However, we doubt that rising religious fundamentalism in a "clash of civilizations" with secular values can adequately explain militancy. The conflict between Islamists and Arab governments, even in the occupied Palestinian territory, is better understood as a class struggle between the disenfranchised poor and the countries' autocratic and corrupt elites. Religion serves as a mobilizing device that gives the poor a moral identity and promises security and certainty in a climate of fear.

Medicalizing a deplorable social condition as a disease—a cancer—that needs to be eradicated, or as a pathological condition to be cured, resonates as an enticing metaphor. What does Tony Blair's phrase of "terrorism as a spreading virus" explain? Medical analogies assume involuntary destiny, which obscures the conscious forces and interests behind specific policies. They do not help to evaluate policy.

Personalizing policy issues and demonizing leaders has a similarly ineffectual result. Merely denouncing Sharon as "the Butcher of Shatila" neglects the reasons underlying his growing appeal to an agitated Israeli electorate. Leaders mainly represent and articulate underlying interests and sentiments. Yet, while leaders are mouthpieces of their constituencies, they also mobilize, instigate, and persuade. It is for this reason that one may speculate whether Sharon may in time mutate into an Israeli de Gaulle or an F. W. de Klerk. The obsession with the late Arafat also testifies to a personalized politics that falsely believes that Arab politics depend on "great men" who manipulate ignorant masses.[10]

While we pay particular attention to the discourse of leaders in influencing the course of conflicts, we also doubt that one can attribute developments to leaders only. Celebrating prominent South African leaders as sole causes of solutions in addition often assumes a selective partisan focus: "Many times in the past it was rational to give up all hope for the future, to assume the nation would decay into a racial holocaust. It did not occur because of the transformative actions of those marvelous leaders Desmond Tutu and Nelson Mandela, confounding the calculus of rationality."[11] The divine power bestowed on these noble figures indeed defies rationality. Even exemplary figures such as Mandela should not be romanticized. One has to question Said's portrayal of Mandela as displaying "profoundly affecting charisma," an "especially eloquent man" who utters "well-crafted words" and always has "something gripping to say."[12] Unlike Gandhi with his ninety-six volumes of collected writings and complex speeches, Mandela cannot be called an intellectual, let alone a philosopher. Far from being an inspiring orator, Mandela delivers the text of his speechwriters in a wooden manner and excites mainly when he ventures into spontaneous sermons. Mandela's achievement lies elsewhere. His acts of embracing his tormentors and his unique sense for unifying gestures of reconciliation almost exonerated whites from their apartheid crimes and made Mandela a hero across the racial divide. The aura of a forgiving president without the expected bitterness after a long incarceration, not innovative leadership, elevated Mandela to a universal icon of peacemaking.

In short, by viewing the Middle East through South African lenses, this study tries to break through the many clichés, such as an "endless cycle of violence," based on "ancient hatreds" in a "tragedy" of inexorable fate that is nobody's fault. In reality, a series of crimes committed can be traced to discernable causes and the initiators should be held accountable.

Our research methods and moral approaches are further illustrated in the following "travel report." As an ethnographic and impressionistic account, the chapter differs from the more "academic" analyses in the rest of the book. The journalistic piece, mainly recording conversations and voices directly, is also meant to whet the appetite of the reader for the analytical reasoning that comes later. Quantitatively oriented researchers normally ridicule such academic tourism as unworthy of inclusion in a sociological account that should report mainly objective, verifiable data and representative surveys. We contend that minute observations and subjective reflections often capture deeper insights than do abstract figures, just as good novelists and journalists often portray social scenes in a more riveting fashion than dry academic analysts are able to achieve. There is something to be gained in the combination.

We also provide first a bit of autobiographical information. Life histories and experiences in different settings shape academic choices and personal values. Exposing those influences allows the reader to evaluate sources of moral judgments.

Acknowledgments

Many colleagues with diverse views have commented extensively on early chapters of this book or discussed the sensitive issues with us at length. Here we mention only the academics and omit the many insights we derived from conversations with our extended family on three continents, comprising lapsed Catholics, secularized Jews, cosmopolitan Hindus, and open-minded Muslims.

In Israel, we have had periodic personal contact with engaged social scientists (listed in alphabetical order) across the political spectrum: Ron Dudai, Avishai Ehrlich, Daphna Golan, Benny Neuberger, Bernie Susser, and Mottie Tamarkin gave us valuable feedback on many occasions. On the Palestinian side, Fouad Moughrabi, Rema Hammami, Andre Mazawi, and Mahdi Abdul Hadi of the Palestinian Society for the Study of International Affairs (PASSIA) have been most helpful in sharing their expertise.

In South Africa, the list of long-standing academic friends who, despite sometimes sharp disagreements, enjoy engaging political discussions includes: Solly Benatar, Alex Boraine, Breyten Breytenbach, André du Toit, Hermann Giliomee, Wilmot James, Michael Savage, Milton Shain, and Van Zyl Slabbert.

Further afield, Ephrahim Nimni and Michael Humphrey in Sydney, Stanley Uys in London, Bodo von Greiff and Hanne Herkommer in Berlin, Joachim Bergman in Frankfurt, Fritz Sack in Hamburg, Wilke Thomssen in Bremen, Pierre van den Berghe and James Banks in Seattle, and George Pavlich in Edmonton should be acknowledged for many stimulating conversations.

At home in Vancouver, Gary Teeple, with his global interests, was always ready to forward dissenting viewpoints. We learned from the related conferences that Pat Marchak and John Torpey, a cosmopolitan, multilingual theorist, had organized at the University of British Columbia (UBC). The valuable input of our graduate students at Simon Fraser University (SFU) and UBC, as well as the annual cohort at the University of Cape Town, particularly the fellows from the Transitional Justice Program, cannot all be individually acknowledged, but Laura Stovel and Tavengwa Runyowa were of special assistance in this project.

An early shorter version of Chapter 4, "The Problematic Israel–South Africa Analogy," was originally published by Heribert Adam as an Occasional Paper 2 of the South African Human Sciences Research Council (HSRC) and formed the framework of the conference "Restoring Hope: Building Peace in Divided Societies," Arabella Sheraton, Hermanus, South Africa, May 4–6, 2003. The meeting of Israeli and Palestinian parliamentarians, academics, and civil society activists with South African public figures was convened with the aim of exposing Middle Eastern opinion makers to lessons from the negotiated South African settlement. Leading representatives of the old and new regime, such as former President F. W. de Klerk, Army Chief General George Meiring, as well as ANC cabinet ministers Kader Asmal and Trevor Manual, together with other South African negotiators and facilitators (Pallo Jordan, Pravin Gordon, Van Zyl Slabbert, Jakes Gerwel) participated in the Ford Foundation– and HSRC-financed exercise. We were encouraged by the general agreement with our reasoning at this conference. We also benefited from responses to our papers presented at a conference on the topic "A South African Conversation on Israel and Palestine" that Mahmood Mamdani had organized at Columbia University, a subsequent seminar at the Truman Instititute at Hebrew University, and a similar lecture at the Palestinian Society for the Study of International Affairs (PASSIA). Andre and Linda Jaquet's contacts with their South African diplomatic colleagues in Ramallah and Tel Aviv facilitated our appointments and checkpoint crossings. Another October 2003 conference of Middle Eastern social scientists, sponsored by the Royal Institute for Inter-Faith Studies in Amman, Jordan, also provided valuable insights. Finally we "workshopped" the themes at our own SFU conference, "Negotiating Compromises in Divided Societies," in October 2004, where several of the above-mentioned South African and Israeli colleagues plus members of the Vancouver public contributed more insights.

Ongoing field research requires funding. Not unexpectedly, the U.S. Institute of Peace turned down our elaborate application for the controversial project, but our more open-minded Canadian reviewers ensured that the Ottawa Social Sciences and Humanities Research Council (SSHRC) continued to support the critical inquiry generously. We are grateful also for the SSHRC conference sponsorship. We are indebted to Temple University's two independent referees, Senior Acquisitions Editor Micah Kleit for unbureaucratic guidance through an elaborate production process, and especially our invaluable copyeditor Lesa Shearer for spotting inconsistencies, calling for clarifications, and proposing more elegant formulations.

Needless to say, we alone should be blamed for the inevitable factual errors and biased judgments, although we always strove for a balanced and realistic account without, however, practicing moral fence sitting.

Introduction

Political Travel through the Holy Land

The Gaze of Outsiders

Our interest in the Middle East dates back to a two-year teaching stint at the American University in Cairo (AUC) in the 1970s when Sadat's Egypt was still a stern Soviet ally in the Cold War. When the Egyptian army turned the superpower competition into a brief hot war in October 1973, we anxiously expected the Israeli bombing to reach our darkened apartment in Dokki on Bolous Hanna near the Nile. However, the respective masters restrained their proxies in afflicting further damage on their innocent, suffering people. From then on, only the propaganda war continued unabated at high pitch, but our hardened colleagues and cynical students at AUC took it mostly as an irrelevant ritual. Occasionally, we escaped the stifling Cairo atmosphere to lively pre–civil war Beirut, but could only visit Israel furtively via Cyprus. Several subsequent conferences about settler societies compared Israel, Northern Ireland, and South Africa, speculating which communal conflict would be easier to resolve.[1] We were also able to interview Shiite and Maronite militia commanders at the height of the Lebanese strife, which the German Goethe Institute in Beirut had arranged for a few curious but naive academics in dangerous circumstances in 1985.[2] In September 2001, we attended the UN World Congress against Racism in Durban where Israel was vociferously assailed as an apartheid state.

Since our "illegal" marriage under the apartheid Immorality Act, we were involved in the South African struggle as both academic analysts and public commentators. Even Mandela in Pollsmoor had read our book *South Africa without Apartheid* and humbly asked in a handwritten letter from prison to have his copy autographed, although we were not allowed to meet him at the time. After *Modernizing Racial Domination* was published, our visa applications for family visits were refused during the 1970s. Intervention with the Pretoria regime by sympathetic Afrikaner colleagues changed this later, and Heribert's subsequent appointment to the Buthelezi Commission in the early 1980s plunged us again into the search for democratic alternatives and blueprints for integration. Research on the banned African National Congress (ANC) and participation in various meetings between open-minded Afrikaners and the ANC in exile, particularly the historic 1987 Dakar encounter, brilliantly conceived and engineered by Van Zyl Slabbert, Alex Boraine, and Breyten Breytenbach, offered lessons in the quest for realistic compromises. At the height of anti-apartheid mobilization (1986–1987), Heribert served as acting director of the University of Cape Town's (UCT) ambitiously named Center for Conflict Resolution, while Kogila was affiliated with UCT's School of Education. Dubbing the university, "Moscow on the Hill," riot squads used stinging gas and truncheons to stop frequent student protest around the lovely campus in Rondebosch. UCT's embattled vice chancellors during the apartheid years, from the principled Sir Richard Luyt to the forthright Stuart Saunders, always appeared to us as models for upholding academic freedoms under adverse political conditions. This marked the beginning of our annual quarterly teaching and research association with the venerable institution.

South Africa's "liberal" English-language universities served as useful barometers measuring the state of race relations. Their academic climate, though shaped by restricted racial access, still differed from the more conformist Afrikaans institutions as well as the even more repressive five ethnic universities for group members only. During the Vorster period, Kogila was fired from her faculty position at the tribal (Indian) university in Durban by the Afrikaner rector S. P. Olivier, following police directives, for associating with the wrong people and not "identifying with your own community." Threatening, anonymous phone calls and visits by security policemen were aimed at intimidation. At the neighboring "open" University of Natal campus, we once received a reprimand from the then rector Owen Horwood (later Minister of Finance)—via an embarrassed department head—that playing "mixed" (meaning interracial) tennis on university grounds was not allowed under Group Areas regulations. Such trite harassment is hardly worth mentioning, considering the lethal fate of others. Years later, our colleague and friend Rick Turner was shot by his ideological foes in his own home in Durban. Nowadays, hardly any of the easy-going students at mixed university campuses—who then were children or not even born at the time of racial repression—associate anything concrete with the abstract notion of apartheid. Unlike the postapartheid climate of apolitical consumerist integration, at least at the elite level, the apartheid atmosphere, particularly in the late 1980s, resembled more the gloomy outlook of Israel twenty years later. Department stores had installed metal detectors and security guards frisked the handbags of shoppers. At frequent police roadblocks, the trunks of suspicious cars were inspected.

With tensions rising and abounding political confusion, many heads of large business corporations also worried about the future. For example, in 1987, Conrad Strauss, the CEO of Standard Bank, and the management of the supermarket chain Pick and Pay asked Heribert, the "objective" foreign academic, unattached to South African political baggage and presumably less constrained by local expectations, to address their subsidiaries throughout the country on likely political developments. His central theme that the release of Mandela would contribute to stability and peace fell as much on deaf ears as did the Sharon government's admonition to negotiate with whoever is left with a following among Palestinians. Sophisticated money handlers argued that Mandela was a dangerous communist demagogue who would incite even more riots. However, it was the white right wing that mostly instigated strife at the time. Indeed, once while discussing the seemingly impossible in the air-conditioned sterility of a darkened Bloemfontein bank hall, a boisterous, ultra-right AWB (Afrikaner Weerstandsbeweging) procession with swastika flags outside drew everyone on the balcony to ponder the impending civil war. Another skeptical audience of supermarket managers in Pretoria before the historic 1994 election mainly wanted to know how they could best defend their stores against looting hordes who would certainly invade properties of white fools not adequately prepared for escape nor stocked up for a long siege. Despite these parochial horizons at the middle management level, several heads of companies, particularly international ones, read the signs of transition correctly. Israelis could learn from some South African corporate executives to seek dialogue with their own internal antagonists, if only to sound them out and prepare themselves for the inevitable changes. Whether at the monthly so-called "Synthesis" meetings in the lavish homes of Johannesburg tycoons or at dozens of foreign-sponsored conferences, white and black local capitalists, nationalists, and socialist unionists could and did engage one another in earnest discussions at all times. In this ideological vacuum of uncertainty, corporate "scenario planning" flourished. Exhortations to take the "Japanese high road" of rapid development in an underdeveloped continent by Anglo-American's persuasive Clem Sunter, for example, did find increasingly appreciative mass audiences, because they showed whites a convincing way out of their malaise. When eventually even conservative businessmen broke the taboo of the prevailing demonization of the liberation movements by openly meeting with the exiled compatriots for the first time in Lusaka in 1986, the academic liberals, social democrats, and moral clerics could no longer be so easily dismissed as Lenin's "useful idiots."[3] Even the U.S. State Department belatedly followed the South African lead, lifted the ban on ANC visits, and received ANC head Oliver Tambo for the first time in Washington in 1988.

Despite our long obsession with South Africa and occasional teaching at the Inter-University in Croatia's magnificent Dubrovnic, our reasoning on ethnic conflicts has been most inspired by our past thirty-five years in Canada. Upon leaving South Africa as a family, neither the imperial, Vietnam-involved United States nor Germany appealed as a future home. While we periodically returned to our countries of origin for short teaching periods and never lost touch with the customs and habits of our upbringing, it was the contrasting Canadian exposure that reshaped our worldview. We write with a proud Canadian identity. Our two daughters were born and socialized in splendid Vancouver, and its two underrated universities off the beaten track provided a congenial intellectual base, the likes of which the still-rigid hierarchical institutions in Germany and British colonial counterparts in Africa can only dream of. The society of immigrants from all corners of the world gradually emerged as our model of mutual multicultural respect. Interracial marriages now make up 15 percent of newlywed couples in Vancouver without anyone batting an eyelid. Forty-five percent of the population indicate multiple identities. Canada annually accepts twice as many immigrants per capita (0.9 percent) compared with the United States or Australia. Canada is the only one of nine Western countries where a majority (74 percent) views immigrants as "having a good influence," whereas in all Western European countries as well as in the United States, majorities responded negatively to newcomers (Editorial, *Globe*, May 31, 2004, A12).

While certainly not without its residual racism and the shameful benign neglect of the indigenous people, the country nevertheless is pioneering in many respects the future global world. United by a superficial anti-Americanism, the historical presence of Quebec has engendered a spirit of compromise in the officially bilingual middle power. The country has overcome separatism through concessions and cooptation internally and takes pride in its peacekeeping and mediation efforts internationally. To our delight, but to the chagrin of many militarists, Canada's military spending of 1 percent of GDP ranks lowest among all Western democracies. Canada, one American writer remarked, "never fought a revolution or a civil war, produced no great world leader, pioneered no great social or political movement and committed no memorable atrocities." But precisely because of this normal record, where the distribution of material spoils rather than moral issues forms the core of political debate, the peaceful polity arrives at decisions through consensus and negotiation. Compared with the emotional intensity of Israel or apartheid South Africa, Canada seems boring. One South African friend mocked it with the witty cliché: "It is a beautiful country to visit, but not for a whole weekend." Pierre Trudeau warned the postmodernist entity not to become "a mere conglomeration of shopping centers." However, it is also a state with a universal, though faltering, health care and welfare system and therefore a safer society with a fraction of the homicide rate of the United States, where the rate of imprisonment is more than six times higher (116 versus 715 per 100,000 residents). After our annual sojourns into the world of intolerance, we long to come home to tranquil, laissez-faire Vancouver and Pender Island.

Our impressions of more polarized politics during one of our research visits to Israel/Palestine from October to November 2002 are detailed in the following report.

In Israel/Palestine, we talked to dozens of colleagues, diplomats, NGO activists, and ordinary people in both camps of a deeply divided society. From relaxed dinners in exceptionally hospitable Jewish and Palestinian homes through joyful iftars breaking the Ramadan fast, from a formal seminar at Hebrew University to a fascinating symposium with professionals at the Palestinian Society for the Study of International Affairs (PASSIA) in East Jerusalem, we oscillated in an intense immersion course of contrasting perceptions between Tel Aviv and Ramallah. Perhaps only innocent foreigners get away with raising the sensitive, controversial questions that underlie the seething resentment behind the self-evident but divergent "truths" perceived on both sides. Outsiders benefit from easy access as well as unsuspicious frankness. The support groups that visit the region often want their own partisanship confirmed and tend to hear only one side, therefore returning even more prejudiced.

We consciously avoided seeking out only people with similar political outlooks. We broke bread with an engaging leader of the now marginalized and dispirited Israeli peace movement as well as a valued colleague who proudly displayed a poster of Sharon on his wall. When we tried to gauge the mutual reaction to the opinion of these adversaries to each other, they both shrugged: "What else do you expect from such lunatics?" The sophisticated Sharon supporter revealed no doubts. He harshly dismissed even the outstanding Israeli daily *Haaretz* as "predictable leftish nonsense." It brought home to us again that the internal political cleavages in Israeli society are at least as deep as the gulf with the Arab "other." These were secularized individuals who probably both consider the 20 percent minority of ultraorthodox Jews in their dark suits yet another separate element. To this division should be added the one million Russian "Jews," who are first of all cultural Russians and mostly political hardliners, and the two hundred thousand ideologically distinct settlers in Palestinian areas, in addition to the two hundred thousand residents in hilltop settlements of subsidized housing on conquered post-1967 Arab land around Jerusalem.

Similar deep internal ideological divisions exist among Palestinians.[4] It was surprising that hardly any of the two dozen or so politically aware Palestinians we spoke to at length displayed any enthusiasm for Arafat's administration and his corrupt security service, let alone for the fundamentalists of Hamas and the smaller Jihad. At the time, nobody dared to dispose of Arafat as the symbolic figurehead of Palestinian liberation, but everybody was aware of his limitations. Yet, exiling him, as Netanyahu advocated, Palestinians unanimously considered as the prelude to their own expulsion. In national opinion polls, 46 percent of Israel's Jewish citizens favor "transferring" Palestinians out of the territories, while 31 percent even support transferring the one million Israeli Arabs out of Israel proper.[5] Referring to the demographic threat, a prominent academic told us: "One Arab is too many!" A Palestinian academic referred to the ongoing "soft transfer" of emigrating professionals as a major problem. Intolerable conditions, from curfews to travel and business restrictions, motivate people with options to emigrate voluntarily. One only has to terrorize a population in order to demoralize and drive out its elites.

Far from being cowed, we sensed an unprecedented confrontational militancy toward the Israeli occupiers among Palestinian youth. The feared Kamikaze pilots of the imperial Japanese army crashed their planes into the U.S. Navy in acts of self-sacrifice. In that case, at least the vicious fighting was confined to two militaries officially at war with each other. Suicide bombers in Israel and Palestine deliberately aim at killing Jews, regardless of whether they are civilians or soldiers, children or adults, left-wingers or right-wingers. Although it is not official policy, when the Israeli army pursues Palestinian militants, many more civilians than gunmen are regularly killed, regardless of whether they are apolitical pacifists or violent activists. In the undeclared war in the holy land, the innocents on both sides are the main victims. As usual, it is also the poor who live in refugee camps or wait at bus stations who are disproportionately at risk and suffer most.

The Israeli-Palestinian conflict bears all the hallmarks of mutual ethnic targeting. You are singled out because you are a Jew. Property of only Palestinians is expropriated, only Arabs with different license plates are checked at numerous roadblocks, and there are roads exclusively for Jews to the West Bank settlements. Randomly, indiscriminately, and unpredictably, life chances are curtailed, just because one is born into a historical label. There is no escape from the bitter history as long as you continue to live in the embattled place. Two hostile people view each other as collective enemies, engage in collective revenge, suspect and demonize all members of the other group, regardless of the widely differing stances of individuals on both sides. This makes the necessary alliances of peace seekers across ethnic lines so difficult. The two most educated and sophisticated peoples in the Middle East stereotype and blame each other in mutual resentment that exceeds anything experienced in other communal conflicts.

"How would you feel if requested to identify the bloodied pieces of your daughter because of some indoctrinated fanatic?" asks our Jewish host in Jerusalem. Most likely, in our unimaginable grief we would also long for collective blame, if not revenge. "Do you expect us to just stand around passively if their settlers confiscate more of our land, uproot more of our olive trees, shoot at us during their curfews and humiliate us in endless waits at their checkpoints?" asks our Palestinian host twenty kilometers away in Ramallah. "They have all the weapons in the world—we have only our bodies and our will to resist their ongoing colonization." Both sides dwell on their legitimate grievances and nurture their respective victimhoods, each as poignantly felt as the other.

The conflict has escalated after hopeful negotiations ceased in January 2001 and extremists on both sides shape events. Apologists on both sides argue endlessly about cause and effect. Palestinians blame blatant settler expansionism on their land. Israelis invoke legitimate security concerns in light of unprecedented attacks on their normal way of life. Both "righteous victims" in Benny Morris' famous book *Righteous Victims* (New York: Vintage Books, 2001), brutalize each other. This undermines all prospects for future peaceful coexistence.

Can the impasse be broken? A similar despair and paralysis prevailed in the seemingly intractable ethnoracial conflict in South Africa during the mid-1980s. Until recently, few expected to ever see the Northern Irish, Cyprus, or Sri Lankan communal strife settled. Yet in all these cases, visionary political leaders on both sides negotiated the seemingly non-negotiable. Can a similar historic compromise between two adversaries be achieved in the religiously charged Middle East atmosphere? What must happen before people get tired of their brutalization and become exhausted from battle fatigue? Can outsiders help, facilitate, build bridges, and restart negotiation politics as honest brokers?

The U.S. administration, which has the most leverage on both sides, has conveniently washed its hands of the matter. Washington lets its hardline Israeli allies determine the course of events. The Canadians, like eager impotent peacemakers everywhere, sit on the sideline, abstain at UN votes, and once proposed to inject peacekeepers into the volatile West Bank under an international trusteeship, even without a peace agreement. However, the extremists on both sides would most likely be gunning for the peacekeepers who would be as helpless as those who were in Bosnia.

Conversations with Palestinians

Outsiders are ill-positioned to give advice to insiders who struggle daily to live normally in a painful situation. Visitors should listen, learn, and observe, but not lecture. Everybody knows a story of earnest consultants in developing countries who fly in from abroad and become instant experts overnight. But what if your hosts turn your questions around and press you for an answer to the question, "What would you do in our situation?" Feigning ignorance or escaping into evasive generalities shirks a moral obligation.

In this dilemma, the thrust of our response to our Palestinian audience was straightforward: "Recapture the moral high ground! Take a public stance against the counterproductive suicide bombings. Intentional killings of innocent civilians is immoral and a crime against humanity under international law. It marginalizes the Israeli peace camp, a much-needed ally. Instead, adopt a Gandhian-style passive resistance, the nonviolence of the first intifada, which was rooted in the popular involvement and protest actions of shopkeepers and school children alike."

In all our conversations we highlighted the stature, philosophies, and successful strategies of Gandhi and Mandela. Gandhi and Mandela, together with Martin Luther King, are celebrated as global historical icons who stand out among political leaders for their appealing moral clarity in the face of great odds, their universalizing message for bridging seemingly unbridgeable divides, their humane vision, as well as their personal charisma. Certainly not infallible and highly autocratic at times, yet personally disciplined spiritually and physically, endowed with great dignity and integrity, Gandhi and Mandela allowed their admirers to project their own desires onto mythical figures. Yet personalizing South Africa's successful transition by attributing it mainly to the reconciling magic of Mandela assumes that the majority of his followers resemble a flock of blind sheep, as Mandela himself has emphasized in reasserting his adherence to the collective ANC decision making.

Gandhi and Mandela succeeded in overcoming superior state forces through the moral blackmail of nonviolence and civil disobedience. They captured the moral high ground by shaming their colonial oppressors rather than defeating them in military terms. In a similar vein, the civil rights struggle involving Martin Luther King invoked the embarrassing gap between the U.S. promise of racial equality and the contrary reality. While Gandhi developed *satyagraha* (a term combining the Hindu words for "truth" and "holding firmly") as a principled strategy, Mandela embraced passive resistance more as an expedient tactic. He later supported "armed struggle," but without intentionally harming civilians. Anti-apartheid activists never used suicide as a weapon; nor did they glorify martyrdom. The ANC officially rejected terrorism, although some cadres engaged in it against orders. During the dying days of apartheid rival militias (Apla), street mobs and state forces committed deeds of killing uninvolved civilians as horrific as those reported daily from Israel/Palestine. In fact, after the unbanning of liberation movements and of general political liberalization between 1990 and 1994, more black people were killed in internecine political violence than during the four decades of apartheid. The success of *satyagraha* relies on the opposing power being susceptible to moral appeals and sharing a similar moral universe. Where a shared value system is absent or the colonized become dehumanized and pathologized (e.g., "barbarian," "terrorist," "mad," "animals"), or are perceived as acting on behalf of a foreign power (e.g., "KGB agents," "Islamist zealots") posing an existential threat to the power holder, moral persuasion tends to fall on deaf ears.

Gandhi and Mandela fought against different forms of colonialism: external and internal colonialism. *External colonialism* ends with the departure of the colonizer and political independence of the colony, although neocolonial economic dependence may continue. *Internal,* or *domestic, colonialism* ends with legal equality and peaceful coexistence. Relinquishing internal colonialism through reconciliation and postconflict reconstruction constitutes a much greater challenge. The legacy of the past strife haunts the common coexistence in the same state. Partition may be the inevitable result of accumulated bitterness and mutual suspicion.

Gandhi's vision of a united India foundered on this historical legacy, while Mandela's ANC succeeded in preventing the ethnic breakup of South Africa. The ideology of colorblind nonracialism as well as the country's economic interdependence facilitated a unitary state with a common dominant Christian religion also binding the disparate elements, in contrast to the much deeper sectarian cleavages in India or the Middle East. Whether the widely hailed two-state solution with "painful concessions" on both sides can be implemented in Israel/Palestine, or a single, binational state ultimately emerges, or one side extinguishes the other through expulsion is still vividly contested and remains an open question.

"What then is a practical lesson we Palestinians can learn for our struggle from Mandela?" a questioner probed. "The most important lesson the Palestinian leadership could draw from Mandela would be how to reassure an adversary that his essential interests will be respected. Mandela's magnanimous gestures of embracing former oppressors, both symbolically and figuratively, never failed to move," we explained. "But don't you think we Palestinians above all need to be reassured, since we are the victims?" "But so was Mandela after twenty-six years' imprisonment," we replied. Quite rightly, the exchange did not persuade our listeners for the simple reason that Mandela assumed power, while Palestinians continue to be at the mercy of a superior occupation force. In addition, Mandela took over an existing state while the Palestinians face the arduous task of building a state from scratch.

Despite our critical rendering of Gandhian and ANC strategies, we could sense our listeners' skepticism when we tried to apply those lessons to the situation in Palestine. We reiterated the crucial difference between the essentially nonviolent protests of the first intifada, which brought global sympathy to the Palestinian cause, and the counterproductive violence of the second intifada. In the first case, Palestinians, as the clear underdog, had then achieved a moral victory with large sections of the Israeli public—similar to Gandhi's gradual capture of liberal metropolitan opinion. Likewise, the ANC's anti-apartheid struggle succeeded because of its appeal to humanitarians the world over and not because of the "armed struggle." However, several Palestinian activists confused the Gandhian approach to liberation with passivity and nonresistance. In reality, *satyagraha*—a principled passive resistance—shames an adversary morally. Using the same violent means used by your colonial oppressor, Gandhi argued, deprives you of your strongest weapon: morally defeating and delegitimizing your materially superior opponent.

In contrast, the second intifada consists of secretive, militarized attacks by autonomous rival militias in a fragile semistate. With Palestinian bombings and shootouts, Israeli opponents are challenged where they are strongest, rather than shamed with moral exposure of expansionism where Israel is weakest. Besides triggering massive retaliation that has destroyed the social fabric of the emerging state, Palestinians have allowed themselves to be branded as terrorists. "Preserve the few institutional gains of Palestinian statehood, rather than facilitate the Israeli right wing to smash you into oblivion," we argued. The crushed ambulance on top of the pile of debris in Arafat's compound appeared to us as a reminder that this is warfare with few rules. After 9/11 at the latest, the militaristic strategy should have been abandoned. Why unwittingly reinforce Israel's insistence that Palestinians are local bin Ladens? We reasoned, "Because you have nothing in common with the dogmatic anti-Americanism of Hezbollah leaders, why don't you say so more often publicly, as some of the Palestinian intellectuals have done internally? Disassociate yourself from al-Queda, which wants to piggyback on your cause for their own ends."

Our Palestinian audience received this pessimistic and critical vision with polite dismissal. Wishful thinking in place of realistic recognition of power differentials knows no bounds if you believe in the justice of your cause. Why did we use the insulting notion of "suicide bombers" instead of the proper term "martyr," one questioner wanted to know. Are we not aware that stone-throwing children did not persuade one settler to leave our land? But failure of nonviolence does not logically mean that violence will succeed, we interjected. Besides, the protest of the first intifada brought Palestinians some tangible gains: the Oslo Accord, down the road a sovereign Palestinian state, as well as global sympathy. But what kind of nonviable, noncontiguous Bantustan is created, insisted our interrogator? Another participant interjected: "We would be the wardens of our own detention camps, completely at the mercy of Israel." Indeed, Sharon has something like this in mind when he talks about "painful concessions": an eventual Palestinian state on 42 percent of the West Bank and Gaza territory under current official Palestinian Authority control, once the Israeli army withdraws.

A Palestinian lawyer questioned:

> After we have already conceded 78 percent of British mandate Palestine to Israel and recognized their right to coexist with us in the 1993 Oslo Accord, how much more displacement and concessions must we tolerate? Colonial settlers are insatiable in their quest for our land and scarce water. While they enact a law of return for all Jews of the world, millions of Palestinian refugees, some still born on this soil, are barred from ever returning.

The return of refugees to their ancestral homes raises the most intractable issue of the conflict. Some Palestinians reject all compromises on this "principle right," including compensation for lost land or symbolic return of limited numbers. For Jewish nationalists from the Right to the Left, the demographic capture of the Jewish state means the end of their dream and the beginning of a nightmare. Apart from a few mavericks, few political thinkers on the Jewish side envisage a bicommunal, federal, and ethnically neutral common state of Jews and Arabs living together in relative multicultural harmony like bilingual Canada or nominally "nonracial" South Africa. Yet, increasingly, some Palestinian intellectuals rethink the goal of a separate state in light of the Israeli occupation. They increasingly redefine their freedom as a civil rights struggle in a *shared* state, rather than national liberation in a separate state.

We have also been reminded that we must choose our words carefully, being mindful of different connotations and that seemingly harmless concepts hold different meanings in different sociopolitical contexts. For example, we validated the term *compromise* in all our discussions. "Compromise" resonates with virtue in the Western liberal tradition, but carries the notion of "sellout" among many politically conscious Palestinians. They argue that genuine compromise occurs only between equals. Because Israelis and Palestinians interact in a grossly unequal power relationship, any compromise from this position amounts to an imposition and a dictate by the stronger party.

Unscrambling History

Attempting to unravel these predicaments amounts to the impossible task of unscrambling history. Few other nationalist movements have succeeded in the way Zionism has established a modern ethnic state, despite the repeated military opposition of its Arab neighbors and the local Palestinian population. The Jewish refugees from European anti-Semitism colonized the barren land not for economic reasons but to establish a safe haven in the form of a normal Jewish state, an endeavor rationalized by the mythology of returning to a holy ancient home. Had there been no Russian pogroms in the 1890s, no Nazi holocaust, or had America welcomed the Jewish outcasts, Israel would not exist. The displaced Palestinians are the indirect victims of European crimes against a vulnerable minority that everyone rejected. Just as other peoples have invoked the right of national self-determination, so did Jews, but clearly *not* in "a land without people for a people without land," as the Zionist cliché asserts.

In private conversations, our Palestinian colleagues largely agreed with our nonviolent advocacy. But they wanted us to understand their own predicament as well as the context of the suicidal resistance. They felt uneasy denigrating the ultimate sacrifice of activists on their behalf. Under conformity pressure to honor the "brave shahids" (martyrs), they also could not publicly disavow them without marginalizing themselves in Palestinian politics. Israeli Palestinians in Jaffa told us about a memorial service for the collateral Palestinian victims of a suicide bombing during which the grieving relatives did not utter any criticism of the bomber. Was this out of fear or support? How long can Israel rely on the loyalty of its 20 percent Arab citizens? These second-class citizens are increasingly alienated, as we sensed during our days in a large Palestinian home in Jaffa. During a tour of dilapidated community facilities, the unequal allocation of public funds for identical taxpayers emerged as a major complaint. From just a look at the potholes and crumbling sidewalks one knows whether one is in a Jewish or Arab quarter in Israel.

While emigration is on many people's minds, without outspoken moral leadership by the community's intellectuals, fragmented and irrational responses to the occupation continue. Palestinian society, as well as Israel's security, is increasingly threatened by autonomous militias outside the control of any political leaders. Among a militant youth with nothing to lose, the functionaries of the Palestinian Authority are discredited because of their perceived personal enrichment and collaboration. Utter powerlessness and frequent personal humiliation produces an all-consuming rage that outsiders can hardly fathom.

We had assumed that religious indoctrination motivates martyrdom but were given quite different explanations. A trusted Palestinian community leader conveyed the story of a well-adjusted high school girl from a secularized liberal family who blew herself up in a supermarket. She told two women in traditional Palestinian dress "to get out" before approaching a group of other female shoppers with children. They were all killed when she exploded. Why did she do this? "Certainly not because she was a religious psychopath!" The teacher explained that he is not worried when one or two girls are missing from his class—but when ten are suddenly absent simultaneously he fears that they compete among themselves about the honor to be the next martyr. "The girls save their own pocket money to buy the belt." He also knows of families who rejected money offered afterward, because "it is no substitute for our beloved child." But who makes and abuses impressionable children as moving bombs?

We asked a twenty-three-year-old Palestinian woman how she experiences "the situation." Her reply boiled down to one concept: humiliation. In her words, she feels symbolically raped by the young men in green uniforms at the many checkpoints and she illustrated this with numerous stories of sheer harassment. We were told of boys whose school bags were emptied and after they had picked up their books, the guard laughingly repeated the harassment.

When entering Israel a second time from Jordan at the Allenby crossing, we saw with our own eyes how Arabs in the line were treated. An elderly dignified couple in their seventies was ordered around with finger-snapping gestures. Their meager household goods in two overstuffed bags were thrown around with contempt, which they then had to pick up and repack themselves. The body language of gun-toting youngsters, including hardened young women, expressed it all. We were traveling with two Canadian-based diplomats, always patient, calm, and polite, who for the first time grew audibly incensed at the unfriendly hassle even they were subjected to at the hour-long procedure. If privileged visitors receive this treatment, how can Israel expect ordinary tourists to return?

In the eerily empty Novotel in the no-man's-land between East and West Jerusalem, the receptionist wears a pistol in his belt and was prepared to drop his room rate to $50 when we hesitated to book. Armed uniformed pensioners guard the university gates and check the garbage cans in the cafeteria continuously. We munched our sandwiches at Tel Aviv University beside a student with an Uzi casually slung over his shoulder. It made us nervous, but Israelis deny that they live on the edge and that nerves are frayed. Generally aggressive driving and horn blowing relieves the pervasive stress. The number of deserters and so-called problem soldiers with posttraumatic stress disorder has risen substantially. These are the hidden, invisible costs of a siege society from which neither side is shielded. The press reported that in one year 40,000 Israeli women sought medical attention arising from domestic violence. The unexpected boom of an air force jet breaking the sound barrier over Jerusalem caused panic below as it sounded like a bomb blast. Restaurants frisk their customers at the entrance. Driving a bus or being employed as a security guard in a shopping mall rank among the riskiest occupations. When 75 percent of Jewish parents want their children to settle abroad, has "the future disappeared," as David Grossman puts it?

Yet at the same time, life continues routinely as if calculating daily survival or forgetting about it is as normal as brushing your teeth in the morning. Our convivial Tel Aviv host showed us proudly his bomb shelter beside the kitchen and drove us to the supermarket a few blocks down to view the site where an explosion had killed people only two days earlier. Fatalistically, both opponents carry on. One underestimates the resilience and generosity of spirit among a beleaguered people that brings out the best and the worst. Israelis have been lauded for their resilience to bombs and their refusal to be terrorized. *Death as a Way of Life* is the apt title of a book by David Grossman, one of the country's most sensitive writers. Yet the quick return to normality after gross human tragedy also indicates a state of numbness, of lapsing into a shock so deep that only seeming indifference to horrible surroundings allows a person to function. Not acknowledging abnormal conditions characterizes even more Palestinian life under occupation. It is romanticized as steadfastness. But what is steadfast when children throw stones at tanks and youngsters attack trigger-happy soldiers with slingshots? The adults who fail to protect their immature offspring from inevitable harm and instead celebrate their infantile adventurism have inured themselves against normal duties. Both abnormal societies mirror each other in their failure to strive for normal life.

Jewish security consciousness seems totally absent in the Arab quarter of Jerusalem where we stayed at the ill-named, but legendary, American Colony Hotel. Frequented mostly by foreign journalists and seasoned TV crews, the stylish meeting place exudes relaxed calm. But most residents of West Jerusalem avoid this part of the city and are even reluctant to pick you up at the hotel, although no hostile incidents have ever been reported here. When you walk as a visible stranger through the chaotic markets of a West Bank town or the narrow alleys of the Muslim quarter in the old city, you feel safe and welcome. Every desperate merchant explains that his prices have been lowered, because of "the situation." When you still resist the amassed religious kitsch and fake antiques, merchants even try a guilt trip with the question: "You don't like to buy from Arabs?"

The Palestinians—both the stateless former commuters in the territories and the residents of East Jerusalem with a special identity card—suffer most from the depressed Israeli economy and the understandable Jewish paranoia. It was a trusted Arab painter, employed for ten years by Hebrew University, who suddenly snapped and placed a remote-controlled bomb in the crowded student cafeteria, which he had painted only the day before. Allegedly to cut costs, and to the protest of a few concerned faculty members, the institution had just laid off most of its Arab cleaning staff. Three hundred thousand migrants from the Balkans, Africa, and Asia replaced the collectively dismissed Palestinian commuters from the territories. Israeli closure policies have increased unemployment in the West Bank and Gaza dramatically. Therein lies a major difference from apartheid. South African rulers wanted to exploit their subordinates; Israel's rulers want to expel Arabs. The very logic of Zionism implies an Arab-free state or, failing that, second-class status for Palestinians in an official Jewish state. Are heightened misery and induced inequality of a suspect minority the keys to the dominant majority's greater security?

What does the future hold? More of the same and worse through a general shift to the right by the Israeli electorate, lament the dwindling left-wingers. Could a strengthened Sharon, under U.S. pressure, mutate into a de Klerk or a de Gaulle, who not only turns against the few Gaza settlers? De Gaulle abandoned a much stronger settler force in Algeria, who considered themselves a betrayed part of the motherland and relied on its protection. But the Algerian settlers lived some distance from France while their Jewish counterparts colonize next door. The Algerian settlers also lacked the messianic convictions about "redeeming" a promised land. Unlike Algeria, Palestinians, Jewish settlers in their midst, and Israel are much more closely intertwined. In their widely acclaimed book, *The Global Political Economy of Israel*, Jonathan Nitzan and Shimshon Bichler state: "Since the Oslo 'peace' agreement of 1993, the various Israeli governments have removed not a single Jewish settlement in the Occupied Territories. On the contrary, they added more." If the settlers cannot be forced out and the Palestinians cannot be "transferred," is then the logical outcome to live together with equal citizenship in a single state?[6] Locked together by history, geography, and economic interdependency, could two hostile people learn to live together equally, if not by choice then by necessity, just as whites and blacks learned to coexist reluctantly in South Africa after centuries of antagonism?

We ended our journey with the banal and tentative conclusion that a sense of hope needs to be restored on both sides. People take risks when they have clear expectations of a better life and a stake in a promising future. Envisaged security—not increased insecurity—changes hardened attitudes. Because the partisan United States is involved as a resented military power in the region, it falls on the European Union (EU) to hold out an alternative. A contingent offer of EU membership for Israel/Palestine could perhaps provide a sufficient inducement for a negotiated settlement. If a divided Cyprus with a large Turkish Muslim population can become an EU member and the admission of Turkey itself is seriously considered for the future, a democratic Israel/Palestine with adherence to Western human rights standards should also qualify. Just as the European states have overcome their historical enmity in common institutions, so the Israelis and Palestinians would be bound together in a supranational arrangement to their mutual benefit.

I

Probing the South African Lessons

In Part I we aim at three interrelated goals: first, to improve understanding of the reasons for failed conflict resolution in Israel/Palestine by contrasting the situation there with successful peacemaking in South Africa; second, to critically probe analogies between the two disparate situations; and third, to draw specific lessons from the South African experience for alternatives in the Middle East.

Analogies with the South African case are increasingly applied to Israel/Palestine for two different purposes: to showcase South Africa as an inspiring model for a negotiated settlement, and to label Israel a "colonial settler state" that should be confronted with similar strategies (i.e., sanctions, boycotts) as were applied against the apartheid regime. Both assumptions are problematic because of the different historical and sociopolitical contexts. Peacemaking resulted in an inclusive democracy in South Africa, while territorial separation into two states is widely hailed as the solution in Israel/Palestine.

Unresolved issues in comparative politics and practical questions for conflict resolution can be clarified from the real-life laboratories of Israel and South Africa. How do fluctuating threat perceptions influence political tolerance, identity, and voting behavior? How can the educational system, the media, and religious communities best prepare their constituencies for peace, counteracting greater in-group identification, militarization, and increased conformity pressure? What roles do civil society and dissenting intellectuals play in a polarizing conflict? In addressing such questions, six central elements of the conflict in both contexts will be compared: economic interdependence, religious divisions, third-party intervention, leadership, political culture, and violence. The main focus will be on the neglected scope of leadership in ethnic conflicts. This account hopes to debunk false analogies, contribute to critical political literacy, and, perhaps, suggest new, realistic visions for negotiating a violent impasse that increasingly spills over to campuses as heatedly as did the anti-apartheid struggle previously in the 1980s and Vietnam in the 1970s.

1

Controversial Issues in Overview

Context

Although Israel and apartheid South Africa are often equated as "colonial settler societies," we argue that the differences outweigh the similarities. This analysis questions these popular analogies.[1] We believe that when policy makers and political activists reach a more nuanced understanding of the two disparate situations, they are likely to turn away from simplistic emulations of anti-apartheid struggles against Israel and search for more realistic compromises. In this respect, the South African model of postconflict reconciliation may indeed inspire revisions of unworkable policies.

For example, we hypothesize on the basis of the South African experience: An end of violence is the outcome of negotiations but should not be a precondition for their start. Only a relatively unified, not a fragmented, adversary guarantees adherence to controversial compromises and prevents populist outbidding. Transparency and bottom-up involvement through voter education must parallel top-down leadership deals. Leaders who are imposed from outside are tainted and acquire legitimacy only through their own constituencies. Each side has to understand the problem of its partner with his or her constituency and should empower the antagonists to deal with it.

In short, on the one hand, important lessons can be learned from South Africa. On the other hand, the simplistic assumption that the South African model readily lends itself to export may actually retard necessary new solutions by clinging to visions or processes of negotiation that may not work in another context. Above all, in South Africa an entire regime had to be changed while in Israel the occupation and the status of the territories are the main contentious issues. However, should mainstream Palestinians turn away from the two-state option, because permanent settler presence and land annexation render a viable state impossible, then the South African solution of one person/one vote in a single state reemerges as an elusive goal. This would amount to the end of the Zionist quest, because Jews would soon find themselves in a numerical minority. We explore how feasible and realistic such a democratic South African alternative is likely to be in the long run, as opposed to a viable Palestinian state, or a Bantustan-like domination, or even expulsion.

Academic and journalistic commentators on the topic can be roughly divided into three groups:

1. The majority is incensed by the very analogy and deplores what it deems its propagandistic goals. Typical of this group would be Harvard President Lawrence Summer who inveighed against the "boycott Israel" campaign with the statement: "Any comparison between South Africa and Israel is implicitly anti-Semitic."[2] Similarly, Ian Buruma, who rejects the comparison as wrong and inflammatory, deplores that for misguided activists, "Israel, in many respects, has become the South Africa of today."[3]
2. The opposing "Israel is Apartheid" advocates include most Palestinians, many Third World academics, and several Jewish post-Zionists who idealistically predict an ultimate South African solution of a common or binational state. Prominent South Africans in this category, like Nobel laureate Desmond Tutu, advocate similar anti-apartheid strategies against Israel and assume that strong pressure would produce similar outcomes. The Israeli activist historian Ilan Pappe (*Green Left Weekly,* September 1, 2004) argues that the nonviolent strategy has no chance, "unless we create an international atmosphere in which Israel is treated as South Africa was." A South African political scientist, Na'eem Jeenah, writes: "Israel is, in fact, an apartheid state.... And I suggest, similar problems within similar contexts can use similar solutions."[4] A British social scientist, Daryl Glaser, starts his moral comparison with: "Most critics of Zionism argue that it is 'like apartheid.' I consider this (for Israel) unflattering claim of likeness to be substantially justified, though those making it rarely provide sophisticated arguments to back it up."[5] Noam Chomsky compares apartheid favorably by asserting that the separation wall is "helping turn Palestinian communities into dungeons, next to which the Bantustans of South Africa look like symbols of freedom, sovereignty and self-determination."[6] Since the 1980s, Uri Davis, focusing on legal arrangements, has argued the case for "Apartheid Israel."[7]

3. A third group diagnoses similarities and differences, but, above all, looks to South Africa for guidance. "Israelis and Palestinians could learn a lot from how South Africa's F. W. de Klerk approached peace," comments *Globe & Mail* columnist Shira Herzog in her article titled "Take South Africa's Lead!"[8] In a similar vein, Tony Judt draws parallels[9] and, like many liberals in this camp, calls upon the United States to impose a solution on the warring factions.

Various political actors also use the South African analogy self-servingly in their exhortations and rationalizations. The Deputy Prime Minister in Sharon's government says: "I shudder to think that liberal Jewish organizations that shouldered the burden of the struggle against apartheid in South Africa will lead the struggle against us."[10] Similarly, former Prime Minister Barak warns of broad international support if the Palestinians turn away from the two-state option and demand a single state "in the spirit of the twenty-first century," as long as there is no acceptable Israeli plan on the table. South African civic democracy haunts the Zionist Left and Right as a nightmare. In Barak's reasoning:

> "One man one vote"? Remind you of something? Yes, South Africa. And that's no accident. It's precisely their intention. And that's their long-term plan. So, we have to say honestly today: the strategic blindness of the Israeli Right and the Sharon government's effort to grab more than it can hold, indeed endanger the future of the Zionist enterprise.[11]

United States rhetorical cautioning, though never followed by action, reinforces a new hegemony of beleaguered siege in Israel. Colin Powell muses: "I don't believe that we can accept a situation that results in anything that one might characterize as apartheid or Bantuism."[12] Because of this political climate, spokespersons of all parties, including Sharon, have repeatedly deplored the occupation and seeming "South Africanization" but have done everything to entrench it. The hypocritical rhetoric masks the successful game of "playing for time" while changing the sociostructural reality. The huge discrepancy between words and deeds simultaneously assuages critics at home and abroad with hope for peace while quietly accommodating settler expansionists with new opportunities.

Uses and Abuses of the Israel–South Africa Comparison

With a slightly different perspective, one could state that comparisons between South Africa and Israel have been employed for three different but interrelated purposes. The first purpose is to contrast forms of domination and resistance of a subjugated population. The second is to focus on ideological similarities, as expressed in the equation of Zionism with racism or the self-concept of some Afrikaners and Jews as "God's Chosen People." The third is to draw strategic lessons from the negotiated settlement in South Africa for the unresolved conflict in the Middle East. The latter is the main focus of this study.

Academic comparisons of Israel and apartheid South Africa mostly invoke the notion of settler societies,[13] focus on similar religious mythologies[14] or deal with interstate relations as an "unnatural alliance."[15] In the colonial settler perspective, alien intruders conquer and displace an indigenous population. They act on behalf of a metropolitan power. The colonial analogy has inspired both Palestinian and South African black resistance. However, settlers also develop their own interests, independent of and often against their sponsor abroad. The colonial concept leaves unanswered when and how settlers become indigenous.[16] As the always-incisive Canadian columnist Rick Salutin comments: "Israel was never just a 'colonial settler-state' like, for instance, South Africa. It was a people who felt they were returning home."[17]

The Israeli sociologist Eliezer Ben-Rafael[18] distinguishes between "colonialism" and "colonization," which he considers a more accurate, though not morally superior, description of Zionism. Ben-Rafael wants to avoid the negative connotations of a vanishing colonialism, feeding into "Israelophobia," while highlighting the frequency of new nations establishing themselves in the modern era. However, if colonization means "a new population" displacing a local one and building up "a society of its own," as Ben-Rafael defines colonization, the distinction is merely semantic and the permanent conquest may actually be worse than temporary economic colonial exploitation for the indigenous people, the frequency and general acceptance of new settler dominance in North and South America notwithstanding.

Yet the right of settlers to coexist with displaced people in the same land has long been conceded by mainstream Palestinian leaders (Oslo Accord) and confirmed by the ANC's Freedom Charter of 1955. Disputed issues are the terms of coexistence, the meaning of equal citizenship, and how to redress the legacy of past injustice.[19] The notion of "settler societies" carries explanatory weight only if their varieties are distinguished. As Canadian historian Donald Akenson has pointed out, "there is scarcely a society in Europe or North and South America that is not a settler society."[20]

Emphasizing the similarities between apartheid and Israeli forms of domination has the effect of delegitimizing Israeli governance. After fascism and African decolonization, the apartheid regime constituted an international pariah state, and equating the Jewish treatment of Palestinians with Bantustans and the suppression of national liberation casts the Jewish state in a similar pariah role. Already in the 1980s, prominent Israelis such as Shlomo Avineri warned that continued control over the West Bank and Gaza "means continued oppression of a million-and-a-half

Palestinians and a slow 'South Africanization' of Israel."[21] Buruma, who doubts the validity of the comparison, nevertheless diagnoses that "Israel, in many respects, has become . . . the litmus test of one's progressive credentials," similar to the Spanish Civil War in the 1930s, Vietnam in the 1960s, Chile in the 1970s, and apartheid in the 1980s.[22]

An obvious difference between Israel proper and apartheid South Africa lies in the universal suffrage. It includes the 20 percent Palestinian Israeli citizens in Israel who have the right to vote for the Knesset. However, if the Palestinian territories under more or less permanent Israeli occupation and settler presence are considered part of the entity under analysis, the comparison between a disenfranchised African population in apartheid South Africa and the three and a half million stateless Palestinians under Israeli domination gains more validity. Most Israeli social scientists treat the two territories as separate issues and thereby avoid drawing some uncomfortable conclusions.

Moreover, the Israeli Palestinians resemble in many ways "Colored" and Indian South Africans. As targets of cooptation, they have been allowed to vote since 1983, albeit for separate parliaments, which held joint sittings with the exclusively white chamber as well. The toy parliaments of the minorities could never outvote their white creators and acquired little legitimacy and voter interest. While the more legitimate Arab parties sometimes hold the balance of power in a split Knesset, they also struggle with widespread apathy of their alienated constituents. Above all, both Israeli Palestinians and Colored and Indian South Africans are restricted to second-class citizen status when another ethnic group monopolizes state power, treats the minorities as intrinsically suspect, and legally prohibits their access to land or allocates civil service position or per capita expenditure on education differentially between dominant and minority citizens. Another example: A 2003 Israeli law forbids Israeli Palestinians newly married to non–Israeli Palestinians to live together in Israel.

Israel's immigration practices clearly parallel differential immigration entitlements under apartheid. South Africa encouraged and subsidized white immigration from any country. Nonwhite immigration was simply not allowed. However, unlike the situation in Israel, security justifications were never used—it was simple and pure racism. The ruling minority had to be strengthened and not "swamped" by more blacks coming in. The closest parallel concerns the one million second- and third-generation Indian minority who customarily imported brides from India. Various linguistic, religious, and caste subgroups practiced traditional endogamy, which required the pool of potential partners to be larger than that available in South Africa. Apartheid outlawed this practice and cut the Indian community off from any contact with India because Indians were supposed to "go back" rather than come in. No exceptions were allowed. Indian South Africans were one of the most law-abiding, well-educated, hard-working, and traditional of South Africa's ethnic communities, yet because they were considered (by blacks and whites alike) eternal "aliens," they were also on the lowest rung of the communal ladder.

Ironically, the apartheid stricture also had the progressive effect of enabling the group to develop a distinctive Indian South African identity, which was more cosmopolitan in nature. Most Western constitutions award families special protection from disruption as they are considered the building stones of healthy states. By splitting up families, Israel does the opposite and does this on a discriminatory ethnic basis, as Jewish citizens are not affected. It amounts to a violation of basic human rights, respected even by European xenophobic states with regard to noncitizen migrants. Whether a self-declared Jewish state in theory and practice, therefore, represents an "ethnic state," an "ethnocracy," an "ethnic democracy," or (if these are oxymorons) no democracy at all, as some Palestinians assert, is endlessly debated among social scientists.

The apartheid analogy is mainly employed to mobilize people and motivate action. The moral comparison, however, yields little insights into specific circumstances that have to be evaluated in their own right. Even commentators who diagnose Israel's human rights abuses realize this. Thus U.S. law professor Dena S. Davis writes:

> The references to South Africa's former government have wasted a lot of time and energy on the pointless question of whether Israel's human rights abuses approach the level of that famously immoral regime. I have absolutely no interest in this question. The questions that interest me are: Do Israel's occupation of the Gaza Strip and the West Bank and its treatment of the Palestinians constitute a serious abuse of human rights? I'd say yes.[23]

The Israeli sociologist Avishai Ehrlich has pointed to the difference between Zionism and other nationalisms: "Zionism is an oddity among modern nationalisms—it did not just call for self-determination in the place where its 'nationals' resided, but shifted its imagined community to a different place. Zionism is thus a colonizatory ideology and project."[24] However, while all other European colonizations were driven primarily by economic motives, the original Labor Zionists moved elsewhere because of persecution and vulnerability. It makes little difference to the displaced indigenous people whether colonization comes out of necessity or out of greed. The newcomers, however, acquire a different relationship to the land, because they have no homeland to return to, unlike economic colonizers. Moreover, once the quest for a safe territory is focused on an imagined ancestral homeland, the guilt of alien intruders is removed. In their perception—or, as others would argue, self-deception—Zionists now reclaimed the land "by right" of return. The later religious zealots of Gush Enumin even invoke divine destiny in occupying their outposts in Eretz Israel. Whatever the historical differences between Zionism and Afrikaner nationalism, their adherents share the notion of their current residential territory as their only homeland, regardless of whether this is accepted by their neighbors.

The Zionist project was further strengthened demographically and ideologically by the expulsion of Jews from most Arab countries. This expulsion was in direct response to the establishment of Israel. These low-status Sephardics and their descendants form the backbone of anti-Arab hostility. These voters for right-wing parties deeply resent their double discrimination by Ashkenazi insiders and Arab outsiders. If there ever is return of or reconciliation with or compensation for displaced Palestinians, an acknowledgment of displaced Jews must be part of the new justice. Similarly, the social base for right-wing Afrikaner parties was predominantly rural people, the lower echelons of the civil service, and the remnants of the Afrikaner working class—all sections that were dropped from state protection by an increasingly self-confident bureaucratic bourgeoisie.

Palestinian refugees from the 1948 war are equally mistreated in Arab countries. Particularly Lebanon has created a foreign underclass by not allowing them to put down roots, acquire citizenship, or improve their life chances. The Palestinians are herded into camps, fed by a UN agency, and treated as outcasts. Under the pretence that Arab states do not want to solve Israel's problems or absolve it of its legal responsibilities, several generations of Palestinians were made into victims. Instead of harnessing the potential and talents of unwelcome newcomers, the shortsighted policy radicalized many of the permanent victims. On the other hand, Palestinians in southern Lebanon also have to blame themselves for their unpopularity. When the PLO formed a semistate within a dependent state in Lebanon in the 1970s, they did not endear themselves to their Shiite neighbors. As Adam Shatz has observed: "The Shiites may despise the Israelis, but they have no love for the Palestinians, who ruled southern Lebanon harshly in the 1970s and often treated Shiites with contempt."[25]

In the ideological battle for legitimacy, most Jewish analysts view their relationship with the Palestinians not as a colonial one, but as a conflict between two competing national entities. In their self-concept, Zionists are simply returning to their ancestral homeland from which they were dispersed two millennia ago. Originally most did not intend to exploit native labor and resources, as colonizers do. As is well known, deep splits about the trade-offs for peace and security, religious notions of sacred places, and the nature of national identity divide Israeli society. Similar deep cleavages occurred when Afrikaner nationalists were confronted with the pressure for reform. Inexplicable perceptions may be labeled false, mythical, irrational, or illegitimate. However, because people give meaning to their lives and interpret their worlds through these diverse ideological prisms, the perceptions are real and have to be taken seriously. People act on the basis of their belief systems.

Probably the only unifying conviction across a deeply divided political spectrum in Israel concerns the preservation of a Jewish state as a response to historical anti-Semitism. Such endorsements of an official ethnic state defy many prescriptions of multicultural citizenship in a liberal democracy. As a perceived sanctuary and guarantor of ethnic survival in a hostile neighborhood, however, it is based on the trauma of collective victimhood. The legacy of the Holocaust cannot be compared with Afrikaner anxieties. From the experience of horrific victimization emanates the tendency to reject any criticism of Israeli policy by outsiders as anti-Semitism.

Understandable outrage about the Israeli occupation and Likud's hard-line policies may well have also triggered latent anti-Semites to express their bigotry openly. Anti-Jewish attitudes sometimes hide under the guise of pro-Palestinian empathy. Therefore, the clear distinction between despicable anti-Jewish sentiments and legitimate criticism of Israeli policy has to be made and underscored. The robust debate among the global Jewish community itself about Israeli policies demonstrates this distinction. Outside commentators should be sensitive about fueling anti-Semitism, which often reveals itself in the almost automatic ascription of negative features to Jewish activities. Jewish names are automatically associated with conspiracies or powerful lobbies. When the Jewish state as a collective is singled out as the only violator of human rights among dozens of ruthless dictatorships (as happened during the UN Durban conference on racism in 2001), this appears as yet another variation of anti-Semitism. Even the Czarist forgery "The Protocol of the Elders of Zion," together with medieval-style blood libels, is frequently resurrected in the discourse of the Arab world. Government-controlled television in Arab countries regularly broadcasts inflammatory sermons in hundreds of mosques praying, "to destroy tyrannical Jews, humiliate infidels, give victory to the *mujahidin* everywhere and liberate the Al-Aqsa mosque from the hands of the usurpers." Shlomo Avineri has asked:

> When suicide bombers receive official state burials by the Palestinian Authority, with a Palestinian police guard of honor, are declared national heroes and their biographies are taught in Palestinian schools as role models—what exactly should the liberal intelligentsia's politically correct response be?[26]

Avineri's rhetorical puzzle raises several strategic questions. More than six hundred prominent Palestinians who signed an appeal against such counterproductive "military operations, which target civilians in Israel" point out that they "kill all possibility for the two peoples to live in peace side by side in two neighboring countries."[27] Answering Avineri can perhaps be best expressed in what morally aware intellectuals should not do: Reinforce the mutual cycle of violence by supporting a policy of escalating revenge, demonize opponents without understanding the historical context of the conflicts, or abandon communication and negotiations until the antagonist surrenders to enunciated conditions.

In positive terms, liberal intellectuals can demystify collective stereotypes about the enemy. They can question their own mythologies of justified action and moral self-righteousness. They can learn realistic lessons from conflicts elsewhere without falling into the trap of uncritically emulating strategies by adopting simplistic comparisons. This danger is exemplified by the calls for an academic boycott of Israeli institutions, or Desmond Tutu's advice to repeat against Israel as a whole the "divestment movement of the 1980s" against apartheid. This falsely assumes that the end of apartheid resulted largely from international pressure. A similar problematic optimism is contained in Judt's exhortation: "Following fifty years of vicious repression and exploitation, white South Africans handed over power to a black majority who replaced them without violence or revenge. Is the Middle East so different?"[28] Yes, it is. The difference is vast and lies specifically in South Africa's economic interdependence, which contrasts with separation in the Middle East; in religion as a moral unifier, which contrasts with religion as a divisive force for competing claims; in moral isolation and erosion, which contrast with international support; in a mutual perception of stalemate, which contrasts with a conviction of victory; and in the utter illegitimacy of institutionalized racial discrimination, which contrasts with the more legitimate ethnic maintenance. After all, most of those who advocate U.S. pressure on Israel wish to preserve the Jewish state, in contrast to the anti-apartheid movement, which rightly aimed at abolishing the whole system of racial governance.

Without abandoning moral judgments or even outrage, intellectuals can propagate painful realism, eschew wishful thinking, and discern a politically feasible compromise solution rather than some morally desirable utopia. Informed by the particularities and uniqueness of each conflict, policy advisors and opinion makers need to be wary of the trap of uncritically emulating recommended strategies. In their political support they could show critical solidarity, rather than follow a "correct line" unquestioned. If this is the lesson to be drawn from analogies with South Africa, then Buruma is wrong when he states, "The comparison with South Africa is intellectually lazy, morally questionable, and possibly even mendacious."[29] Despite the earlier-noted differences, probing the Israel–South Africa analogy does furnish insights into conflict resolution and obstacles to a negotiated settlement, while at the same time revealing the limits of such comparisons.

The Relevance of the Middle East for South Africa

Because much has been written about the important U.S.-Israel relations and the role of the Jewish diaspora in influencing policy, we will use the lesser known South African case to illuminate the relevancy of the

Middle East beyond its borders. The South African discourse may well be representative of other multiethnic societies with Muslim and Jewish communities.

Apart from the moral and political issues at stake, developments in the Middle East affect South Africa for three main reasons. The first reason is that increased polarization in Israel/Palestine could potentially spill over into intergroup relations in South Africa. Traditionally, strong identifications with Israel by the 80,000 anxious Jewish South Africans is resented by the eight times stronger Muslim community that champions—with equal fervor—the Palestinian cause. Such conflicts could threaten South Africa's hard-won social cohesion. Whatever progress has been made in harmonious race relations, reconciliation, and national unity could be undermined by new partisan stances triggered from the outside.

In this vein, a respected mainstream religious body, the Muslim Judicial Council (MJC), announced in March 2002 that it had abandoned its conciliatory stance on the Middle East conflict and now supported the Islamic groups Hamas, Islamic Jihad, and Hezbollah, although the MJC also notes it does not support terrorism. "We recognize those groups as legitimate freedom fighters for the liberation of Palestine. We view them in the same light as people view the role of the ANC and PAC in the liberation struggle of this country," the MJC's deputy president, Moulana Ighsaan Hendricks, is quoted as saying.[30] In response, Philip Krawitz, chairman of the South African Jewish Board of Deputies' Cape Council, pointed out that the supported organizations "by their words and deeds have made it clear that their aim is not to come to any final status agreement with Israel but to destroy Israel altogether" by any means necessary. The Hamas rhetoric of eliminating the Jewish state as well as the organization's sectarian anti-Semitism also runs counter to the widely accepted South African government policy that peace in the Middle East necessitates creating a Palestinian state, existing side by side with the state of Israel in security with its neighbors. "The Board believes that the conflict in the Middle East should remain there and not negatively impact on the good relations between Muslims and Jews in South Africa."[31]

With instant global communication, however, political emotions cannot be confined to one place. They easily jump borders, as dozens of placard demonstrations, protest marches, and prayer sessions in South Africa have shown. In such a charged atmosphere, the more violent methods of Middle East confrontations may also find emulators in South Africa. These prospects were somewhat diffused by the publicity surrounding a manifesto, "Not in our name," initiated by Minister Ronnie Kasrils and ANC MLA (Member of Provincial Legislature) Max Ozinsky. The initiative demonstrated that those of Jewish ancestry maintain diverse positions in a wide spectrum of opinion.[32] With its direct criticism of Israeli policy, however, it disturbed the supposed Jewish consensus and led to a robust debate within the community. The overwhelming majority of Jewish South Africans dissociated themselves from Kasril's document, which attracted only three hundred signatures. Kasril's stance is, however, unequivocally supported by the ANC. The ANC's Gauteng general secretary, David Makhura, called the reoccupation of Palestinian-controlled territories "a blatant violation of human rights," amounting to "an act of state terrorism by the Israeli government."[33] Other commentators have remarked on the contradiction when the South African government criticizes Israel but is not prepared to apply the same standards of behavior to its neighbor Zimbabwe.

After the assassinations of Hamas spiritual leader Sheikh Yassin in March 2004, several South African newspapers urged Jewish South Africans to speak out against "Sharon's policy of mindless reprisals, and to press for peaceful solutions."[34] A flood of furious responses accused the papers of "impudence and moral arrogance." The national chairperson of the South African Jewish Board of Deputies complained about "a modern-day version of classic Jew-baiting, a pernicious form of collective harassment" that tries to "emotionally blackmail South African Jewry into denouncing the actions of co-religionists."[35] UCT academic Milton Shain labeled the act of singling out Jews collectively for not criticizing Israel as "anti-Semitic in effect, if not in intent."[36] He asks why Russians in South Africa are not called upon "to condemn the Putin government for its extra-judicial assassinations of Chechens . . . and all Muslims in South Africa to condemn their co-religionists for what is being done in the Sudan by Muslims to Christians and animists, or what is being done in the name of al-Qaeda"? Good questions, indeed, because human rights violations everywhere should be assailed, and not only by concerned fellow ethnics. Nonetheless, turning a blind eye to abuses by other groups, as hypocritical as it is, should not justify doing the same.

No other diaspora cultivates such close bonds to its imagined homeland as does the roughly two-thirds of the twelve million self-identified Jews outside Israel. In contrast to emigrants who left other countries for many reasons, most Jews abroad have never lived in or even visited Israel, yet paradoxically they feel an unparalleled affinity to the country as a sanctuary or religious heartland. At the Passover Seder, millions of Jews around the world celebrate the exodus from Egypt, the redemption of the slaves, and the liberation from bondage. Each believer is obligated to see himself or herself as if he or she personally went out of Egypt. Even if the holiday ritual is largely emptied of its historical origin, the clarion call, "next year in Jerusalem," resonates, even with secular members of the group. Marriages and bar mitzvahs invoke the land of Moses. No such reminders of religious bonds exist for Russians, Irish, or Indians abroad. Even Muslims who pray in the direction of Mecca or undertake a hadj hardly feel connected with the affairs of the Saudi state. There is no Muslim state or authority that speaks for all coreligionists. Only Israel claims to be the home of all Jews who receive instant citizenship upon immigration. An "in gathering" of Christians of all varieties occurs in the afterlife, not in Rome or Moscow.

In addition to these religious invocations, organized Jewry in the form of the executives of the South African Jewish Board of Deputies, South African Zionist Federation, South African Union for Progressive Judaism, and the Chief Rabbi identify themselves collectively as supporters of Israel: "South African Jews are overwhelming Zionist and are born Zionist. Those Jews who actively denounce Zionism are in the extreme minority and are on the fringe of the community."[37] In such a statement, Jews are not singled out but are self-professed. Why should it be "sinister" and anti-Semitic to criticize such uncritical organized support? Real anti-Semites are keen to destroy Israel, but not "to press for peaceful solutions," as argued in the *Mail & Guardian* editorial that provoked the ire. The real friends of Israel try to save it from itself, yet are denounced as Jew haters. Those who acquiesce in Israel's self-destructive policies are hailed as the country's true friends. An ironic reversal of solidarity, indeed!

Coreligionists' reluctance to take a stance against extremist acts seems to afflict Jews and Muslims alike. After 9/11, the bombings in Bali, and the bombings of the synagogues in Tunis and Turkey and trains in Madrid by self-declared jihadists, one could have expected the vast majority of moderate Muslims in every country to publicly distance themselves from such deeds, if for no other reason than to rescue religion from being besmirched by terrorists. Yet nowhere did Islamist street demonstrations take place, particularly in Arab countries. A few unrepresentative local leaders uttered ambiguous explanations, but the majority of believers remained silent and facilitated the false impression of terrorist sympathy. Aggressive Zionism is at least challenged by peace-oriented, dissident Jews within Israel and abroad. Where are the organized Muslim voices that challenge a mindless religious "Kulturkampf"? Where is an Islamist "Not in my name" movement? Why do Muslim elites allow themselves to be perceived as supporters of terrorism?

This perception is reinforced when Muslims all over the world do demonstrate, namely against Israel. But why is the justified protest often accompanied with grotesque images of militancy and Judeophobia? In this vein, reports of a march in front of the Israeli embassy in Pretoria showed a man, carrying his six-year-old child, with a fake explosive belt on his back. The father is quoted as saying that his son wants to be a shahid (martyr). When anti-Israel protesters display swastikas or break up Holocaust discussions and denounce them as pro-Israel propaganda, as happened at the UN conference in Durban in 2001, one could almost suspect a Zionist lobby behind the macabre spectacle, were it not for real. Another example of Muslim and Jewish unquestioning commitment to their respective causes stems from two personal experiences, albeit separated by many years: both camps' willingness to serve militarily as ideological mercenaries.

In 1967, while teaching undergraduates at the University of Natal, many South African Jewish students suddenly absented themselves, because they had joined the Six-Day War in Israel. Almost forty years later, in April 2004, a female Muslim student in a graduate class at the University of Cape Town reported in her weekly diary assignment: "At last week's Khutbahs (sermons) a number of Mosques in Cape Town called on young men to go to Palestine to defend Al-Aqsa Mosque and to fight the Israelis." However, she also added a telling personal comment, which signals hope and change during the four decades of hot and cold warfare:

> I find this concept laughable. For most middle-class Muslim men the worst thing that would happen to them is for their BMWs to get damaged. There is no way that these men could pick up arms and fight, most of them are paralyzed by the thought of crime in South Africa; there is only a very slim chance that they would last in combat.

The South African Jewish BMW drivers who shun the Israeli army also mirror their Islamic counterparts. However, while minority consumerism may dampen militarism, majority poverty and insecurity seek identity in ideological commitment.

The second way in which developments in the Middle East affect South Africa is that South African politicians are eager to share the lessons of peaceful conflict resolution and Middle Eastern activists often visit South Africa to learn from anti-apartheid struggles. South African politicians justifiably pride themselves on their negotiated settlement. In May 2002, a contingent of Israeli reservists, who refused military service in the occupied territories, met with members of the former End Conscription Campaign to learn from their tactics. At a January 2002 conference near Cape Town, President Mbeki and other leading members of the old and new order spent three days conveying to four Palestinian ministers and several former Israeli office holders the secrets of the South African success story. Since then, regular mutual visits and conferences by South Africans and Israeli/Palestinians have deepened the contacts across the political spectrum. A distinguished South African law professor, John Dugard, serves as the UN's special rapporteur for the occupied Palestinian territories. When ANC chief negotiator Cyril Ramaphosa was nominated as a member of a UN team to investigate the human rights situation in the territories, all editorials wallowed in praise and celebrated the wise choice. "Given the seemingly intractable problems SA faced prior to Nelson Mandela's release from prison in 1990, and the manner in which we resolved them, our citizens are especially well placed to share experiences with Palestinians and Israelis."[38] South Africa was again ready to solve the apparently unsolvable.

The third way in which developments in the Middle East affect South Africa is that apart from the South African government's increased role in international forums, the postapartheid state frequently hosts international conferences at which controversial global issues dominate the agenda. On such occasions, public opinion is often mobilized with slogans and simplistic analogies. A prime example was the UN World Conference against Racism, Xenophobia and Related Intolerances in Durban in September 2001. A majority of the 10,000 delegates and non-governmental organization (NGO) participants endorsed the long-discarded notion that "Zionism is racism." They were unable to distinguish Jewish nationalism (Zionism) from apartheid racism. Serious discussions of anti-Semitism as a classical form of historical racism were broken up by enraged activists, who considered any mention of the Holocaust an apology for Israel, as previously discussed.

False Analogies and Theoretical Approaches

Against this background, the following analysis examines the usefulness of the comparison between South Africa and Israel by probing some commonly held stereotypes and false analogies on both sides. Israeli policy on the West Bank cannot be compared with the Nazi occupation of France, as some Palestinians assert, nor was Arafat another Hitler, as some Israelis insist.

At the same time, the simplistic equations of Palestinian resistance strategies with South African liberation struggles are critiqued not only for those strategies' counterproductive ineffectiveness,but also for their inexcusable assault on innocent civilians. Instead of winning over Israeli opinion for a just settlement, the attacks on civilians have marginalized the once stronger Israeli peace camp. The assumed "softening" of Israeli public opinion has resulted instead in a hardening. Recent research has also shown that South Africans similarly display heightened intolerance in the face of increased threats.[39] As the ANC leadership gradually realized, the success of its liberation struggle lay not in "out-fighting" the opponent, but in what the ANC called "armed propaganda." Such a strategy was aimed at "out-legitimizing" and morally isolating the adversary, both domestically and internationally. Particularly with suicide attacks against civilians, the Palestinian militants achieved the opposite: They reinforced Israel's contention that after escaping Nazi extermination Jews are again the victims and have to guard their survival by all means possible, rather than confront Palestinian suffering and dispossession.

In short, by looking at the Middle East conflict through South African lenses and experiences, a better comparative understanding of two major global predicaments may be achieved. There are lessons for Israeli/Palestinian peace activists, and South Africans may gain a more realistic appreciation of their accomplishments by revisiting the falsely labeled "miracle." No blueprints or solutions are offered, yet clarifying the issues comparatively could prove helpful for achieving the desired outcomes.

The literature on protracted conflicts assumes that violence begets counterviolence in a spiraling escalation until a "hurting stalemate" is reached or an outside power intervenes. This conventional wisdom needs to be reexamined. Following I. W. Zartman's extensive work, much of the literature on negotiations is dominated by an abstract discussion of the "ripeness" of a conflict to be settled.[40] Some authors construct complex mathematical dyads of "bilateral reciprocity"[41] others emphasize threat perceptions[42] in "mutually hurting" or bearable stalemates that affect morale maintenance and "battle fatigue."[43] South Africa and Israel lend themselves as testing grounds for these theories. At the end of apartheid at least, neither side seemed "fatigued," but both anticipated a future weakened position for different reasons if they did not negotiate from a current position of relative strength. Yet there are limits to rational choice approaches and cost-benefit calculations to the analysis of ethnic conflicts. As aptly formulated by Robert Rothstein: "What is missing from interest-based analysis is the emotional depth of the conflict, the intensity of hatred, mistrust, and contempt that has developed and deepened over time."[44] German philosopher Jürgen Habermas' "discourse rationality" and "communicative competence" fade under these conditions.[45] Ofer Grosbard seems more persuasive—"the peace process is, fundamentally, an emotional process."[46]

This study focuses on six areas of comparison: economic interdependence, religion, third-party intervention, leadership, political culture, and violence. In all six areas, the differences between apartheid South Africa and Israel/Palestine outweigh the similarities. These six conditions may have favored peace building in South Africa but mostly they serve as impediments to compromise in the Middle East. Nevertheless, it would be unjustified to conclude that the Middle East cannot learn lessons from the South African negotiation process. For a small minority of Jews and Palestinians, the most crucial achievement of the South African settlement—an inclusive, democratic, secular, common state—stands as a utopian ideal. However, the vast majority of Jewish and Palestinian nationalists now favor partition into two nation-states. This solution is the opposite of the South African settlement and, one would expect on first reflection, is easier to achieve than peaceful coexistence in an integrated state. However, there is strong disagreement as to what constitutes a viable Palestinian state, what are legitimate security and identity concerns, and what amounts to a fair compromise in a long-standing conflict in which both hostile people have rights to ancestral land, sacred places, and scarce resources.

Recent literature on the South African transition emphasizes the structural factors (demographic changes, sanctions cost of insurrection, end of cold war) that "forced" the minority to change course.[47] This deterministic focus underrates the role played by political leaders and intellectuals in interpreting objective developments, as aptly highlighted by Hermann Giliomee in his magisterial study of the Afrikaners.[48] Such interpretations differ widely in an ethnic regime that is never a monolithic bloc. When ethnic conformists follow trustingly a political leadership, regardless of radical policy changes, the stature and vision of leaders would appear far more important than social scientists commonly tend to admit, although successful leaders must also be in tune with major material and ideal interests of their constituencies.

Conventional explanations of policy change focus on turning points when rising costs outweigh benefits. These rational choice explanations underestimate leadership agency. Leaders, however, are rarely only shrewdly calculating individuals, but always come with their own idiosyncrasies. Even a major change in the political environment—such as the collapse of the Soviet Union that finally triggered the South African transition—might not have been sufficient to have led a Conservative Party in power to similar shifts. Equally important: Without a conciliatory Mandela counseling reconciliation and assisting the Afrikaner leap into another order, the settlement may have gone off the rail. In his intriguing comparison of Israeli "ethnic policing" with Serbian "ethnic cleansing" in different institutional settings, McGill sociologist James Ron quotes an Israeli senior official: "Israel's greatest nightmare is that one day, there will appear a Palestinian Nelson Mandela in the West Bank who will demand 'one man, one vote.' That will be the end of Israel as a Jewish democracy."[49] It remains to be seen whether Sharon acquires the foresight of an F. W. de Klerk. There is no de Gaulle in sight in Washington who could impose a solution on embittered antagonists. When Judt concludes: "There is only one possible peaceful outcome, everyone knows what it entails, and it is going to have to be imposed from the outside, the sooner the better"[50]—he is waiting for Godot.

Our analysis revisits "the miracle" of the negotiated settlement in South Africa when almost everybody predicted a racial civil war.[51] Why did a privileged South African ruling group "surrender without defeat"?[52] What divisions occurred and how were internal cleavages handled? How was the historic compromise marketed to a skeptical constituency and ideas of reconciliation disseminated (media, schools)? We look anew at the players who negotiated the thirty-four principles of the Interim Constitution, including party representatives who initially boycotted the assembly (AZAPO, PAC, IFP, Afrikaner right wing). With hindsight, what advice would they give their Middle East counterparts in drawing in all factions that could wreck a compromise?

In Israel we explore whether a moral erosion of a Zionist consensus can be realistically expected, similar to the defection of Afrikaner intellectuals from the nationalist cause. In 1986, only 3 percent of whites supported black rule, according to Giliomee,[53] yet barely a decade later most wonder why they had not made that mind change earlier. Despite a secularized majority, the challenges to religious instruction and programs for tolerance and peace building would seem particularly important for the Islamist and Jewish ultraorthodox sectors. Do the sermons and publications of faith leaders reflect the need for nonviolent compromise or indoctrinate in mutual demonization? What support to whom can be expected from the international community and diaspora? How is international opinion influenced by local adversaries? What are the benefits and pitfalls of outside funding of NGOs pre-, during, and posttransition?

The role of the security establishment and the rivalries between different security agencies is crucial in times of heightened anxieties. How are military, police, and freelance militias brought and kept under political control? In South Africa, the business sector responded to the escalating crisis proactively by mobilizing resources both in support of and in opposition to the status quo. Can the costs of instability for globalizing corporations, the brain drain by mobile professionals, or the decline of tourism in Israel lead to similar business pressure for a settlement? The success of economic sanctions is often overrated. Blanket economic and moral penalties can also lead to a hardening, now-we-have-to-go-it-alone stance. Therefore, what kind of specific third-party intervention would be most effective under which circumstances? Is the stalled "road map" or the similar Geneva Accord a way out of Israel's "apartheid dilemma"? Is the United States performing a "balancing act"[54] or acting as a "dishonest broker"?[55] Optimistically, despite the sharp swing to the Right and hawkish actions on both sides since September 2000, the collapse of the 1993 Oslo Accord, and the failure of the Camp David/Taba negotiations,[56] support for the longtime peace process remains among a majority of both Palestinians and Jewish Israelis alike. However, as the Steinmetz survey of December 2004 concluded for Israelis: "The intensity of the wish for a permanent settlement with the Palestinians is much greater (75%) than the belief that it is attainable (32%)."

2

Nationalism, Patriotism, and Multiculturalism Revisited

Ultra-Nationalism in Defiance of Universal Norms

Authors writing about divided societies need to clarify their position on four contested concepts with multiple meanings, particularly for a North American audience: nationalism, patriotism, multiculturalism, and cosmopolitanism.

As is well known, two versions of *nationalism* need to be distinguished: civic and ethnic nationalism. *Civic* nationalism is based on citizenship and allocates equal rights to all residents of a state. Provided they are legal citizens, their ethnic origin, race, or religion does not matter in these terms. Western liberal democracies have embraced civic nationalism as their constitutive principle, although an unofficial and informal ethnic hierarchy and social discrimination continues to various degrees.

Ethnic nationalism, on the other hand, elevates origin, descent, or religion to the crucial criteria of belonging. An ethnic state privileges one group with the "right" features over other citizens with the "different" markers. Some states exclude some longtime residents from citizenship altogether or relegate them to second-class citizens. In short, while civic nationalism is *inclusive,* ethnic nationalism is largely *exclusive* to various degrees in any given case.

As an official Jewish state, Israel could be labeled a typical ethnic state. So are most Arab states, which have made Islam and Islamic law the official state religion where citizens of other faiths are merely tolerated at best, or ghettoized and marginalized at worst. Are the European nation-states not also ethnic states? It needs to be reiterated that the distinguishing criteria between an ethnic state and a civic state is not the absence of social discrimination, which exists in both varieties, but whether formal equality of citizens is at least enshrined in law. In this regard, the European countries, as well as the immigrant societies of North America and Australia are not ethnic states. New residents may face various obstacles to acquire citizenship, but once they have their cherished passports, they are entitled to the same rights and privileges as native citizens. In contrast, when ethnic nationalism is propagated by the state and preference written in its self-concept, national symbols, and official policy, minorities experience rejection and nonrecognition. Ethnic nationalism feeds internal conflict, because minorities or "others" are suspected to be "fifth columns." They are considered outsiders who do not really belong to an imagined community of insiders.

The danger of ethnic nationalism can be demonstrated with extreme Zionism. While Jewish nationalism (Zionism) comes in many varieties and conflicting visions, its extreme form shows no qualms about uprooting other inhabitants in the interest of its own group expansion. On the other side on the spectrum of nationalism are located the Liberal Zionists, who support Jewish self-determination with equal rights for non-Jewish minorities, or Labor Zionists, with yet another agenda of a "normal" community, let alone anti-Zionists and post-Zionists, who deny the need for such an exclusive ethnic home or who advocate a single, binational state. Their perspective is best expressed in the famous 1946 statement of Hebrew University President Judah L. Magnes: "I am not ready to achieve justice to the Jew through injustice to the Arab."[1]

In short, Zionism should not be used as a term of opprobrium. Unfortunately, the label is frequently bandied around both for legitimate criticism of Jewish nationalism as well as a substitute for illegitimate anti-Semitism. Like any other nationalism, the Jewish one (Zionism) displays good and bad features. Among the positive markers of nationalism rank the quest for self-determination, sharing and caring for members in true solidarity with a kinship community, and the readiness to subordinate selfish individual goals for a common good. The problematic and dangerous tendencies of nationalism comprise parochialism, arrogant contempt for nonmembers, and potential aggression toward outsiders. Nationalism evolves into racism only in this second aspect of exclusion and subordination of others. Hence, Zionism per se cannot be equated with racism, as an ill-fated UN resolution once did. However, when nationalism is advocated at any cost, including the conquest and displacement of another people, nationalism evolves into racism in effect, if not in intent.

The case of an eminent, sophisticated Israeli historian, Benny Morris, the author of the acclaimed classic *The Birth of the Palestinian Refugee Problem, 1947–1949*, can best illustrate the logic of extreme ethnic nationalism. In a remarkable frank interview, Morris places nationalist self-preservation explicitly above human rights.[2] "Preserving my people is more important than universal moral concepts." The notion that everything is justified when a threat to survival is perceived has found increased acceptance in the West after September 11. A new morality of realism substitutes for the old morality of idealism, as specified in international law or UN conventions. Because Morris exemplifies this widespread mentality with unusual clarity, it is worth exploring his views in depth.

In "Notes on Nationalism," George Orwell wrote that not only does the nationalist not disapprove of atrocities committed by his own side, but he also has a remarkable capacity for not hearing about them. Yet in Morris, Zionism found a nationalist who discovered and documented atrocities of his own side as nobody else before him, but nonetheless now identifies with and makes allowances for abuses without engaging in Orwell's ethnocentric deafness. Does the full awareness of a crime aggravate its justification? Morris uses the very knowledge of the historical circumstances for acquitting fellow perpetrators or at least "understanding" them: "There are circumstances in history that justify ethnic cleansing. . . . When the choice is between ethnic cleansing and genocide—the annihilation of your people—I prefer ethnic cleansing." Morris blames the founding Israeli president Ben Gurion for getting "cold feet during the war. If he was already engaged in expulsion, maybe he should have done a complete job." Had Ben Gurion "cleansed the whole country—the whole land of Israel, as far as the Jordan River—he would have stabilized the State of Israel for generations."

Ethnic nationalism thrives on the "us-and-them" dichotomy. The search for common ground is abandoned, because the enemy is irredeemable. Even the Arab Israeli citizens, who in their overwhelming majority prefer to live in Israel despite their inferior status, are defined as a deadly threat. "The Israeli Arabs are a time bomb. Their slide into complete Palestinization has made them an emissary of the enemy that is among us." Once defined as a threat, they are not spared the wrath of the superior power. "If the threat to Israel is existential, expulsion will be justified." That shifts in political attitudes of a minority depend on how it is treated does not occur to the nationalist. In line with Harvard's Samuel Huntington's clashing civilizations, Morris adopts the essentialist definition of an Islamic cultural deficit. Islamic cultural values are incompatible with Jewish visions, because "the Arab world as it is today is barbarian."

Such views rest on a monolithic perception of the adversary without differentiating between deeply divided factions, between secularists and Islamists or between pragmatic reformers and ideological zealots. According to Morris, Palestinian society as a whole "is a very sick society. It should be treated the way we treat individuals who are serial killers." The imagined enemy is not only pathologized but also dehumanized as a "wild animal that has to be locked up in one way or another." Reading such familiar stereotypes one wonders whether the anti-Semitic sloganeering of Europe has infected its victims who now assume the role of victimizers.

In his reply to his critics, Morris merely digs himself deeper into moral confusion by invoking other examples of ethnic cleansing as justification.

Ethnic nationalists of his type not only think in collective categories about their adversaries and homogenize "the Palestinians," they also arrogate to themselves the right to decide what is good for other people. "Was not the expulsion of the Sudeten Germans after World War II justified? And didn't it contribute, in the end, to their happiness, and certainly to the happiness of the Czech people?" If ethnic cleansing contributes to the happiness of people, what prevents Islamist zealots from using the same amoral logic to rid the area of Jews? Ironically, the Czech government and President Vaclav Havel apologized for the unjustified collective punishment of Germans during which several hundred thousand refugees perished, including innocent children, women, and the elderly.

In summary, the Morris argument lends itself to troubling conclusions. Terrorism—whether in the form of suicide attacks or state-sponsored assassinations in which usually more civilians than combatants are killed—not only destroys the potential for coexistence of two people. It also negates any communicative understanding. Habermas' "discursive rationality" rests on a nonviolent settling of differences. With mutual terrorism, not only dialogical reasoning but also universal morality is abandoned and targets fall back on legitimizing own-group crimes as self-defense. When Morris deplores that the founders of Israel did not complete ethnic cleansing, or when he contemplates circumstances in which the remaining "strangers" could be expelled, he underwrites the principle that the ethnic state, when threatened, can and should act beyond any moral rules or legal constraints. This is the same leading historian who answers the question of how many acts of Israeli massacre were perpetrated in 1948, honestly and precisely, in contrast to the Zionist founding myth of voluntary exit:

> Twenty-four. In some cases four or five people were executed, in others 70, 80, 100. There was also a great deal of arbitrary killing. Two old men are spotted walking in a field—they are shot. A woman is found in an abandoned village—she is shot. There are cases such as the village of Dawayima, in which a column entered the village with all guns blazing and killed anything that moved. . . . In Operation Hiram there was an unusually high concentration of executions of people against a wall or next to a well in an orderly fashion. . . . Apparently, various officers who took part in the operation understood that the expulsion order they received permitted them to do these deeds in order to encourage the population to take to the roads. The fact is that no one was punished for these acts of murder. Ben-Gurion silenced the matter.

Morris, too, justifies it by stating: "Ben-Gurion was right" in uprooting in the interest of the fragile new state. With this doctrine, the victims of anti-Semitism change into perpetrators and repeat on others their own victimization.

In the interest of establishing a nation state, the ultra-nationalist not only disregards the plight of outsiders, but even the death of his own kind. Ben Gurion's famous 1938 remark about the costs to secure a Jewish state exemplifies this attitude: "If I knew it was possible to save all [Jewish] children of

Germany by their transfer to England and only half of them by transferring them to the Land of Israel, I would choose the latter, because we are faced not only with the accounting of these children but also with the historical accounting of the Jewish people."[3] Death is calculated as an inevitable sacrifice for the glory of the nation. In light of this tradition, it is not surprising that some messianic claimants of "Eretz Israel" callously consider a few thousand more casualties as the necessary price to be paid for achieving the dream in the future. What incentive does peace provide to this mindset? Rationally emphasizing peace dividends based on compromise and coexistence falls on deaf ears. It amounts to a betrayal of higher goals. Particularly once the opponent is demonized as a Nazi-type mortal threat, seeking accommodation equals Chamberlain-like appeasement. Against perceived modern-day Arab Nazis any aggression can be justified as mere self-defense. A decontextualized Holocaust memorialization of Jews as eternal victims everywhere adds to this collective anxiety. Arab rhetoric about an illegitimate Jewish state reinforces this nationalist propaganda. In reality, most Palestinians, including surviving Hamas leaders, now realize that they must come to terms with the existence of Israel. Nazis possessed power to wipe out peoples and states; Palestinians are powerless to threaten Israel's existence. In the meantime, a massive educational effort awaits both antagonists before peace stands a chance.

Morris aligns Israel with similar post-9/11 thinking in the U.S. administration, but alienates it further from a post-Holocaust Europe that finally drew the opposite lessons from its past crimes. The clearest expression of this lesson was Joshka Fischer's "Never Again Auschwitz!" with which he justified the NATO bombing of Serbia in 1998. The globalization of justice, embodied in the new International Criminal Court (ICC), directly clashes with a doctrine that elevates national self-interest above universal human rights. It is therefore not surprising that the United States and Israel oppose the ICC, which interferes with the sovereignty of states when their nationals commit war crimes.

The ethnocentric mind decides without hesitation the fate of an entire people in the totalitarian rationalization that the noble end justifies the ignoble means. Previously Morris had argued, but now regrets: "Even the great American democracy could not have been created without the annihilation of the Indians." Besides being factually wrong (since the stateless hunting and gathering indigenous societies were never an existential threat to the superior intruding Europeans), the implicit moral callousness belatedly struck him as problematic. Yet one should be thankful to Morris for his frankness. Taken to its conclusion, powerless people everywhere were made aware of their fragile status, unprotected by law or convention if need arises, as perceived by the power holder. Morris explicitly does not support "transfer" at present and considers it improbable, unrealistic, and even undesirable, but he crosses a red line by making expulsion thinkable and respectable under certain conditions.

In light of the appeal of ethnic nationalism the world over, minorities are better advised to anticipate potential human rights abuses rather than deceive themselves with the naïve trust that civil rights would never disappear in a liberal democracy, which Israel claims to be. In some states, such as the United States, rights long taken for granted were suddenly restricted after 9/11 and respected civil rights lawyers, like Harvard's Alan Dershowitz, even legitimize torture if deemed necessary. In other states, authoritarianism lurks under the surface, ready to jettison the soft pretences of humanism at the slightest provocations, and few societies can be considered truly immunized against the temptations of official despotism.

Israel in a state of permanent warfare teaches the world how thin the veneer of universal rights turns out when people seek security through coercion of a threatening adversary. Moral amnesia then no longer represents an extremist fringe position, but is articulated by the best intellectuals. Yet it would be wrong to blame the chilling sentiment solely on misguided and "sick" individuals, as Morris' critics have charged. The widespread support for the depressing apocalyptic vision of "living by the sword" eternally also points to the failure of the Arab adversary to persuade the Israeli public of its readiness for peaceful coexistence. As long as fashionable, self-serving, anti-Zionist rhetoric is peddled among Arab policy makers and intellectuals, the Israeli peace movement lacks credible allies on the other side.

Critical Patriotism

Patriotism manifests itself in the collective rituals that express pride in one's country. Singing the national anthem or displaying the flag signals loyalty. Compared with Europe, the United States is widely considered a particularly patriotic nation, despite (or because of) the fact that the state is historically made up of immigrants from all parts of the world. Newcomers from different traditions are politically assimilated through unifying patriotic symbols. Patriotism is usually associated with nation building in pluralist, multination states. South Africa moved from ethnoracial nationalism under white minority rule to a nominal civic nationalism and officially propagated patriotism under majority rule. With a simultaneous "Africanization" of the civil service and corporate world through affirmative action and equity legislation, rhetorical nonracial nation building has not persuaded all skilled minority members to sign on. Many professionals with options abroad still emigrate for many reasons while others understand the necessity of measures to compensate for long-standing discrimination and exclusion of the majority black population. Yet a majority in all groups cooperates smoothly, some grudgingly and out of necessity, most without the friction and animosities that cultural differences are supposed to engender, according to ethnic nationalists. Whether Palestinians and Jews can travel a similar road in Israel remains the question.

Insofar as patriotism engenders collective solidarity with fellow citizens and loyalty to the laws and democratic constitution, it is a positive and useful attitude. True patriotism fosters social responsibility and civic courage to defend the rights and freedoms that a democratic political culture bestows. Habermas speaks of "constitutional patriotism" as a guarantee against tyranny and exclusion, because all citizens are equally entitled and protected by the constitution. Problems arise when one group of residents claim themselves to be the "true patriots" or citizens and aim at discriminating against or dominating others as untrustworthy "traitors" or foreigners.

In this situation, patriotism becomes a double-edged sword that comprises both positive and dangerously negative attitudes. In the name of "true patriotism," intolerance of dissent is frequently propagated, freedom of speech is restricted, and an arbitrary consensus is imposed. The very accusation of "unpatriotic behavior" intimidates teachers and students into self-censorship. They bow to conformity pressure that emanates from powerful media and authority prescriptions of what is legitimate and what is out of bounds and "politically incorrect." Nobody likes to be ostracized and marginalized as an outsider to the national consensus. However, particularly after the national trauma of 9/11 and the Patriot Act, many members of certain religious and ethnic minorities suddenly found themselves labeled suspects, regardless of their individual loyalties. During the 1950s, Senator Joseph McCarthy went on a similar indiscriminate witch hunt against suspected traitors in the ensuing Cold War. False patriotism usually assumes that one's own nation surpasses others. In the United States, William Bennett's "superior goodness of the American way of life" resembles the infamous German ideology "am deutschen Wesen soll die Welt genesen" ("the German character ought to cure the world"). When this ethnocentric conviction combines with military might to impose "superior" values on unwilling people, love of country fuses into aggressive nationalism.

To guard against such abuse of patriotism, one need not shy away from fostering national identity, let alone embrace Samuel Johnson's dictum that love of country is "the last refuge of a scoundrel." Teachers need to emphasize critical patriotism. This approach eschews the fashionable "My country, right or wrong!" Critical patriots have learned to love as well as hate their country. The very foundation of an open society is based on critical discourse in which nobody can claim a monopoly of truth and patriotism. Teachers therefore require not only knowledge in social studies or even tolerance of unpopular opinions, but also an attitude that nurtures autonomy and questioning of conventional wisdom among their subjects. As Henry Giroux has persuasively argued: "The real crisis in schools and youth culture may not be about censorship, freedom of speech, or other alleged evils of political correctness, but whether students are learning how to think critically, engage larger social issues, take risks, and develop a sense of social responsibility and civic courage."[4]

In superpatriotic countries such as Israel, critical patriotism encounters hostility and accusations of betrayal. Dissidents that resist conformity pressure are ostracized, even by their potential ideological allies on the Left. Israeli conscientious objectors to military service in the occupied territories are not supported by any political party. In contrast, the more numerous South African whites, who skipped the draft, could also expect much more understanding and sympathy, at least among the English community. Yossi Sarid, the former leader of the left-wing Meretz Party, self-critically speaks of "the 'disease of patriotism' from which we are unable to cure ourselves."[5] Using his own example, Sarid wonders why "even those who, like me, feel the Sharon government is an Israeli tragedy, are usually also infected with the patriotic germ, which dissuades them from collaborating with outside parties in the struggle against the evils committed by the government of Israel."[6] For the ethnocentric patriot, all outsiders are suspect. The image of a hostile world extends to respected judicial institutions, such as the International Court of Justice in The Hague. Even before the court's (14 to 1) judgment on the separation barrier, 69 percent of the Israeli public believed it to be biased in favor of the Arab position, according to the January 2004 Steinmetz Peace Index (although a smaller majority supported Israel's attendance for public relations reasons).

Collective introspection is hardly fostered when a community feels besieged. Scapegoats are readily found. The dehumanized enemy is written off as biologically marred. Israeli deputy defense minister Ze'ev Boim asks whether it is "some sort of cultural deficiency or is it a genetic defect" that causes Palestinian violence? Another Likud MK (Member of Knesset), Yehiel Hazan, answers: "This is something in their blood. It is genetic.... You can't trust an Arab even after 40 years in the grave."[7] If such remarks about Jews had been made in any Western parliament, the member would have been forced to resign immediately. Gush Shalom noted that in the state of "the survivors of racism," racism has now become routine. However, all states harbor extremists fringe groups, and Israel is no exception. The problem arises when extremists assume power and a passive public allows this to happen without holding the racists to account. It is in such discourses that critical patriots need to intervene and at least delegitimize hate speech, even though it is impossible to legislate attitudes and outlaw prejudice.

Israeli political scientist Neve Gordon, using a 2003 survey of the Israeli Democracy Institute, found an even more tenuous hold of democratic habits in public attitudes than was diagnosed for the unconsolidated democracy in South Africa. Gordon reports:

> Only 77 percent of the Jewish population support the statement that "democracy is the best form of government," the lowest percentage (alongside Poland) among the 32 countries for which there is available data. Over half the

> population (56%) is of the opinion that "strong leaders can be more useful to the state than all the deliberations and laws." Fifty percent concur that if there is a conflict between security interests and the preservation of the rule of law, the former should take precedence.[8]

Whites in apartheid South Africa proudly displayed their minority "democracy." Just as millions of South African blacks were disenfranchised, Israelis have become used to maintaining territorial control over three and a half million persons not possessing the vote and yet calling its system democratic. Even the 20 percent non-Jewish citizens in Israel proper are threatened by public attitudes that do not support their equal status.

And, according to Gordon:

> More than half of the Jews in Israel (53%) state that they are against full equality for the Arabs; 77 percent say there should be a Jewish majority on crucial political decisions; less than a third (31%) support having Arab political parties in the government; and the majority (57%) think that the Arabs should be encouraged to emigrate. Not only is the majority of the Jewish population against the provision of equal rights for Arab citizens, half of the Jews are even unwilling to face up to the fact that Palestinian citizens of Israel are discriminated against.[9]

Another survey by Haifa University's Center for the Study of National Security found that 63.7 percent of Jewish respondents said the government should encourage Arab Israelis to emigrate. Almost half of the Jewish respondents—48.6 percent—said the treatment that Arabs in Israel receive from the government is too sympathetic. A majority think Arab Israelis endanger the state's security and 45.3 percent support depriving Arab Israelis of the right to vote and to be elected.[10] The Palestinian writer Omar Barghouti characterizes such attitudes as "relative humanity."[11] Relative humanity assumes that Palestinian Israeli citizens neither can nor should have equal needs and rights as do Jewish Israelis. Equal human worth is subordinated to the aspirations of the stronger party.

With increased threat perceptions, the trends toward authoritarianism and intolerance toward outsiders clearly strengthened and the democratic demise accelerated. However, it is problematic to speak of a "recent drift toward fascism," or characterize the state as a "semifascist regime," as the Israeli sociologist Baruch Kimmerling does.[12] For one, if Israel were fascist, such outspoken dissent would have been silenced long ago. And if everything is fascism or genocide, including discriminatory systems such as apartheid South Africa or Israel, then the term becomes so wide as to be meaningless.

Multiculturalism and Cosmopolitanism

Multiculturalism has been adopted as the official state policy in Canada and Australia since the 1970s. It developed as a reaction against colonial assimilationist pressure in the two immigrant societies. In the United States, the multicultural discussion has mainly been confined to broadening a Eurocentric curriculum with a smattering of other perspectives. New immigrants objected to the erasure of their heritage resulting from adopting the cultural habits and values of the founding nation.

Insofar as multiculturalism levels a social hierarchy between earlier arrivals and newcomers and extends recognition and state subsidies to all ethnic communities, including indigenous people ("First Nations"), it amounts to a progressive policy. Fears that multiculturalism undermines national unity and encourages separatism are unfounded. In Canada, multiculturalism has strengthened national cohesion together with maximal federalist regional autonomy, particularly in Quebec. Separatism among French speakers has declined through cooptation policies and devolution of centralist powers.

Critics of multiculturalism bemoan the policy's initial focus on *lifestyles* at the expense of *life chances.* In response, the policy is now also concerned with ethnic "representivity" and issues of political power. An antiracism program together with anti-hate legislation has also been added.

Both Israel and South Africa practice limited forms of multiculturalism without calling the policy by this name. In Israel, the state recognizes differential family laws among Arab communities as well as Orthodox Jews' exemptions from certain civic duties. In South Africa, customary law in rural areas coexists with civic law, and eleven official languages are recognized. However, the state to all intents and purposes promotes English as the sole lingua franca to the chagrin of minority-language speakers, particularly previously dominant Afrikaners, who feel marginalized.

Cosmopolitanism refers to a mindset curious about the world everywhere, an orientation of openness and broadmindedness that transcends the narrow confines of one's own group, be it locality, religion, ethnicity, or nationality. Cosmopolitans perceive themselves as citizens of the world. Martha Nussbaum defines their primary allegiance "to the community of human beings in the entire world" rather than their own national citizens. Cosmopolitans are ready to immerse themselves in other cultures, engage with difference and acquire diverse "cultural capital."[13]

Nussbaum contrasts cosmopolitan universalism and internationalism with parochial ethnocentrism and inward-looking patriotism. She extends "an invitation to be an exile from the comfort of patriotism and its easy sentiments."[14] In opposition to Richard Rorty's emphasis on shared American traditions, these cosmopolitans do not "rejoice in our American identity," but celebrate a "politics of difference."[15]

Advocates of cosmopolitanism rightly inveigh against an education system that at best leaves students indifferent toward others beyond national borders and at worst ignorant about the outside world. Eighty-two percent of adult Americans do not own a passport and obviously have little desire to explore other countries. However, cosmopolitanism need not be opposed to a critical patriotism. Pride in one's own heritage can be reconciled with appreciating other traditions. A reflective national or ethnic identity does not exclude a cosmopolitan outlook, but may even be a prerequisite for a broader perspective. Politically, the slogan "Think globally, Act locally" best expresses a useful strategic synthesis.

The case for cosmopolitanism can be argued on moral as well as on pragmatic utilitarian grounds in an intertwined world. In the Kantian tradition, cosmopolitans universalize moral obligations and advocate international solidarity. In Nussbaum's words: "If we really believe that all human beings are created equal and endowed with certain inalienable rights, we are morally required to think about what that conception requires us to do with and for the rest of the world."[16]

Cosmopolitanism in practice, as opposed to this noble, idealistic theory, however, faces two major obstacles: First, despite economic globalization, the world is still organized into nation-states. None of the two hundred sovereign states has open borders that would allow people from everywhere to live anywhere without passports and permissions. Rich societies refuse to share their wealth with their poorer neighbors out of sheer greed. Our institutions militate against international solidarity and shape mindsets, which are focused on the national good, the locality, the ethnicity, or the family.

Second, if sociobiologists are correct, this selfishness of our species rests on evolutionary conditioning. According to this controversial view, people always prefer kin over non-kin, because such nepotism provided an evolutionary advantage in the competition for scarce resources. Survival depended on looking after your own first in this perspective.

It is doubtful, however, whether nationalist and ethnocentrist attitudes serve the same useful purposes in a modern integrated world, where events in the remotest parts affect the rest of the globe. When tropical forests are denuded, the climate everywhere changes. New diseases, like SARS, spread rapidly and indiscriminately. Pollution of the air, terrorism, or migration out of poverty and civil wars do not stop at artificial borders. Global institutions like the World Bank and the International Monetary Fund have to bail out failing economies in Asia or Africa. Isolationism is an option no longer, particularly for the United States, as the sole global superpower.

This interconnectedness of the modern world requires international cooperation and global planning. People with a cosmopolitan mindset are better equipped for these complex tasks than are parochial persons, who are unilingual and proud of it, are comfortable only in their own culture, and are oblivious to other people's thinking. Americans are inexorably entangled with the rest of the world. In their own self-interest, there is much to commend the mastery of a cosmopolitan cultural and political competence to deal with this role with moral responsibility and strategic savvy.

3

A Brief History of South Africa and Apartheid

This introduction to South Africa is meant for readers who are not familiar with the history of the country and apartheid. The brief overview summarizes turning points and sociopolitical developments well known to area experts who may wish to skip this chapter. However, because the Middle East is being compared with the South African transition, a minimal understanding of the historical background and the evolution of apartheid is essential for grasping differences and similarities.

The History of South African Colonialism

Old South African history books date the country's beginning to the arrival of the first Europeans at the tip of the continent in 1652. The Dutch East India Company needed a refreshment station for its ships while sailing around Africa to trade with its empire in Batavia (Indonesia). However, when Jan Van Riebeeck founded the settlement called the Cape of Good Hope, the first three dozen company employees did not raise cattle and grow fruits and vegetables on empty territory. Like European colonialists everywhere else, they encountered indigenous people who had lived on the land from time immemorial. The story of South Africa is the dispossession, resistance, and economic cooperation, liberation, and ultimate reconciliation of foreign intruders with indigenous inhabitants. When and how the colonialists themselves become indigenous—in short, whether there can be white Africans with equal rights and privileges, despite the colonial legacy—is largely settled nowadays.

In this analysis, the common label of *African* for the black majority does not preclude that the members of other groups are also African in the political sense of citizens belonging to the

African continent as their only home and origin. In contrast to the Middle East, all parties in South Africa have accepted this status of original "settlers." Therefore, not all Africans are black, and not all blacks are Africans. It should also be noted that since the rise of the Black Consciousness movement in the late 1960s, *black* had become a proud political term, comprising politically conscious members of all three disenfranchised groups, including South Africans of Indian descent and those of mixed origin ("Coloreds").

In the Western Cape there were two distinct aboriginal groups, (1) the Khoikhoi, semi-nomadic herders, and (2) San speakers, hunting and gathering people, whom the Europeans derogatively named "Bushmen." A hundred years later and 500 kilometers further east, the expanding settlers clashed with a third indigenous people, who spoke yet another language and practiced a different way of life: (3) agriculturalists who lived from subsistence farming and were Nguni speakers called *Bantu* (people), or what in modern times are labeled *blacks* or *Africans.*

Because Africans were more numerous and were better organized in rudimentary states with chiefs and kings, they offered the stiffest and longest resistance to European colonization of all three indigenous groups. However, they were also weakened by their own infighting, superstition, technological underdevelopment, and the colonial policy of divide and rule. Yet, unlike the Xhosa subgroup in the Eastern Cape (from which Mandela originates), the related Zulus in Natal were only subdued by the British colonial army in drawn out battles as recently as 1900. The first democratic election in 1994 reversed this colonial conquest, by replacing 350 years of minority racial domination with majority political rule. Currently, 77 percent of South African voters belong to the African group, while 11 percent are classified as "white."

The weakest San speakers befell the worst fate—near genocide. Like wild game, they were often shot on sight by special raiding parties under the pretense of being habitual cattle thieves. A cattle-herding economy of sedentary farmers increasingly penetrated the hunting grounds of the San and rendered the two modes of survival incompatible. Today only about thirty thousand San people survive in the whole of Southern Africa, mainly in neighboring Botswana and Namibia, where they are still treated as second-class citizens and are relegated to state parks or reservations. Were it not for the manufactured tourist attraction they provide or the tracking services they offered to the South African army during the war, most of those descendants from a different age might have vanished altogether.

The Cape settlers initially established an uneasy bartering relationship with the Khoikhoi; their rebellious chiefs were incarcerated at Robben Island, but most of the people gradually became absorbed into the feudal Cape economy as farm laborers or domestic servants. Missionaries converted the majority of Khoikhoi to Calvinism; many Khoikhoi women consorted with European men or had children from rape or relationships out of wedlock. Descendants of this group are today known as *Coloreds,* of whom the overwhelming majority speak Afrikaans as their mother tongue and who make up about 9 percent of the total South African population of forty-four million.

The ethnic mix of South Africa was further complicated by the importation of slaves from Angola, Indonesia, Malaysia, Madagascar, and elsewhere a mere ten years after the foundation of the Cape colony. During the first hundred years, the Cape colony barely grew through additional immigration from Europe, yet the outpost needed a dependent labor force. The huge gender imbalance among the Europeans—three men to one woman—encouraged sexual liaisons across the groups. The leading South African historian Hermann Giliomee probably understates the sexual violence and exploitation in the colonial status hierarchy when he points out: "There was also large-scale miscegenation in the form of casual sex, especially in the slave lodge frequented by European men as well as sailors and soldiers."[1] Because some children from those encounters were absorbed into the Afrikaner society and others grew up in the free black and slave community, the racial consciousness and assertions of racial purity during the later apartheid period appear particularly absurd. Social science research across cultures has revealed that insistence on exclusive racial or ethnic identity is particularly strong among people who have an insecure self-concept and are not sure about their own identity. Sigmund Freud called this phenomenon "the narcissism of small difference." Ironically, the early Cape society seemed to be more color blind and free of racially defined life chances than the frozen twentieth-century legislated race classifications of apartheid.

Among the European colonial powers, South Africa became a desired possession and the Cape colony several times changed hands between the Dutch and British who feared the French under Napoleon. Unlike the earlier freelance immigration by Dutch and German unemployed adventurers and a few hundred religiously persecuted French Huguenots, large-scale immigration from Britain started only in the early nineteenth century. These were largely government-selected immigrants with crafts and skills who came with their families. Most settled on the Eastern seaboard, particularly in Natal. British control of the Cape and the abolition of slavery are usually mentioned as the reasons for the "Great Trek" of Afrikaner farmers beyond the Cape frontier into the interior in the second quarter of the nineteenth century. Giliomee sees diverse causes in "a lack of land, labour and security, coupled with a pervasive sense of being marginalized."[2] The effect of the trek left Afrikaners dispersed throughout the country. The Orange Free State and Transvaal emerged as the two new independent Boer Republics.

The British influence and influx was also supplemented from 1860 by immigrants from British India on five-year contracts as indentured laborers for the sugar plantations and market gardens around Durban. Most of these poor labor migrants stayed in South Africa after the expirations of their contracts, brought their families over, and gradually prospered on the basis of close kinship solidarity and emphasis on education for their children, despite severe discrimination. This middle minority faced animosity from the dominant whites as well as the subordinate blacks. During the 1949 Durban riots, 150 Indians were killed until the army restored order belatedly. Unlike the wealthy Indian trading minorities in East Africa, the Indian community in Natal consists mostly of working-class people. This did not prevent them from becoming scapegoats and targets of resentment by the Zulu population in the competition for jobs and scarce resources.

About 75 percent of the 1.3 million Indian population are Hindus from various Indian linguistic groups; 20 percent are Muslims. Together with the so-called Malay Coloreds, the eight hundred thousand Muslims comprise about 2 percent of the South African population. The majority of the South African population professes to belong to various mainstream Christian denominations while about 30 percent claim membership in independent (Zionist) churches.

The Rise of Afrikaner Nationalism

The discovery of diamonds in Kimberley and rich gold reserves around Johannesburg in the second half of the nineteenth century again changed the course of South African history. It laid the foundations for the only industrialized country in Africa. Deep-level mining required long-term capital investments that only British imperialists were prepared to supply. Unlike colonies of exploitation where a few temporary colonists export their profits to the European metropole, the permanent settler colony of South Africa reinvested its profit inside the colony for further economic expansion. That presupposed political control over the territory, which Cecil Rhodes and other British rubber barons needed to wrest from the Boer republics.

Imperialist greed and the arrogant assumptions of a colonial superpower were the simple reasons for the Boer war at the turn of the century. The outgunned Boers in their guerrilla war against superior English forces enjoyed widespread global support, including from Lenin, in what was considered the first anticolonial war of Africa. The Boers lost this war and about 10 percent of the Afrikaner population was killed in the two republics. In the bitter struggle, the ruthless British army practiced a scorched-earth policy against the rural civilian population and established for the first time concentration camps in which many women and children died from starvation and disease. The Nazis later claimed this precedent, although the German colonial army undertook a similar campaign of genocide against the Hereros in then South West Africa.

The trauma led to a quest for revenge and the emergence of Afrikaner nationalism. British colonial policy everywhere aimed at the Anglicization of culturally different groups. The public use of their language was discouraged, outlawed in public, and penalized in schools. British cultural arrogance denigrated different cultural practices. Very much as in Quebec, English speakers dominated the economy and only English speakers could hope for a career. This forced assimilation triggered a counternationalism that clamored for equality of an impoverished people with their English overlords. The Afrikaner intellectual ethnic mobilizers stressed pride in the now fully developed new Afrikaans language. They encouraged Afrikaner capital accumulation in their own insurance companies. About 90 percent of Afrikaners in the 1890s lived in rural areas, many drifted as landless, unskilled "bywoners" (tenants) into the cities in search of work. They competed with African work seekers who were preferred by English employers, because they were cheaper and considered less rebellious and more pliable. About 25 percent of Afrikaners were classified as "poor whites" at the time.

The government of the time consisted of an English-Afrikaner United Party under the highly reputed General Smuts. In 1939, it joined the war against Nazi Germany on the British side, which most nationalist Afrikaners opposed, mainly because of anti-British sentiments but also because of residual sympathies for German ideologies and anti-Semitic sentiments. Many alienated Afrikaners considered Jewish owners of the large Anglo American gold and diamond corporation to be local oppressors and exploiters.

Because Afrikaners constituted 60 percent of the white voting population (as compared with 40 percent English speakers) and only a few Cape "nonwhites" were enfranchised, the Afrikaner National Party surprisingly won the 1948 general election. Capturing state control marked the triumph of Afrikaner nationalism. It now could use the state apparatus for patronage of Afrikaner interests and to keep English competitors at bay and black labor cheap. The English United Party also practiced racist segregation, but less openly than Afrikaners. The National Party replaced segregation with *apartheid,* an unprecedented project of statutory racial reordering. Its main architect was the new charismatic leader of the National Party, Hendrik Verwoerd.

In short, Afrikaner nationalism, with exclusive control of the South African state, institutionalized the informal Anglo segregation policy into formal, legalized aparthcid. This grand experiment of race-based social engineering eschewed any assimilation and instead fostered ethnic difference among the black population. "Separate development"—as the ideology of divide and rule was euphemistically labeled—attempted to ethnicize the black majority and racialize the white minority comprised of different cultural origins. Thereby it tried to unify "Europeans" (particularly the Afrikaans and English speakers of the white minority) into a "white nation," but fragment Africans into nine "tribal" national groups. The imagined white nation was built on race and biology. The envisaged black nations were based on partially invented or exaggerated ethnic and cultural differences. The fate of the two middle groups (Coloreds and Indians) was left undecided initially, but changed into open cooptation strategies in the early 1980s. Coloreds and Indians were enfranchised on separate voter's rolls for separate parliaments with limited powers that could not threaten white overall domination. The attempt backfired because of the exclusion of the majority black African population. Apartheid imposed a state-decreed identity on different groups and disallowed people to define their own identity. In all other ethnic conflicts around the world, people belong and identify with their group because of self-association.

The Many Faces of Apartheid

The American sociologist Pierre van den Berghe[3] has distinguished three forms of apartheid:

1. *Microapartheid* or *petty apartheid,* which segregated people from birth to death in daily life. Whites and nonwhites had to use separate facilities, from hospitals to cemeteries, from elevators to toilets, from restaurants to park benches, from buses to beaches, from post office counters to railway coaches. All facilities were of superior quality for whites and, if provided at all, of inferior quality for blacks, Indians, and Coloreds.
2. *Mesoapartheid* denotes the residential segregation enforced under the Group Areas Act. Cities, which had once been integrated, were forcibly segregated during the late 1960s and nonwhites deported to outlying areas. Today, we call this "ethnic cleansing." The four racial groups were allocated different residential areas of their own. Whites could generally remain in the better parts of the city while houses and shops were expropriated (particularly from Indians and Coloreds) and the owners forced to relocate far from city centers. This eliminated competition for white traders and amounted to the confiscation of valuable real estate. The policy was justified with the slogan of "slum clearing." However, when the slum was cleared the owners were not allowed back to rebuild.
3. *Macroapartheid* was the designation of the country into nine tribal "homelands" on 13 percent of the land, while the rest was declared white territory. Blacks could live in "white South Africa" only with special permission, if they were needed as labor. Slightly more than half of the total black population fell into this category. Some of the black "homelands"—also called *Bantustans*—declared themselves politically independent with their own flags and border controls, but their alleged sovereignty was recognized only by white South Africa. The government in Pretoria heavily subsidized its homeland creations, because they were supposed to be the answer to the anticolonial African independence movements occurring throughout the rest of the continent.

Apartheid constituted domestic or internal colonialism. Generally corrupt and unpopular black appointees of the white government in the capital Pretoria were designated to administer their own poverty and police themselves. The minority Afrikaner central government wanted to shed territory and responsibility for people considered useless, costly, and politically undesirable. Because all blacks would have acquired citizenship in their own independent "states" there would be no need to grant them a vote in the white state. They would have been legally denationalized in their country of birth. Only a few black Bantustan leaders, prominently the Zulu chief Mangosutho Buthelezi, refused to go along with this charade. His Inkatha movement had broken away from the African National Congress (ANC) in 1979 and decided to oppose apartheid legally from within.

Economically, a labor aristocracy of whites benefited from job reservation, differential salaries for work of the same kind, or preferential promotion in a system that officially called itself a "civilized labor policy." Afrikaner poor whites enjoyed the most successful affirmative action policy. They found jobs on the railways, at the post office, or in state corporations, whether they were qualified or not. Forty-five percent of economically active Afrikaners were employed in the civil service, in what comprised a unique nation of bureaucrats. Better-qualified professionals were looked after by the secret *Broederbond,* an ethnic male employment agency that ensured that suitable brothers and not English competitors filled the most influential positions in the universities, media, or senior civil service. The 12,000-elitist-member organization simultaneously functioned as a think tank and clearinghouse for new strategies of Afrikaner nationalism. Together with the founding of several new Afrikaner universities and the expansion of several old ones, those patronage activities ensured that Afrikaners gradually closed the wide educational and income gap with their English counterparts. Especially after Anglo American allowed Afrikaner capital entry into the mining sector in the 1960s, the traditional ethnic divisions in the nation's boardrooms faded. Beyond the continuing ethnic particularities, Afrikaner and English capital shared basic common interests in defending the country against sanctions, perceived ANC communists abroad, and increasingly militant trade unions at home.

The majority of rural blacks were deprived of the right to seek work in urban areas through *pass laws.* These restrictions exiled the elderly, women, and children to the desolate countryside, in order to save the system the social costs of education, unemployment, and old age. Eventually all black South Africans were supposed to become foreigners in the country of their birth by acquiring citizenship in one of nine ethnic homelands. They would be "guest workers" without rights in 87 percent of the land, unable to own property or acquire a sense of a permanent home and belonging.

Colonialism everywhere operated on the distinction between citizens and subjects.[4] Just as women in Europe were variously disenfranchised until the first half of the twentieth century, so indigenous subject populations (both in Africa or North America) were treated as "trustees" of the state, unworthy or incapable of participating in public affairs as equal citizens. A peculiar condescending paternalism confronted the alleged childlike underlings when they demanded their rights—rights that they were told first had to be earned through abilities demonstrated during a slow process of "growing" equal. Colonial ideologues declared this the "burden of the white man" who had assumed a "civilizing mission" to primitive natives in Africa.

Segregated education with different curricula and differential allocation of resources was one of the main tools with which this policy was to be achieved. Bantu education was shaped by essentialized notions of what the black mind was capable of and what kind of lower skills were needed in an industrializing economy. Depoliticized attitudes ensuring compliance, acquiescence, and acceptance of the status quo as the natural orders of things were the expected products of the system. More open and progressive missionary schools were brought under state control. The few nonwhite students who attended the liberal white universities were channeled into new own-group tribal colleges, all located in remote rural areas with the exception of the Coloured University of the Western Cape and the Indian University of Durban–Westville. Most faculty members at these ethnic institutions were initially conservative Afrikaner civil servants. Little did the apartheid planners envisage that these colleges would gradually evolve into hotbeds of black nationalism and anti-apartheid resistance.

Ethnically based apartheid education, although imposed and resented, nevertheless built on entrenched traditions and linguistic backgrounds that are alive and relevant among the African rural population. Even in the cities, every black South African speaks an African language; more often it is polyglot, although the medium of the public discourse is almost exclusively English, despite eleven official languages. Yet English, poorly taught as a second language, severely disadvantages many African learners in the competition for good grades and jobs.[5]

Even today, those living in the rural areas under the authority of traditional chiefs are further handicapped by customary law. Officially recognized as a concession to powerful traditional leaders, customary law does not sit well with liberal notions of equality and individual freedom. An unresolved contradiction exists between individualistic notions of citizenship and community-based rights and customs. The authority of chiefs does not rest on democratic legitimacy. Traditional leaders insist on inherited, dynastic rights. Women, in particular, suffer under communal obligations and status inequalities. Mamphela Ramphele speaks of a "dual citizenship that creates tensions between loyalty to the nation and to one's own group, however defined."[6] The tensions remain unresolved, and glaring discrepancies exist between the constitution and customary law. For example, the postapartheid constitution insists on gender equality, but under customary law, rural African women cannot inherit property. Precolonial African society tends to be romanticized as communal decision making by consensus, but the monopoly of power in the hands of male elders and male chiefs can hardly be called democratic.

Resistance and Liberation

European penetration of the African hinterland had destroyed most of the traditional African subsistence economy. Squeezed into ever more overcrowded reserves, its inhabitants increasingly relied on remittances of migrant workers in the cities. At the beginning of industrialization, Africans had to be forced into poorly paid work on the mines through head and hut taxes, which British administrators first introduced in the Eastern Cape. Later, it was sheer rural poverty that drove blacks into the city slums, dormitories, and compounds. Migrant labor not only destroyed the African peasantry but also undermined the traditional family. The competition among ethnically housed migrants in the insecure urban settings encouraged tribalism as a form of kinship solidarity and own-group protection in a tough struggle for survival.

In 1910, the ANC was founded. Among the first goals of the ANC was the battle for African unity against tribalism. Under the influence of supportive white and Indian liberals and communists, this priority was later extended to color-blind nonracialism. A moderate black elite, educated at Christian missionary schools, repeatedly pleaded with the government for recognition. A much-celebrated Freedom Charter of 1955 claimed the right of all South Africans to the land of their birth. A Gandhian-type civil disobedience campaign against new pass laws was tried in Natal, but failed when the government simply imprisoned the peaceful protesters. The National Party government responded with ever more repressive legislation. The 1960 Sharpeville massacre of more than sixty protesters marked a turning point. The ANC and its rival, the more radical Pan African Congress (PAC), decided to go underground, revert to sabotage without intentionally hurting civilians, and establish an exile presence for the anti-apartheid struggle after they were outlawed inside the country. After a few years in hiding, Mandela and his comrades were caught and sentenced to life imprisonment to be freed only after twenty-seven years on Robben Island in 1990.

In 1983, the National Party had split and shed its conservative wing. In 1989, the hardline president P. W. Botha was replaced with a new National Party leader, F. W. de Klerk, who had finally realized that apartheid was not sustainable. The costs outweighed the benefits. Influx control of blacks into the cities had failed; business needed ever more skilled employees who also had to be politically satisfied; a powerful union movement had taken over from the banned political organizations since the late 1970s; restless townships could not be stabilized, despite permanent states of emergencies;

demographic ratios changed in favor of blacks, with more whites emigrating and draining the country of skills and investments; the costs of global sanctions, particularly loan refusals, and moral ostracism of the pariah state were felt. The collapse of communism and the end of the Cold War in 1989 provided the final straw for the normalization of South Africa. The National Party decided to negotiate a historic compromise from a position of relative strength while the whites were still ahead. With the loss of Eastern European support, the ANC also had to turn away from the armed struggle and seek a political solution. A perception of stalemate on both sides prepared the ground for a constitutionally mandated agreement to share power for five years. The first free democratic elections in 1994, 1999, and 2004 provided the ANC with a two-thirds majority.

The compromise for whites involved handing over political power to the black majority, but in return leaving the economic order essentially intact. The ANC abandoned its socialist platform of "capturing the commanding heights of the economy," and turned into a right-of-center social democratic party with neoconservative fiscal and privatization policies that suited the powerful business community. A rapidly growing "patriotic bourgeoisie" has happily joined its white counterpart in defending nonracial capitalism.[7] Whereas the white–black income gap has narrowed, however, the inequality within each racial group has widened. Black empowerment programs and affirmative action policies have mainly favored an already-privileged elite, but have barely addressed the increased mass unemployment and poverty.

The ANC has to ask itself: What happens when the liberation euphoria wears off? Currently black frustration has turned inward: A spiraling crime rate, sexual violence, and escalating HIV infection rates, resulting from inexplicable government stalling on available counterstrategies, affect the physical well-being of the postapartheid generation even more so than their parents under apartheid. Despite one-third female representation in the South African parliament, African women are not yet empowered in the private sphere dominated by a highly patriarchal system. Although the government has made substantial progress in supplying new housing, electricity, water, and health and educational services to the needy, it has also wasted precious resources on unnecessary arms purchases. Several high-profile corruption scandals have raised eyebrows. The quiet ANC support for a tyrannical Mugabe regime in Zimbabwe has done little to reassure jittery minorities that their long-term interests are safe in South Africa. Commercial farmers in particular worry about frequent criminal attacks on farmers and potential land confiscations along the Zimbabwe model.

Uncertainty of members of ethnic minorities is reinforced by a new government emphasis on "Africanization." Transformation has been interpreted as racial representivity, which contradicts the goal of color-blind emphasis on individual merit. Racial representativeness in every institution as a policy disadvantages members of minority groups, particularly whites and

South Africans of Indian origin who are historically better qualified than the majority African group. Similar to the U.S. debate about affirmative action, opponents inveigh against elevating "demography into destiny." Unlike the U.S. practice of assisting a disadvantaged minority, the South African "equity legislation" aims at improving the opportunities of a previously disadvantaged majority and thereby unwittingly perpetuates the very state-imposed racial classifications that the anti-apartheid struggle sought to abolish.

The cherished South African constitutionalism has not yet been tested in a real crisis of good governance, although the democratic record of the postapartheid government cannot be faulted. Yet trends toward authoritarianism and highly centralized decision making undermine democratic grassroot participation. Most constitutionally independent institutions are headed by ANC loyalists. This switch has weakened parliamentary oversight, traditionally a reserve for opposition parties to keep government accountable. Authoritarianism, similar to the old order, originates not from overwhelming governance, but on the contrary, from the widespread crisis of authority and the inability to enforce order. The country lacks the institutional capacity for effective governance in many realms. An admirable human rights culture and fledgling democracy faces its most severe challenges from both the citizen's cynical withdrawal into the private realm and support for a strong hand to impose order and economic progress without debate. A fragile civil society in South Africa is no guarantee that democracy will prevail in a crisis when even black and white business might side with the stability and predictability that a more authoritarian order promises.

The celebrated Truth & Reconciliation Commission (TRC), to be analyzed in detail later, has affirmed victims and made some perpetrators confess because of the unique reward of amnesty after full disclosure of past crimes. It has, however, only achieved symbolic reconciliation. By focusing only on perpetrators and a few thousand individual victims of gross human rights violations, the TRC has ignored the millions of ordinary people who suffered under apartheid. It has also let the local and international business beneficiaries off the hook. Claims for reparations are still being debated.

Was apartheid genocide or a crime against humanity? If we define *genocide* as the planned and premeditated physical elimination of a people on the basis of their group membership, apartheid did not constitute genocide. Whites depended on blacks for cheap labor. However, depriving a people of fundamental human rights on the basis of their race and origin, stifling and wasting untold talents through arbitrary restrictions of advancement and differential resource allocation, or systematically insulting the dignity and equal recognition of citizens because of their descent certainly constitutes a crime against humanity. That atrocities also happened in countries that were among the harshest critics of apartheid South Africa does not excuse the crimes of apartheid. While it is inaccurate to label the perpetrators "the Nazis of Africa," the paternalistic motivations and actions of apartheid ideologues do not exonerate them. Although guilt cannot be collectively ascribed and there were also many brave dissidents and human rights activists among the dominant group, the white community bears responsibility for the continuing legacy of the crimes committed in its name. All South African whites have benefited—willingly or unwillingly—from a horrendous legalized racial system, whether they supported it or not. Many victims of apartheid to this day bear visible and invisible scars. That these historical legacies are acknowledged by all sides and serious efforts made to redress those wounds should be self-evident to all politically literate South Africans.

4

The Problematic Israel–South Africa Analogy

Economic Interdependence

In both the South African and Israeli conflicts, the economic power imbalance is the most striking aspect. Economically, both Palestinians and black South Africans are far weaker than their wealthier and resource-rich antagonists. Common asymmetrical power notwithstanding, the difference between Jewish Israelis and white South Africans, however, lies in the extent of their dependence on their opponents. The Israeli economy can do without Palestinian labor. Only in agriculture and construction do Palestinian workers constitute a significant minority workforce. Even in these sectors they are easily substituted with Asian and Balkan guest workers. The frequent closures of Gaza and the West Bank harmed mainly one side: The Palestinian economy grew more impoverished and individual Palestinian commuters suffered disproportionately by being cut off from their livelihoods. Collective economic punishment inconvenienced only a few Israeli employers, but caused considerable hardship to Palestinians.

In contrast, frequent strikes and lockouts in apartheid South Africa affected both sides. In terms of lost production and profits, white-owned businesses were arguably more affected than were unpaid workers, for whom survival along the bare poverty line had become a way of life anyway. Banning unions and strikes, however, ceased to be options after the mid-1970s, when Natal employers were confronted with leaderless strikers, despite the outlawing of strikes. The Wiehan Commission reluctantly legalized unions, because business and the state needed a credible negotiating partner to facilitate stability and predictability.

The subsequent emergence of a strong union movement socialized South Africa in negotiation politics. Trade-offs were practiced and the art of compromise was learned through hundreds of labor confrontations every year. Politicized unions served as substitutes for outlawed political organizations; their role therefore extended beyond bread and butter issues. Political and community concerns figured as prominently on union agendas as wages and dismissals. As a result, the welfare of workers beyond the factory gates also became a concern for employers. They adopted the notion of corporate social responsibility, in part to generate a positive public image in the competition to look "progressive," and in part to cultivate a contented labor force. Many businesses attempted to prevent a spillover of the chaotic township conditions into their enterprises. This meant intervening with local police officials or protest organizers when too many "stay-at-home" calls curbed production. Some companies provided company housing, day care, or bursaries for the children of selected employees. When a firm has invested heavily in the training of its skilled personnel, it cannot afford to replace them in a crisis. Despite implacable antagonism, the groundwork for consensual decision making and hard bargaining was born out of necessity in the course of two decades of escalating labor confrontations.

In the immediate post-Oslo years, the Palestinian economy also improved considerably. The promise of a Palestinian state encouraged investment and trade and increased integration with the Israeli economy. However, the economic optimism was soon stifled by political regression through settler expansionism, Rabin's assassination, and a corresponding Palestinian impatience about Israeli intransigence on the promised state.

In contrast to the current deteriorating Palestinian economic situation, in South Africa the huge black–white wage gap had narrowed somewhat long before equality of opportunity and equity legislation aimed at reversing the privilege of the "historically advantaged." With black purchasing power rising and a better-educated lower-middle class gradually increasing in a society in which the proportion of whites had shrunk to 11 percent, the economic absurdity of racial discrimination became ever more obvious. No company could justify paying differential salaries based on skin color to employees with the same qualifications. Individual productivity, which depends in part on identification with a firm and its work requirements, is undermined by alienated and discontented employees.

All-white companies, squeezed between the political intransigence of the state and the militancy of workers, had to act as honest brokers, even if their own sympathies lay elsewhere. While South African business managers met this challenge to varying degrees, most were aware that in the delicate political climate, negotiated compromises proved superior to unilateral dictates. In a gradual learning process, both sides realized that even unfavorable judgments of a Labor Court were preferable to bloody street confrontations. Bargaining was institutionalized and became a legitimate form of conflict resolution long before legalized racism was abolished.

In short, mutual dependency limited ruthlessness on both sides. Despite disparities in power, the powerless disenfranchised could exercise the nonviolent pressure that Palestinians lack. In the Israeli–Palestinian conflict, two separate economies survive side by side; South Africa has only one integrated economy that forces antagonists to coexist with one another reluctantly, even if their attitudes favor separation. While Palestinian economic dependence on Israel has increased since 1967, this has been a comparatively one-sided process that has mostly benefited Israel by creating new markets, consumers, and taxpayers in the occupied territories. Palestinians working in Israel constituted around 6 percent of all employees in Israel but amounted to about 36 percent of the Palestinian workforce by the late 1980s. Therefore, work prohibitions in Israel have hurt the Palestinians disproportionately. Still, the two economies are inextricably linked. Most of the imports to the Palestinian territories come from Israel and vice versa. After the European Union and the United States, the Palestinian entity is Israel's most important trading area.

After a visit to the region, a South African cabinet minister and Jewish peace activist, Ronnie Kasrils, focused on the labor exploitation in both contexts:

> Clear parallels arise with the border industries of the apartheid system which drew on labor from the Bantustans. Adjacent to Gaza and the West Bank are plans for at least five industrial parks in Israel to be situated close to gates in the wall. Once the West Bank and Gaza economies are ruined, the unemployed farmers and workers will have no choice but to sell their labor in the Israeli industrial zones.[1]

Indeed, daily commuters who live in a "foreign" entity, are the cheapest form of labor, because the host system saves all the social services (i.e., health, education) and welfare benefits, supposedly supplied by the territory of residence. From a cost perspective, commuter labor may even be preferable to international migrants who need housing and want their families to join for additional costs.

Apartheid planners' subsidized border industries failed because the already-industrialized cities provided better employment opportunities. New investors and existing enterprises were reluctant to relocate, despite tax incentives. Influx control measures and stringent pass laws in the 1960s and 1970s were unable to stem the steady stream of African work seekers into so-called white areas. The much more sizeable homeland reservations could not be fenced in as in Palestine, and "illegals" could only be "endorsed out" with declining success. The apartheid state also continued to pay small pensions and salaries to their Bantustan creations, to keep both the fiction of developing independent states as well as an impoverished population alive. Israel avoids these costs of occupation, which are mainly born by the international community and a comparatively more-developed and self-sufficient Palestinian economy.

The destruction of this relatively self-reliant Palestinian economy through land confiscations and security restrictions condemns Palestinians to work for poverty wages in the dozens of industrial estates planned along the separation barrier. Built on the Israeli site of the separation wall, but on Palestinian land, the industrial zones are exempt from Israeli labor laws. On average, Palestinians in the industrial estates earn a third of the Israeli minimum wage. Industrialists calculate production costs at 70 percent less than they would be in Israel, thanks to low wages and low rent. The industrial estates along the wall are envisaged as Israel's answer to the trend of investment relocation to the Far East. Moreover, Israel's strict environmental laws do not apply in these industrial zones. Polluting factories, like Geshuri's pesticide and chemical production, once unacceptable in the coastal city Netanya, moved to Tulkarem on the West Bank with the same smell. Through adjoining gates in the wall, the industrial estates operate under exclusive Israeli control and thereby avoid the time-consuming and costly checks of the products from enterprises inside the Palestinian areas, once envisaged in the Oslo agreement.[2]

The creation of an atomized, low-cost Palestinian proletariat under tight control of its employers is hardly recognized when the separation barrier is condemned as land grab, allegedly solely motivated by nationalism or religion. Proletarianization results from neither religious beliefs nor security anxieties, but from profit considerations. The Israeli version resembles the late nineteenth-century production of an African proletariat through head taxes and willful destruction of a subsistence economy in South Africa's overcrowded reserves. However, there is one significant difference with the imperial mining magnates of Kimberly and Johannesburg. A few Palestinian entrepreneurs, frequently through joint ventures, also benefit from the cheap labor of their fellow countrymen, which legitimizes the exploitation as progressive employment creation. The beneficiaries praise themselves as having found the most effective weapon against terrorism by providing work to combat "dietary insecurity" when a large proportion goes hungry and almost half of the population lives below the poverty line of $2.10 a day.

The pessimistic analogies, however, ignore a more optimistic dialectic. Assuming Kasrils' predictions come true, and the planned industrial zones do rely on Palestinians rather than on foreign migrants, the dependency of unemployed Palestinians will not remain one-sided for long. If apartheid developments are any guide, employment—even at low wages—also gradually empowers the powerless. Employers, in their own profit interest, have to invest in skills training and productivity-raising incentives. A disgruntled, unmotivated work force would contradict the prescriptions of all modern management manuals. Mass dismissals and easy replacements become costly and disruptive practices of a bygone period, particularly when employees have acquired minimal legal rights and are organized. Risking repeated strikes, let alone sabotage, would harm not only the company accounts, but also the image of Israeli business. Israeli multinationals would not be operating in a Chinese-type closed authoritarian system, even if they long for sweatshop conditions. Under the scrutiny of global NGOs, Israeli enterprises depend on minimal labor standards and favorable public relations in their market at home and abroad. These interwoven trends favor an economic interdependency that in time may well spill over into the social and political realm, as occurred in South Africa.

Economic interdependence ultimately defeated partition in South Africa. Both conservative *Boerestaat* (Afrikaner state) advocates and Zulu traditionalists flirted with the Palestinian/Jewish option of secession. The grand apartheid model of different homelands for different ethnic groups presented such a blueprint. All ultimately faltered on their problematic economic feasibility. Attaching ethnicity to territory by attempting to create halfway homogeneous new states would have meant the forced removal of millions of people.

While such an outcome was not inconceivable, as the ethnic cleansing in Bosnia and elsewhere has shown, the dispersed Afrikaners preferred a racial compromise that allowed them to maintain their material security. In contrast to Israel, the South African historic compromise was also enabled by the increased self-confidence of a ruling Afrikaner group that had economically drawn even with its historic English victor and had thus shed the victim mentality. Such a collective self-perception is still cultivated in Israel.

Unifying versus Divisive Religion

Opting for an inclusive state in South Africa was facilitated by the absence of religious tensions that would seem a major obstacle for a secularized common Jewish/Palestinian entity in the Middle East. While the conflict in the Middle East is not primarily about religious differences, leaders on both sides legitimize their actions and mobilize influential constituencies in the name of religion and historical religious persecution. Influential sections on both sides claim each other's territory as sacred ancestral ground. The stronger party monopolizes scarce water resources and fertile land. In South Africa, the ownership and control of ample space never acquired the same conflictual dimension as in a densely populated small terrain, bestowed with cherished landmarks, sacred beliefs, and meaningful mythologies.

Unlike Jews in Israel, whites under apartheid rarely felt existentially threatened. To be sure, various anxieties about black rule prevailed, particularly among the less educated. Concern about physical safety and molestation of white women ranked high. Among the elite and more affluent, however, fear about loss of political power was equated more with material redistribution, declining living standards, and reverse discrimination.[3] Among Afrikaners, "survival" meant protection of the Afrikaner language and culture and a "civilized" way of life. Collective annihilation rarely figured in the Afrikaner discourse. Although Afrikaners were defeated and severely mistreated in the Anglo-Boer war at the turn of the century, this loss never constituted quite the same historical trauma as anti-Semitism has for Jews. The British scorched-earth policy and the internment camps for the Boer civilian population cannot be compared with the Nazi death factories, although the label *concentration camp* is often used for both.

The Zionist quest for a Jewish homeland preceded Hitler and the Dreyfus affair in France and took off after the 1881 pogroms in Russia and Ukraine with subsequent immigration into British Palestine. However, Nazi actions led to instant recognition of the new Jewish state in 1948, even by Stalin, who wanted to weaken British dominance in the Middle East. While Jews were direct victims of the Nazis, the Palestinians they displaced may be considered indirect casualties of the German atrocities as well. The near extermination of European Jews confirmed the previous Zionist critique of Jewish vulnerability and cemented the founding rationale for the sanctuary in British Palestine. Without this nightmarish past and its later religious overtones, Jewish nationalism might have developed the same type of pragmatic accommodation of adversaries that Afrikaner nationalism eventually achieved. Instead, initially secular—even "socialist"—Zionism, was increasingly identified with expansion, new territory, and symbolic sites, legitimized with religious mythology, in contrast to the expedient turn of Afrikaner nationalism. While both religious Jews and Afrikaners claimed to be God's chosen people,[4] the Calvinist version sometimes had a hollow ring to it and was increasingly less credible even to its own ideologues.

Despite its denominational diversity and widespread adherence, religion in South Africa served as a point of commonality for blacks and whites alike. Anglican Archbishop Desmond Tutu in ecclesiastical garb successfully mobilized Christian ontology for reconciliation through his Truth Commission, in which theological assumptions about healing and forgiveness predominated. Previously, Catholic Archbishop Denis Hurley in Durban and the Council of (Protestant) Churches played a prominent role in opposing apartheid, often joined at protest marches by Cape Town's Imams—but never by Jewish religious representatives, although secularized Left Jewish South Africans played a leading role in the anti-apartheid movement. Prominent Dutch-reformed church ministers, such as Beyers Naude, had defected to the anti-apartheid camp early on. Even the main Calvinist churches, after an agonizing decade-long debate, eventually declared apartheid a sin and heresy. This amounted to an ideological death knell for racial-minority rule long before it was formally abolished in 1994.

In Israel, on the other hand, a religious minority of about 20 percent holds the balance of power. Orthodox Jews of widely different outlooks have succeeded in imposing religious prescriptions on a multireligious state that defines itself officially as Jewish, although the majority of Jewish Israelis are nonobservant and one million Israeli citizens of Arab descent

(20%) belong to Muslim, Christian, or Druze denominations. Confronted with an equally adamant religious adversary in the Muslims, symbolic sites like the Dome of the Rock and the Western Wall beneath it have become an uncompromising battleground. Instead of internationalizing Jerusalem by granting all religions access to holy sites, both Jews and Muslims insist on exclusive sovereignty. For example, during the July 2000 Camp David talks involving Clinton, Barak, and Arafat on who should control Haram el Sharif or the Temple Mount, two participants report that:

> The Americans spent countless hours seeking imaginative formulations to finesse the issue of which party would enjoy sovereignty over this sacred place—a coalition of nations, the United Nations, the Security Council, even God himself was proposed. In the end, the Palestinians would have nothing of it; the agreement had to give them sovereignty, or there would be no agreement at all.[5]

Symbolic transgressions, such as the creeping Jewish annexation of East Jerusalem after 1967; reported attempts by Jewish extremists to blow up the Islamic holy site and rebuild the temple on its ancient revered location; or Sharon's provocative, electioneering September 2000 march onto sacred Muslim ground, inflamed Arab opinion more than any economic discrimination.[6]

Compared with the vexing question of the return of Palestinian refugees, Jerusalem may be an even more difficult question to resolve. Avishai Margalit writes: "The core now concerns neither the Palestinian refugees nor the Jewish settlers. It does not involve the issues of security and water. It is Jerusalem."[7] Jerusalem embodies a nationalist commitment and historical identity for both sides, which has no equivalent in South Africa. The politicization of archaeology can illustrate this antiquarian competition about the "symbolic heart" of the Middle East conflict. Neil Silberman has shown how legitimate archaeological research and preservation efforts were exploited by both sides for partisan ends.[8] In 1996, with predictable deadly consequences, Prime Minister Netanyahu opened the Western Wall tunnels, whose outlet was in the Muslim Quarter of the Old City. He declared the tunnels "the bedrock of our national existence." Palestinians considered such politically inspired acts further evidence of "Judaization" and added their own damage through unprofessional large-scale excavation work in the context of the renovation of a mosque in the underground halls of "Solomon's Stables." Silberman writes that instead of attempting to understand "the natural process of demolition, eradication, rebuilding, evasion and ideological reinterpretation that has permitted ancient rulers and modern groups to claim exclusive possession," archaeologists joined the fray of partisan memory. Instrumental in the struggle for Jerusalem's past, a seemingly objective science exacerbates rather than ameliorates a nationalist dispute. Silberman concludes: "The digging continues. Claims and counterclaims about exclusive historical 'ownership' weave together the random acts of violence in a bloody fabric of bifurcated collective memory." Both sides remain prisoners of their mythologized past.[9]

No such disputed holy ground exists in South Africa. Even during the Group Areas Act of ethnic cleansing of integrated city neighborhoods during the late 1960s, the bulldozers that demolished the alleged slum areas of District Six in Cape Town or Cato Manor in Durban left the mosques, churches, and Hindu temples standing amidst the deserted debris. Rudimentary respect for the beliefs of others characterized the Calvinist and Huguenot traditions, perhaps due to their own origin as persecuted heretics in seventeenth-century Europe. Afrikaner nationalism, its many intolerances notwithstanding, lacked the manifest destiny elements of ultraorthodox Judaism. In contrast to the nonproselytizing Jews, Calvinism as a missionary enterprise also had to cultivate minimal empathy for its colored "sister" congregations. As a political justification for segregation, a Calvinist nationalism developed more into a blueprint of expedience than a dogmatic ideology of dedication. This is not to suggest that mainstream Calvinism practiced religious tolerance or Christian moral equality in its treatment of difference. Paternalistic tutelage toward blacks, if not outright scientific racism, inspired the original formulations of apartheid. The absence of religious friction should not be ascribed to an intrinsically more tolerant Christianity, but to a more watered-down, worldly, secularized, and universalistic form of religious morality in South Africa, particularly in its Anglican and Methodist versions. In Jerusalem, on the other hand, as Pierre van den Berghe has pointed out:

> You have the perfect meeting ground for all the religiously committed fundamentalists of the three most intolerant religions in the world. This is not limited to Jewish and Muslim believers. Just look at the disputes between Catholics, Orthodox, Armenians, Copts, etc. within the confines of the Holy Sepulchre and other fetishized places. Give them AK-47s, and they would start shooting at each other too.[10]

Israeli sociologists, such as Sammy Smooha, once predicted a decline of religious influence and the spread of individualistic, hedonistic, and materialistic attitudes.[11] Instead, the power of the religious bloc has substantially increased, despite the influx of a million largely secular Russian immigrants into Israel. In Israel's three-tiered educational system—state/secular, state/religious, and autonomous ultraorthodox schools—40 percent of the entire Jewish school population is currently exposed to religious instruction and indoctrination.

Because Israel's steadily dwindling two main parties—Likud and Labor—need coalition partners, even a Labor-led government would now be deadlocked on compromises with the Palestinians. The Israeli electoral system of proportional representation allows small sectarian parties to blackmail the bigger blocs, usually only for educational subsidies, but often for divisive ideological concessions. A clear example of this predicament is the faster expansion of settlements under the Labor government of Ehud Barak than under the tenure of his right-wing predecessor Netanyahu. In an interview with Benny Morris, Barak himself has conceded that this was done in order to "mollify the Israeli right" which he needed to be quiescent.[12]

In Israel, the degree of religiosity correlates strongly with antagonism toward Arabs.[13] It also serves as a better indicator of "left" and "right" self-identification than does economic policy preference. Statistically, the more orthodox and religious individual voters are, the less trust they express in Palestinians and the more they reject the entire peace process ("land for peace"). Many in the orthodox religious parties (comprising about 20% of the electorate) would rather contemplate civil war than allow meaningful concessions. Israeli sociologist Avishai Ehrlich concludes: "The strength of the religious community within the electorate has been the major cause for the inability of Israel to offer the requisite conditions for a historic compromise."[14] A Jewish internal struggle between the secular and the religious was supposed to be triggered by the seemingly inevitable peace process and the dismantling of settlements. Instead, the very peace process has been abandoned for the time being.

In South Africa, the ultra-right conservative parties—Conservative Party (CP), Afrikaner Weerstandsbeweging (AWB), Freedom Front (FF)—were the equivalent of the religious right in Israel. However, they could never block the National Party (NP) politically. The NP always enjoyed a majority, narrowly within the Afrikaner electorate and nationally with the growing support of more liberal English voters. Religiosity did not correlate with party support or right/left orientations in South Africa. In addition, the former Westminster "winner-takes-all" electoral system facilitated a strong and stable ruling party that could ignore its opposition as long as it held the majority in parliament. A reforming National Party could easily substitute its defecting right-wing constituency with conservative English voters.

Clearly, Israeli settlers do not form a monolithic bloc. An assessment of settler influence and reactions to pressure must take note of the manifold divisions among them. Settlers comprise a minority of less than 4 percent of the Israeli population; the ideological zealots, frequently recent American immigrants, constitute an even smaller minority among the minority. The primarily commercial motives of the 7,500 Gaza settlers differ from some more religiously driven counterparts on the West Bank who view the Gaza abandonment as a precedent of their own. Compared with the more numerous Afrikaner ultra-right after the split of the National Party during the last decade of apartheid, the Israeli extremists would seem a negligible force. Conventional wisdom holds that most settlers are primarily motivated by economic subsidies and cheaper housing, that the overwhelming majority would comply with state orders to evacuate, that others could be coopted and bought out with sufficient incentives, and only a few diehards would need to be coerced if the government were serious about a viable Palestinian state.

However, the Likud majority vote against its leader on the proposed Gaza evacuation in May 2004, although with less than half of party members participating, also proved that a determined and disciplined minority can be a stumbling block for leadership designs, which merely rely on a passive constituency. At the same time, the right-wing opposition to Sharon's disengagement, paradoxically enhanced his credibility among previous skeptics, similar to the changing image of the conservative de Klerk under attack by his hardliners. Unlike the racist Afrikaner right-wing, cut off from state and outside funding, the Israeli settlers command resources and influence. While the Afrikaner ideologues were gradually pushed out of state institutions and the Broederbond by the rival National Party, the settler-sympathetic ruling Likud opened the doors. Sharon for a long time acted as guardian and godfather of the settlers. As a knowledgeable analyst has observed:

> In the course of the decades, the settlers have set up an extensive apparatus of control and propaganda. Patiently, they have infiltrated the army, where they now occupy the key positions once held by Kibbutzniks. Their independent media are expanding, while the Left has in the course of the years given up literally all their independent media. The settlers are in possession of huge funds, not only the money that flows to them through hundreds of channels from the state coffers, and not only the lavish donations from American Jewish multi-millionaires, but also from the plentiful resources of the American Christian evangelists.[15]

Not one of the Afrikaans newspapers or state-controlled SABC TV and radio outlets, let alone the English South African media, supported the Conservative Party or the even more purist Herstigte Nasionale Party (HNP). The ostracized Right outside the National Party had to rely on its own small organ, *Die Patriot*. Unlike the Jewish ideological hardcore in Shiloh, Beit El, Elon Moreh, or Hebron, the Afrikaner *verkramptes* also had to raise their own campaign funds, as neither local nor international business would want to be seen in the company of forces that opposed reform. Moreover, the even more dogmatic factions of the AWB with an alcoholic agitator like Eugene Terre'Blanche at its helm had thoroughly discredited the anti-reform camp with their antics of uniformed storm-troopers and swastika flags. These ultranationalists were ridiculed and despised by the more sober Afrikaner conservatives who considered them uneducated, lower-class rabble-rousers.

In contrast, the Israeli settlers are subconsciously admired as austere, uncorrupted pioneers by many local and foreign empathetic onlookers, despite or because of their resistance to pragmatic compromises. The settler's historic claim to the whole of Palestine and messianic vision, if not entirely shared, at least finds sympathy in large sections of the Israeli public. The Steinmetz survey of Israeli public opinion by Ephraim Yaar and Tamar Hermann (*Haaretz*, May 13, 2004), conducted after the Likud referendum, indicates that "the proportion of those who describe their attitude toward the settlers as sympathetic or very sympathetic, in light of the possibility that the plan is implemented and the Gaza settlers are evacuated from their homes, is much larger than the proportion of those who express a lack of sympathy or indifference toward them." Yet, paradoxically, the majority also favors a forced evacuation—including the use of military force—if some residents of the settlements actively resist.

However, the minority religious settlers also embody a disruptive potential that does not necessarily comply with state action, even by their patron Sharon. Because the religious zealots strongly believe that "God is watching over us," even imminent danger is no deterrent. The death of a child merely "sanctifies God's name," which sentiment mirrors the Islamist cult of the shahid. Since, in the Bible, the borders of a state are drawn by divine edict, the Israeli settlers claim exclusive right to holy territory in Judea and Samaria just as vehemently as some Muslim extremists will not tolerate infidels on sacred Islamist territory. Both groups defy attempts to disentangle Jews and Palestinians. In an illuminating account, Jeffrey Goldberg has observed: "The most hardcore settlers are impatient messianists, who profess indifference, even scorn for the state; a faith in vigilantism; and loathing for the Arabs. They are free of doubt, seeing themselves as taking orders from God, and are an unusually cohesive segment of Israeli society."[16] Believing that one only *obeys* God, but does not *negotiate* with God, these zealots live beyond rational persuasion.

Much of this characterization also holds true for the Afrikaner right-wing in the 1980s, except that they lacked the deep religious conviction. While also citing the fear of atheist communism, they were racist nationalists first, and Calvinist adherents second, if religiously motivated at all. They had no eschatological vision of a theocracy. They shared the terrorist potential with their Jewish counterparts and some practiced it occasionally against blacks and fellow Afrikaner "traitors" alike, but they did not act in such a religiously charged environment as is Jerusalem. South Africa, too, tottered at the brink of a civil war when, in 1993, a right-winger shot the second most popular black leader Chris Hani in his own driveway one Easter morning. When the Brooklyn physician Baruch Goldstein mowed down twenty-nine Muslims praying in the Tomb of the Patriarchs in Hebron, it had a different impact. Goldstein is still openly celebrated as a saintly hero among the followers of Meir Kahane, another rabbi from Brooklyn who agitated for "transfer." The killers of Hani linger widely despised in jail, while Meier Kahane's advocates of expulsion of Arabs gain support. If Jewish fanatics ever were to succeed in blowing up the Al Aqsa Mosque above the ancient Jewish temple, it could trigger a worldwide upheaval of Muslims.

In short, while religion played a unifying role in settling the South African conflict peacefully, religion divides intransigent adherents in the Middle East. Religious absolutes negate the very idea of bargaining. The South African strife was about relative power and privilege, which allowed trade-offs. In conflicts perceived as being about fundamental values, the negotiation of compromises is much more difficult. The conflict becomes more intractable, unless solved by the total defeat of one opponent or intervention by a strong outside force.

Unlike apartheid South Africa with its openly racist regime, negotiations about Israel always contain the burden of history. Narratives about Jewish ancient rights over places of veneration or Muslim relations with the crusaders draw on deep historical and mythical wells that did not burden South African negotiations. The Zionist movement, while originally secular and semi-socialist, has been able to mobilize Western support with such religious references and holy monuments. Afrikaner Calvinism lacked these antecedents, despite the feeble invocation of biblical support for racial segregation. In the United States, evangelical Republicans support Israel more strongly than any other social grouping, while most secular Democrats have also joined the uncritical pro-Israel camp under the pressure of support groups.[17]

In contrast, mobilized Christian constituencies in the United States were more likely to oppose apartheid domination than to weigh in on behalf of the supposed "bastion of Western Christian civilization."

Third-Party Intervention

A crucial difference between the South African and Israeli conflicts obviously lies in the differing nature of outside support. In terms of global legitimacy, Israel differs fundamentally from the pariah apartheid state. Apartheid faced a hostile world opinion, although it enjoyed subterfuge assistance from key powers. Thatcher's Britain, the Swiss banks, and German car manufacturers never stopped investing in or trading with the apartheid state. Since the mid-197Os, Israel itself cultivated close military and technical links with the pariah state.[18] After the Organization of African Unity (OAU) turned its back on Israel, Rabin even invited the South African once Nazi-supporting Prime Minister John Vorster for a state visit. Apartheid's foreign supporters, however, had to conceal their ties or justify them with promoting reform through economic growth. Under pressure from various domestic constituencies, even the Reagan administration reluctantly embraced the sanctions movement in 1988. "Constructive engagement," as the controversial policy was labeled, continued but with more sticks than carrots. In short, apartheid South Africa lacked a supportive diaspora or protective kin-state that would lend assistance to domestic policy.

Much has been written about the fluctuating degrees of support that Israel receives, particularly from the United States, regardless of the administration in charge in Washington. The diaspora nationalism and emotional ties with the Jewish state run so deep that they almost define who is a Jew and who has abandoned this ethnic self-conception among "Jews" abroad. Among the many committed, support of Israel does not depend on Israeli policy or the party in power but is unconditional and total. Israeli behavior may even be severely criticized, but that does not detract from the underlying identification when called upon to take sides. None of this supportive relationship characterizes South African white expatriates. On the contrary, they were often found among the apartheid opposition or were motivated to migrate due to dissatisfaction with South Africa's political system or high crime rate. In contrast, outside support for Israel is motivated by a shared belief in the need for a Jewish state.

From the global legitimacy of a struggle against the South African pariah state, emanated the certainty of eventual victory. This clarity about the outcome of a common democratic state was backed by the power of numbers. The end of white minority rule might have taken some time, but was widely considered inevitable. Even the Afrikaner rulers conceded the need for permanent reform in order to postpone the loss of power. Already in the 1970s, Vorster talked about "adapt or die." Hermann Giliomee writes that "Afrikaner history embodies a fatalistic anticipation of inevitable collective defeat."[19] The opposite seems the case in Israel. Anxieties about survival are countered by an optimistic militarism. No matter what the future holds, that Jewish military power will not be defeated is an overwhelming belief in Israel.

In contrast, for Palestinians the outcome of the Middle East conflict remains uncertain. Possible scenarios range from expulsion, to ongoing subjugation, to two states, to a common multicultural democracy. The uncertainty weakens resistance. With a perceived gloomy future ahead, many Palestinian professionals have elected to emigrate. In South Africa, a few thousand political activists exiled themselves, but only temporarily. While many members of the three minority groups left, few of the African majority sought permanent betterment abroad. Emigration of scarce skills constitutes an important part of the rising costs of an ongoing conflict. However, in Israel, those costs are ameliorated by subsidies and some immigration, although the previous influx is fading. As long as the United States bankrolls the Jewish client state, material losses from an ongoing war are bearable. The kinds of crises that ultimately enticed the Afrikaner bourgeoisie to reconsider its racist policies and embrace meaningful negotiations are likely to have a limited impact in Israel.

Whether a state faces a hostile or supportive diaspora does not necessarily determine whether there will be negotiated or confrontational conflict management. In the South African case, economic sanctions have often been overestimated as causal factors of compromise. Withdrawal of foreign firms initially even strengthened domestic intransigence, as the absconding companies were bought out by South African capital at bargain prices. Many local firms acted as less generous employers as they were under less scrutiny for good corporate citizenship. Boycotts of South African goods abroad were easily circumvented by false labeling, establishing subsidiaries in neighboring countries, or developing new markets in Asia, the Middle East, and Latin America following the virtual closure of traditional export destinations in Western Europe and North America. The boycott was estimated to add an average export tax of 10 percent on commodities, which South African businesses considered bearable. Sanctions hurt most when they blocked access to capital markets abroad. The public and private sectors' inability to raise long-term foreign loans hampered the development of infrastructural projects and added to domestic inflation.

The widespread foreign perception of South Africa as a potentially unstable high-risk economy significantly undermined domestic economic confidence. It was in this psychological realm, rather than through unbearable cost increases, that sanctions contributed to a readiness to entertain negotiated solutions to escalating unrest. Paradoxically, the moral sanctions of ostracism by supposedly anti-Communist Western allies bothered the Afrikaner politicians more than the economic losses. Sanctions did not achieve the expected deepening split between business and government. On the contrary, because apartheid South Africa could now be viewed as truly under siege by a hostile outside world, the more liberal business section was pressured to join in to beat sanctions as a patriotic duty. Most corporate leaders duly complied.

In short, if applied unwisely, outside pressures for a negotiated settlement can sometimes be counterproductive. Sanctions can help solidify a fragmented regime when they contribute to poverty and unemployment. Cultural and academic boycotts, for example, assist the work of the censor in authoritarian environments. Instead of opening minds to progressive alternatives and new visions, they serve simply to assuage the moral egos of their sponsors. In the case of South Africa, paradoxically, the sports boycott applied the most successful pressure, as sports-obsessed South Africans quickly integrated segregated teams in order to make their country acceptable for international competitions. Successful sports integration, however, is also the least consequential in sociopolitical terms.

Stanley Cohen writes that "the essence of white consciousness in apartheid South Africa was a continuous shutting out of what seemed 'obvious' to any outsider."[20] If "shutting out" implies a conscious effort to repress contradictory information, the statement is problematic. On the contrary, at least the elite of regime apologists showed a keen interest in what the maligned opposition was arguing, particularly when it was written in Afrikaans. One could visit government offices in Pretoria for interviews, and senior bureaucrats or generals often had Hermann Giliomee and Andre du Toit's *Die Suid-Afrikaan* or Max du Preez's *Vrye Weekblad* on their desks. Because the critical views were expressed by respectable fellow Afrikaners (and not by despised English liberals), they weighed more heavily, particularly because a compliant party media hardly ever exposed government scandals. The successful patient erosion of a political hegemony by ethnic insiders cannot be quantified and also has never been recognized by

South Africa's new rulers. Israeli and Palestinian peace activists can draw important lessons from this precedent. Those with the most impact on recalcitrant regimes are neither the "moral crusaders" who merely express outrage, and ridicule and condemn the political actors, nor the "polarizing militants" who have joined the "enemy camp" unreservedly. Their critical line is predictable and instantly dismissed. But when a "strategic dissenter" speaks out and engages the regime apologists with feasible alternatives and their own moral follies, the critique originates from a credible source—and therefore hits home.

Critical visitors and outsiders who cannot be instantly labeled "supporters" or "opponents" can play a similar subversive role. For the colonized minds of apartheid South Africans—Afrikaners and blacks alike—anything imported from abroad, from fashion to academic expertise, carried a mythical quality and undeserved prestige. Most of the ethnic Afrikaner intelligentsia were keen to have their world views of "the communist threat" or the fickle nature of hostile world opinion or the "moral decay of liberal America" confirmed by the foreign visitor. There was little cognitive retreat from disturbing news—the average Afrikaner adult did not mind discussing with visitors delicate subjects plainly or even admitting their own racist atrocities. Non–South Africans were generally viewed as biased or misled, and National Party supporters went out of their way to enlighten the assumed ignorant foreigners and show them "the real South Africa." Unfortunately, few liberal intellectuals from abroad took the opportunity to engage their hosts critically. Instead of sowing doubts and shattering the complacent myths of apartheid indoctrination, they boycotted the pariah state. Reaffirming their own purity and pseudo-radical credentials seemed more important to many foreign academics than achieving an impact. The underlying assumption that racist and fascist minds were totally closed overlooked the quest for moral recognition by a shunned outcast people. Similar to the uncritical solidarity groups on pilgrimage to Israel, conservative foreigners filled the need of justifying the unjustifiable. Paradoxically, when liberal intellectuals broke the ill-considered cultural boycott, as did the renowned Irish academic Connor Cruise O'Brien in 1987, they were hounded out of South Africa by the very activists whose cause they supported.

Can the outside pressure for a negotiated settlement in South Africa provide any lessons for negotiating a compromise in Israel? It is difficult to envision a worldwide sanction movement against Israeli intransigence on Palestinian rights or against the Palestinian campaign of suicide attacks against Israeli civilians. Palestinians, however, risk being abandoned by outside powers. Since 1972, half of all Security Council resolutions on Palestine have been vetoed by the United States, including resolutions ordering Israel to stop building illegal Jewish settlements on occupied land or proposals to dispatch UN monitors.[21] The American and Canadian presses are less critical of Israel than are the Israeli media that are much more geared to the conflict. As Edward Said and Peter Novick have shown, Israel skillfully exploits Western guilt and devotes significant resources ("Hasbarah") to deflect and neutralize criticism by invoking the Holocaust or by tweaking the uneasy conscience of diaspora Jews for abandoning the homeland.[22]

Israel's dependence on U.S. backing makes it acutely vulnerable to outside dictates. A reduction of the $3 billion annual U.S. aid (one sixth of total U.S. foreign aid) would severely hurt the Jewish state. While not exactly in a total patron–client relationship, the self-declared Western outpost has to take shifting Washington policies seriously. Despite its overwhelming military superiority, Israel always has to weigh its military measures against its impact on world opinion. As underdogs, Palestinians do enjoy some global empathy beyond the Arab world, particularly in Europe, and especially after the Israeli military invasion and reoccupation of Palestinian territory in 2002.

Many analysts have pointed out how poorly the Palestinian case is represented in the Western media. Lamenting the bias of the media or blaming an all-powerful pro-Israel lobby overlooks the Arab/Palestinian failure to mount a persuasive educational campaign. Edward Said rightly argued that a "Palestinian victory will be won in the U.S.." Said suggests that Palestinians have "not at all understood the politics of nonviolence" or grasped the "immense, diffusionary, insistent and repetitive power of the images broadcast by CNN."[23] Instead of trying to influence public opinion abroad, the Palestinian voices have berated, caricatured, or begged America, according to Said, "cursing it in one breath, asking for help in another, all in miserably inadequate, fractured English."[24] Saddled with the stigma of terrorists, Israel has succeeded in making Palestinian militants into local bin Ladens. The Israeli state not only claims military but also propagandistic superiority, although many Israelis complain about a hostile foreign media, particularly in Europe. There is a "Mitleidseffekt" (empathy) for Palestinians, which has nothing to do with anti-Semitism, but has reduced the moral standing of Israel. The underestimated impact of spreading personal media (Web sites and Internet) has partially countered the influence of the official media. In the North American press and TV, Palestinian society is often pathologized. The West Bank and Gaza is portrayed as a zoo, in which the Israeli wardens guard animal-like killers. Thus a popular columnist in a national Canadian daily writes:

> Arab society in the West Bank and Gaza is pathological and self-destructive—a horrible stew of anti-Semitism, self-delusion, jihadi ideology, tribalism, Saddam-worship, clan rivalries and Saudi cash. Sharon realizes that neither he nor any other Israeli leader can prevent such a society from generating killers. All he can do is set them amongst themselves and hope they eventually become exhausted.[25]

The few Palestinian supporters, on the other hand, mirror this accumulation of negative stereotypes with an equally simplistic collection of positive images. When thoughtful Palestinians themselves debate how best to end the counterproductive intifada, foreigners pontificate: "First, we have to build support for the Intifada and ensure a defeat of Israeli militarism in the region."[26] How Israeli militarism is to be defeated is not mentioned. At best, the counterparts to the pathologizing commentators romanticize and idealize Palestinians. The less power they exercise, the more their imagined power is glorified. In this vein, Canadian activist Mordecai Briemberg asks: "What do you think has been the most powerful anti-war movement against the Bush gang? Who has most impeded their unilateralism?"[27] Briemberg's answer is that

> the Palestinian people of the post-1967 Israeli occupied territories. These targets of Israeli barbarism; these people burdened with "leadership" neither capable nor sincere; these combatants almost entirely without weapons; these refugees huddled in their dense hovels and trapped inside smaller and smaller segregated pockets of their homeland; these "wretched of the earth" have shown such resilience, determination and furious resistance that they shake the political structures of the entire region, raising a spectre of regional chaos that scares even imperial masters and has divided them amongst themselves over their war plans.[28]

Only wishful thinking imagines that the U.S. administration will be "scared" into questioning their warmongering and the Arab world will be "in revolt explicitly over Israel's tormenting of the Palestinians."[29] In reality, most Arab states have long abandoned their Palestinian counterparts and merely pay lip service to their cause while secretly welcoming imperial patronage against an ever more frustrated populace. If Palestinians had the power and support that empty words suggest, they would not have been relentlessly crushed.

In contrast, the South African liberation movements slowly captured world opinion, although they also had to overcome ingrained, unspoken racist skepticism perpetuated through black–white imagery. Against these odds, the ANC succeeded in mobilizing even conservatives in Europe and North America to isolate the apartheid government as a morally unacceptable regime. This almost universal condemnation owes much to the politics of inclusion and nonracialism the ANC espouses. The Palestinians have not communicated convincingly their policy of coexistence, and according to Said, "Neither have we understood the power of trying to address Israelis directly, the way the ANC addressed the white South Africans."[30] Here lies a clear lesson to be drawn.

Short of an unlikely military intervention, South Africa remained relatively immune to imposed outside prescriptions. Like the conflicts in Northern Ireland or other marginalized areas, apartheid also ranked low in terms of global geopolitical importance. But in the Middle East, access to oil and the West's standing in the Arab/Islamic world is at stake, now particularly crucial in terms of the fragile post–September 11 global coalition against terrorism. In the ideological competition of the Cold War, apartheid's racial capitalism remained a mere embarrassment to the West. With the end of that era and its proxy wars, Africa receded in geopolitical significance. Meanwhile, the unresolved Israel/Palestinian crisis and the instability of autocratic Arabic regimes advanced on the world agenda.

Andre Jacquet, a veteran South African diplomat deeply involved in negotiations on Namibian independence in 1990, made the point that "The Namibian solution was crucial for the subsequent settlement in South Africa. It convinced the hardliners in Pretoria that you could talk to 'terrorists' and achieve a mutually satisfactory result."[31] The recognition accord between Egypt (Sadat) and Israel (Begin) might have had a similar demonstrative effect, particularly for the hostile Arab rejectionists. However, the subsequent assassination of Sadat by Islamic extremists only confirmed that peace overtures enjoyed little support in Egypt, let alone in other Arab states. In the wake of the accord, many curious Israelis traveled to Cairo for the first time, but few Egyptians reciprocated and the anti-Zionist sloganeering in the public discourse was soon revived.

The end of the Cold War affected the Israeli–Palestinian conflict differently and less directly, while it was decisive in spurring South African negotiations. The collapse of the Soviet Union deprived the ANC of diplomatic and Eastern bloc military support, forcing it to refocus on the political road to power. Perceiving a weakened ANC, Afrikaner elites negotiated because they anticipated a declining power base, combined with a shrinking demographic ratio, and intended to use their remaining strength to secure a good deal and orderly transition. In the Middle East, Israel's overwhelming military superiority has removed any incentive for meaningful compromise, despite an increasing sense of personal insecurity. Similarly, the historic 1993 Oslo Accord came about, in part, because the Palestinian cause had been weakened by the Palestine Liberation Organization (PLO) support of Iraq during the First Gulf War in 1991 and the withdrawal of Russia from Syria.

Israel's history and location in the Arab world and the presence of Palestinian refugees in many countries made the Middle East conflict an international issue, requiring an international solution beyond a mere Israeli settlement. South Africa, in contrast, was widely perceived as a national, one-country problem. South Africa solved its transition with minimal outside interference. Once negotiations had started, both the ANC and the National Party shunned international mediation and arbitration. An Inkatha-inspired attempt to have an international commission under Henry Kissinger pronounce on a dispute about federalism quickly ended with the departure of the foreigners after three days in the country, as did a previous futile mission by a Commonwealth "Eminent Persons Group" to get negotiations under way in the first place.

Many European states assisted the struggling democracy movement with financial subsidies, which sometimes went directly to the ANC or to thinly disguised front organizations. However, European assistance never approached the magnitude of American aid to Israel or the annual $250 million European Union (EU) contribution in addition to Arab funds to the Palestinian Authority. Outside help for the anti-apartheid movement proved most useful in areas such as providing for the legal defense of political activists on trial, the direct support of small NGOs and alternative media outlets, and the occasional provision of conference support, such as for the important ANC/Afrikaner conference at Dakar in 1987. This type of tangible assistance by sympathetic governments and foreign philanthropists, such as George Soros, strengthened South Africa's civil society and provided psychological encouragement in a hostile domestic climate. Frequently, however, well-intentioned foreign donors trusted their clients blindly and failed to insist on proper standards of accountability. This oversight encouraged corruption as well as a tendency to neglect reliance on internal support. The eclipse of the Palestinian Authority by Hamas stems partly from similar widespread fiscal irregularities and abuse of power, as a result of which the welfare services of Hamas outperform those of the official institutions.

For foreign supporters of open and democratic societies, the lessons from South Africa lie in resisting the easy route of channeling funds to government and official institutions. Instead, democratic grassroots organizations should be sought out for direct support that comes without imperialist dictates but with firm insistence on transparency and accountability.

Embattled Leadership in Controversial Compromises

In South Africa, the middle ground always enjoyed majority support among whites and blacks alike. The white ultra-right slogan "bullets instead of ballots" had been as marginalized as the Pan African Congress/Azanian People's Liberation Army (PAC/APLA) call for "one settler one bullet," despite the ongoing mobilization for armed struggle by the ANC.

How a moderate leadership can minimize the ever-present danger of outbidding depends equally on its own performance and on the behavior of the opponent. Negotiation leaders must maintain credibility with their constituencies in order to sell a controversial compromise. In South Africa, de Klerk secured the consent of his white constituency for negotiations through a referendum on 17 March 1992. A surprising 68.7 percent of South Africa's whites supported a negotiated abolition of their minority rule through a likely nonracial majority rule, although they had no inkling how much white power their trusted government would eventually agree to relinquish. The National Party campaign slogan "negotiation yes, surrender no," was cleverly crafted to give the leadership an open-ended mandate.

They disagreed among themselves about what was open for negotiations, how long the process should last, who the interlocutors should be, and how it would all end. Vague notions floated around, including a rotating black and white presidency, consociational power sharing, and constitutionally entrenched ethnic group rights. In the end, none of these minority guarantees materialized or even mattered. More important was the mandate that de Klerk had sought and received. The historical success of the party-stalwart de Klerk lies in defeating hardline rivals and preventing a mutiny among sections of his security establishment and the threatened civil service. De Klerk invoked legitimacy within the Afrikaner constituency among whom the National Party held a slight majority at all times. This was helped by the conservative image that de Klerk had acquired in the past.

The authoritarian Afrikaner culture places great trust in legitimate ethnic leaders, unlike the more quarrelsome, individualistic, and fragmented Jewish political scene. Even most disaffected right wingers would respect the legitimacy of democratically elected incumbents of office, despite their deep disenchantment and distrust. A few months before de Klerk unbanned the liberation movements, little breakdown of ethnic cohesion had taken place. A comprehensive survey among several thousand white Afrikaner and English students across the country by Stellenbosch political scientist Jannie Gagiano in mid-1989 revealed solid sympathy toward public authority with only 6 percent of Afrikaans-speaking whites unsympathetic, but 41 percent of English speakers. Less than 10 percent of Afrikaner males (as opposed to 35.5% of English speakers) would consider refusing to do military service and only 6 percent of Afrikaners expressed unsympathetic attitudes toward the security establishment (21% among English students). What Gagiano calls the "repression potential" amounted to more than 90 percent among Afrikaners; the author concludes: "The state need have no inordinate fear that repression will be seriously resisted by strategic sections within the white community."[32] Gagiano, unfortunately, does not explain what accounts for the "symbolically very significant and previously unthinkable, defections from the Afrikaner community to the ranks of the liberation movements" within the course of a year. Ethnic conformists who trustingly follow a political leadership—regardless of major policy changes—would seem to provide a large part of the answer. If that is the case, the quality and vision of leaders in ethnic democracies would appear far more important than is usually assumed.

The ANC also enjoyed the advantage of relative internal cohesion, partly based on an authoritarian organizational exile culture and partly on the unblemished reputation of honored leaders. Nelson Mandela, who had been imprisoned for so long; Joe Slovo, a demonized, lifelong communist, or Cyril Ramaphosa, a savvy negotiator with impeccable militant union credentials: In popular perceptions, these men would never betray the struggle. Their judgment carried weight with a skeptical constituency. Even when they declared controversial decisions nonnegotiable, as Mandela did on several occasions, their authority did not suffer. The cessation of the armed struggle or, later, the dramatic shift in economic policy from social-democratic to neo-liberal principles could only be managed by strong leadership. In its turn, internal democracy was marginalized and the input of civil society in government decisions minimized. These turnarounds were facilitated by the alliance with the Congress of South African Trade Unions (COSATU) and the South African Communist Party (SACP), both of which could credibly present controversial concessions as interim stages in the ongoing political struggle to achieve a socialist society. In this regard, ANC conservatives benefited from the communists at least as much as the weakened Left relied on the government payroll for individual careers and legislative pacifiers in the form of protective labor laws for collective justification.

An idealized myth praises the South Africans for their transparent negotiations while reprimanding the Middle East adversaries for their secrecy. Thus Shira Herzog recommends "openness" as a first lesson from South Africa:

> White and black leaders realized that involving their own people was essential for negotiations to succeed. Even before the formal negotiation process, an extensive bottom-up process engaged broad sectors of the population and complemented the talks at the top-down leadership level. . . . As early as the 1993 Oslo Accord, negotiators on both sides failed to appreciate the importance of legitimizing a deal within their own constituencies and didn't believe in transparency and inclusiveness.[33]

In reality, the ANC did not need to legitimize its compromises because its leaders enjoyed wide legitimacy. Insofar as the ANC elite imposed its policy on an increasingly demobilized constituency, so did the National Party with its bewildered voters. Involving "the people" by inviting them to submit their ideas about the new constitution amounted to a mere public relations exercise rather than a serious grassroot input. The essential compromises had long been clarified in a series of expert meetings that were held in various European and African cities before the unbanning of the liberation movements in 1990 and continued afterward in the same elitist manner inside the country. The old United Democratic Front (UDF) stricture of seeking a mandate for all major decisions had long been abandoned. Negotiating controversial compromises out of the limelight in closed meetings ensures that the politicians do not primarily address the gallery. It also deprives populist demagogues of immediate ammunition, as long as the voters are regularly informed and educated about the reasons for startling developments. Both the South African and the Middle East adversaries could have done much more to prepare their following for necessary new political developments. Arafat as well as Barak at the time never fully explained their failed Camp David negotiation strategies, apart from blaming each other. In South Africa, at least the well-funded business campaigns for political reforms—

with scenario futurologists alleviating anxieties and spreading optimism among bewildered whites—discredited the advocates of continuing racist supremacy.

In contrast to the hegemonic ANC/UDF ideology and legitimacy of leaders, the Palestinian negotiators at the 2000 Camp David meetings lacked cohesion, despite the far more autocratic Palestinian Authority structures. Malley and Agha in their participatory analysis report that tensions among the dozen Palestinian negotiators, never far from the surface, had grown as the stakes rose, with the possibility of a final deal and the coming struggle for succession:

> The negotiators looked over their shoulders, fearful of adopting positions that would undermine them back home. Appearing to act disparately and without a central purpose, each Palestinian negotiator gave pre-eminence to a particular issue, making virtually impossible the kinds of trade-offs that, inevitably, a compromise would entail.[34]

Neither the ANC negotiators nor their NP counterparts with their 1992 mandate were plagued by similar concerns about rival actors. Both used the lurking presence of extremists to propagate the advantages of their own moderation. If parties to negotiations must avoid treating the adversary as a monolithic entity with no internal politics, the ANC and NP were far more successful at this than were the Middle East combatants. The Palestinians failed to exploit deep cleavages in the Israeli political system and the Jewish state always holds Palestinians collectively responsible, as if the leadership could control every individual.

Within both the ANC and the PLO simmered a cleavage between exiles and internal activists. The split proved deeper in the Palestinian camp than in the ANC. With the return of the exiles to South Africa in 1990, local resistance groups were reluctantly dissolved, marginalized, or coopted into an essentially exile-dominated leadership. At all times the locals had taken their cues from the ANC headquarters in Lusaka and deferred to the leadership abroad, apart from the 1979 split by Buthelezi's Inkatha which henceforth competed with the ANC as a separate, independent organization.

In the Palestinian case, the relationship between exiles and internals proved the reverse. Internal opposition influenced the leadership in Tunisia much more profoundly. When the "Tunisians" returned in 1994, as part of the new Palestinian Authority (PA) under the Oslo Accord, they frequently clashed with the indigenous resistance. The internals' suffering under curfews and "administrative detention" contrasted sharply with the luxury lives of the exiles in Tunisian villas. Although Arafat offered senior indigenous members positions in the PA security apparatus, some refused to give up their guns. The Fatah Hawks in Nablus, for example, carried on independently, even though they had marched beneath Arafat's picture before. The new PA lacked the legitimacy to reign in dissidents from its own ranks, let alone more militant groups. In addition, initially rival sectarian organizations like Hamas were secretly supported by the United States and Israel as a counterweight against the then more threatening nationalist and secular PLO.

In short, the ANC, particularly with an icon like Mandela at the head, could discipline opposing forces with the sheer moral weight of its struggle credentials. Unlike the corrupt, autocratic, and opportunistic PLO in power, the new ANC officeholders could invoke wide legitimacy in their struggle with the old bureaucracy. In both cases, though, the "virtues" of exile survival (secrecy, distrust, conspiracy) do not easily transform into democratic habits of transparency, accountability, and mandate politics. Much of the problematic patronage and cronyism of undeserving individuals in both the ANC and PLO can be attributed to loyalties and habits formed in exile.

A Militarized Political Culture

As a catchphrase for many of the issues analyzed, *political culture* comprises collective attitudes, intergroup relations, hegemonic discourses, and cultural traditions that deserve special attention as facilitators of—and obstacles to—negotiations.

At the grassroots level, a striking paradox marks the two political cultures under study. In integrated Israel, an external observer would soon note a relative lack of personal contact between the adversaries. The segregated South Africa of the apartheid era, on the other hand, was characterized by comparatively close personal interactions. After the unification of Jerusalem, writes Amos Elon, "Between Palestinians and Jews there was little if any social intercourse, no intermarriage, no economic cooperation to speak of except, perhaps, in the underworld or between the Israeli security services and their paid collaborators and spies."[35] In South Africa, most white households employed black servants; many had their children looked after by an African nanny; most menial work was done by blacks; the black elite always sent their offspring to integrated white private schools; and the country's universities increasingly reflected the racial mix of their surroundings. Even the tribal colleges for specific ethnic groups were dominated by white staff. While this inter-racial intimacy in the workplace never approached equal status contact, mutual familiarity softened attitudes, blocked demonization of the other, and gave rise to a prevailing paternalism on the part of the dominant group. Paternalistic condescension toward racialized childlike underlings differs from the chauvinistic social distance and mutual animosity characteristic of relations between Jews and Palestinians. While the Israeli and Palestinian leaders negotiate as formal equals, elite perceptions and street sentiments differ much more than in South Africa. Nationalist indoctrination also hampers the possibility of accepting painful trade-offs.

Apartheid rulers were always aware that a political—not military—solution would ultimately have to be found. This was the case even at the height of the war against the exiled ANC during the 1980s, when the military itself preached the doctrine that the fight against the "total onslaught" is 80 percent political and 20 percent military. Despite the everyday brutality of racial humiliation, official policy aimed to win the "hearts and minds" of moderate blacks through economic betterment schemes. In contrast, the right-of-center Israeli parties view Palestinians as a collective threat, meting out collective punishment, which forces a unity on the adversary that apartheid rulers tried to avoid at all costs. In 1988, General C. J. Lloyd, the Secretary of the South African State Security Council, stressed that in "eliminating" the small number of ANC revolutionaries in the townships the security forces must take care not to "incur the wrath of the masses" by harming uncommitted, nonrevolutionary members of the community "by accident." A long-retired apartheid general described to us in an interview (11 May 2002) his once close collaboration with his Israeli colleagues, whom he now considers "doing everything wrong in the book." He mentioned that the main advice of the Israelis to the South African military was to be "more assertive toward blacks" and go with tanks into Soweto and "take the terrorists out." The South African military, according to him, declined: "No, we cannot declare war on fellow South Africans." It was impossible to ascertain whether this comment amounted to a rationalization with hindsight. Perceiving a collective Arab enemy as an outsider to be battled is undoubtedly greater in Israel than it was in apartheid South Africa.

Like the Peace Now movement in Israel, South Africa's liberal anti-apartheid opposition always advocated political appeasement through negotiations. However, unlike the Israeli Left, this small opposition succeeded in instilling an increasing sense of moral doubt and even illegitimacy among leading National Party supporters. The Israeli peace camp, on the other hand, shares the same sense of ethnic identity and nationalism as the rest of the country, an identification that the white, mostly English, opposition never shared with the Afrikaner ruling party in South Africa. The majority of the 40 percent English-speaking whites perceived the Afrikaner government almost as a foreign ethnic ruling class from whose racial policies they benefited and for whom many voted, but with whom they had little else in common. In this ideological identification with their state lies one of the crucial differences between the anti-apartheid and internal Israeli opposition. For example, the English-speaking youth who chose the path of conscientious objection to compulsory military service rejected the entire racial system. The few hundreds who risk jail in Israel by refusing to serve in the occupied territories are still firm in their Zionism and would defend Israel proper at any time, if the state's survival were threatened. They are soldiers who have served before, with many holding rank. Unlike the South African activists in the End Conscription Campaign, the Israeli objectors cannot be accused of opportunistic cowardice, although in Israel they are denounced as traitors. Their impact lies not in weakening the Israeli military but in reviving the credibility of Israel in the perception of disillusioned Palestinians.

As Steven Friedman has perceptively commented: "Just as whites refusing to fight for apartheid may have strengthened the black leadership's non-racialism, so the Israeli objectors may send a message to Palestinians who see Israelis purely as occupiers."[36] Michael Sfard, a lawyer for the protesting conscripts, has vividly described the brutalization of a society that similarly plagued some South Africans who refused to serve in the army. It is worth quoting the essential moral concerns of the ostracized dissidents at length:

> The occupation corrupted Israeli culture, it eroded our code of ethics, and it even contaminated the Hebrew language. In the name of the fight against the murderous and unforgivable terror that struck Israeli cities and towns we grew accustomed to manning check-points in which thousands of Palestinians are being detained for hours and humiliated by young soldiers. We grew accustomed to pointing our rifles at children and women. We became tolerant to large-scale demolition of houses ("surface uncovering" in military jargon). Finally we accepted a state-sponsored policy of assassinations, neatly labeled by Israeli spokesmen as "focused prevention." We learned how to distinguish between roads for settlers (Jews) and roads for "locals" (Palestinians), and we were asked to implement discriminatory laws for the sake of illegal settlements that have trapped our country in an endless messianic war. A war that the vast majority of Israelis never wanted. As soldiers who witnessed, first-hand, the corrosive effect of the occupation on ordinary Israelis and Palestinians we could no longer bear its destructive implications for what we were raised to believe were Israeli values—respect for human life and dignity. The occupation chiseled out unequal relations between Palestinians and Israelis. It planted in many a seed of racism against Arabs.[37]

Academic rational choice analysts often overestimate cost-benefit calculations and underrate the moral unease that also motivates people to strive for alternatives despite pressure to conform.

Some of the brightest Afrikaner academics defected from the ruling camp early on and a vague feeling of guilt among the politically conscious always paralleled feudal labor exploitation. In what is arguably the best account of the complex South African transition, Patti Waldmeier perhaps overgeneralizes, but diagnoses correctly: "By the mid-1970s, Afrikaners had begun to recognize the impossibilities foisted on them by apartheid. They were motivated, at least in part, by morality. Gently, almost imperceptibly, apartheid had begun to prick the Afrikaner conscience; the spiritual comfort vital to the national psyche had been disturbed."[38]

This unease under pressure to justify the unjustifiable ultimately culminated in a slow erosion of the will to rule without substantial reforms. When these attempts of reformist cooptation through a Tricameral Parliament in 1982 proved counterproductive, the vision of a genuine democracy emerged.

In Israel, a collective guilt toward stateless Palestinians in the occupied territories is either totally absent or overwhelmed by a collective sense of victimhood through Palestinian suicidal resistance and perceived Islamist threats to Israel's very existence. The Israeli journalist and reputed author Amos Elon points out that "Among Israelis there is only very rarely a shadow of guilt over the fact that their astounding material, social, and international success had come at the price of rendering millions of Palestinians homeless."[39] Most Israelis would reject this direct attribution of their higher living standards to the displacement of Palestinians. The links between the privileges of a ruling group and the disadvantages of the rest are much clearer in South Africa. Indeed, early Zionists shunned employing non-Jewish labor and aimed at an economically self-reliant community until Dayan officially lifted the taboo on hiring Palestinian labor in the 1970s. Among "post-Zionist" intellectuals there exists also a genuine desire to work for a fair deal for Palestinians, similar to the few Afrikaner voices that called for "rule with justice." With heightened polarization, however, such reasoning becomes increasingly marginalized and stigmatized as fraternizing with the mortal enemy. Elon speaks of a "moral myopia," that is unable to resolve the painful paradox of steadily increasing military power and steadily decreasing national security. When two irreconcilable chauvinisms confront each other, neither side acknowledges the harm caused by its own stance.

Afrikaners were as dispersed inside South Africa as are Jews in the global diaspora. Not one of the three hundred magisterial districts in apartheid South Africa contained an Afrikaner majority. They also entertained anxieties about a future under black rule, and a minority seriously flirted with establishing a "volksstaat" along the Jewish model. The dream failed to garner support not only because of economic interdependence. Unlike diaspora Jews, the ruling Afrikaners did not feel particularly vulnerable and had not faced persecution from blacks. Despite all the anxieties about "black numbers swamping whites," "white women being molested," or "administrative chaos erupting," the Afrikaner paternalistic mindset did not believe that blacks collectively were inclined to or even capable of seriously harming their white overlords. To be sure, there was the occasional bombing of Wimpy bars and supermarkets or mines on remote farm roads. Many civilians were maimed when the air force headquarters in a busy Pretoria street was targeted or later when a black fringe group attacked a Cape Town church and an Eastern Cape golf club. Still, most Afrikaners dismissed the "armed struggle" as the work of a few misguided communist terrorists. The signs of growing militancy did not shake the average bystander out of the customary complacency. Ordinary Afrikaners lived complacently in their cocooned suburbs. They continued to attend the Saturday afternoon rugby games and trusted their government to handle the occasional disturbances. Personal security was perceived as protection from individual black criminals rather than the rage of an entire population as in Israel. When, during a provocative invasion of Bophuthatswana, a few surrendering white right-wingers were finally shot in revenge by black policemen before rolling cameras, the event caused a traumatizing shock in the Afrikaner community.

It is the differential experience of vulnerability between Zionists and Afrikaner nationalists that accounts, in part, for the different responses of separate versus common states. As obvious beneficiaries of racial minority rule, Afrikaners could hardly portray themselves as victims the way both Israelis and Palestinians sanctify victimhood. Israelis are far more convinced of their own rationalizations than Afrikaner nationalists ever were. Suzanne Goldenberg, a long-time foreign correspondent, observes that "Israelis and Palestinians appear to suffer not from doubts, but from certainties." Afrikaners never idealized their society or elevated their army into a "moral force" the way Israelis think their country operates on higher ethical standards.[40]

One of the world's leading criminologists, Stanley Cohen, in his perceptive book *States of Denial*, has compared different bystander motivations under Nazi rule, in Communist Eastern Europe and in Israel and South Africa.[41] Unlike the compliance out of fear in the totalitarian Nazi and communist regimes, Cohen diagnoses as voluntary the conformity with government policy in the ethnic democracies of Israel and white South Africa. "But denial of the injustices and injuries inflicted on the Palestinians is built into the social fabric. The Jewish public's assent to official propaganda, myth and self-righteousness results from willing identification."[42] The real threat to life and limb through suicide bombers has of course, reinforced a "defensive self-image and a character armor of insecurity and permanent victimhood." Cohen traces the different idioms of denial in Israel that afflict even critical visitors: "The same American Jews who are outspoken critics of human rights violations everywhere from El Salvador to Tibet now change from sophisticated observers into dumbed-down collective victims. Their fellow Jews who criticize the Israeli treatment of Palestinians too strongly or openly are denounced as 'self-hating Jews' or as having a 'Diaspora mentality.'"[43]

Paul Arthur, writing about the Anglo-Irish peace process, illustrates how communities can become prisoners of their past by cultivating a "narcissism of victimisation."[44] Arthur talks about a "victim-bonded society in which memories of past injustice and humiliation are so firmly entrenched in both communities and the sense of entrapment so complete that the hunger strikers (of 1980–81) are a metaphor for the entrapment of the larger society."[45]

It would seem that a similar insistence on victimhood is shared by Israeli and Palestinian societies in their insistence on their exclusive suffering. In such a situation, people are unable to develop what could be called an "anticipatory memory." The South African parties achieved this by projecting images of future liberation from past conflicts. Acknowledging past crimes by all parties, including themselves, inaugurated a necessary break with a deadening past.

In Israel, the military and politics are closely intertwined. Battle heroes frequently become prime ministers (Rabin, Barak, Sharon), and politicians depend on their security advisors. In a society under siege, the high status of military leaders comes as no surprise. That does not mean that all generals are uncompromisingly hawkish. In fact, Labor Party affinities once dominated in the secular Israeli top military hierarchy, with few sympathies for religious nationalists. Often the generals stopped the more extreme zealots from further inflaming Palestinian militancy and undermining Israeli security. Former generals Rabin and Barak advocated the greatest concessions to the Palestinians. In South Africa, too, it was the former head of the army, Constand Viljoen, who almost single-handedly averted civil war by persuading large sections of his military men to join him in following a political route to realizing the dream of an Afrikaner homeland. Having experienced the horrors of war first hand, military leaders are often more pragmatic than civilian ideologues are when it comes to avoiding casualties in renewed conflicts. Had the Afrikaner military leadership not succeeded in reigning in the band of two thousand ultra–right-wingers who invaded Bophuthatswana to set up an anti-ANC base, or had Mandela failed to calm the black rage after Chris Hani's assassination on Easter 1993, the country may well have descended into civil war. In short, the South African opponents intentionally assisted each other in achieving a peaceful outcome. In the Middle East, however, war-mongering factions on both sides intentionally sabotage peace efforts.

Apartheid South Africa has always been dominated by civilian politicians. Even under President P. W. Botha, who as a former minister of defense relied on the military as his main support base and employed a hardline military man (Magnus Malan) as his own defense minister, generals carried out political decisions but hardly shaped them. A British tradition of apolitical military professionalism prevailed. With the exception of General Smuts before 1948 and Constand Viljoen as party leader in the post-apartheid era, few prominent Afrikaner military figures switched into politics in modern times, let alone sat in the cabinet. While Afrikaner lawyers, civil servants, academics, and churchmen in the top echelons of the National Party listened to the police and military advice and gave these institutions a free hand to pursue the enemies of the state, security issues did not necessarily top the political agenda, even at the height of township confrontations. Economic cost-benefit calculations were at least equally important, as white privilege depended on black labor and investment perceptions abroad. In white South Africa, racial animosity and prejudice steadily softened with rising costs, as dozens of opinion surveys during the 1970s and 1980s revealed. Conversely, with military superiority and solid outside support in the face of suicide missions and a seemingly self-destructive adversary, Israeli prejudicial attitudes hardened. Both apartheid South Africa and Israel have rightly been described as "societies under siege." South African whites broke out of their siege mentality by embracing risky negotiations. Israel, faced with a more existential threat, a more uncompromising adversary, and strong outside endorsement, has united in rejecting further compromises in a political culture of defiance.

Unlike apartheid South Africa, where the military and police remained background players—even in the State Security Council during the state of emergency periods in the 1980s—in Israel retired generals not only dominate national politics, but private business, public companies, and big city administrations alike. The general staff of the IDF, analysts have noted, serves as a finishing school for all kinds of top managers, equivalent to corporate CEOs trained at Harvard, MIT, and Stanford, but only cheaper since they all receive an additional army pension. Richard Ben Cramer who stresses this point in his insightful book *How Israel Lost* also sketches what these generals have in common, despite tactical and political differences:

> It's a shared experience—by retirement age, it's a world view. The cardinal ethic is to fight to a win—and never give up ground. For twenty years, at least they have faced fear and inspired fear—it's what they know. Force has been their calling card, and the normal solution to problems they confronted. (There's an old army saying: "If force doesn't work, try more force.") And no one gets to general in the IDF without understanding that Arabs are the enemy. No one gets a star on his collar without buying into the conflict. It made them the big guys they are.[46]

However, confronted with new problems as private entrepreneurs, whether selling soap, cell phones, or even dealing in arms, the authoritarian military style of commanding unquestioning compliance may not work in eliciting voluntary orders in a competitive consumer market. Some generals discover that what is good for the narrow confines of an army does not necessarily work in a global business world. They develop a wider and strategic political vision. Obsessions with security thinking give way to socioeconomic calculations as a priority. Given the unquestioned prestige and moral authority that the army enjoys in Israel, its generals paradoxically could also develop into catalysts of change. In several ways the dissident generals, conscientious objectors, and moral refuseniks are Israel's saving grace and hope. From this perspective, the internal debates in the secret intelligence departments acquire particular importance.

While the intelligence services of a besieged state normally present themselves as a closed world, their disputes and rivalries can trigger important reassessments and policy shifts. For this to happen it is necessary that the disagreements become public and transparent, so that opposition politicians can use these professional rifts for counter strategies. In apartheid South Africa, it was well known that Army Intelligence and the National Intelligence Agency (NSI) differed fundamentally in their threat perceptions. The former advocated weakening ANC combatants abroad with military raids, while the latter located the main threat as originating from within, resulting in a more political strategy toward the enemy. Secret official contacts with the imprisoned Mandela and exiles started when the second assessment gradually prevailed. In Israel, similar cleavages were revealed in the heated 2004 disputes between Amos Gilad, the national assessor for cabinet, and his former superior Amos Malka who questioned the conventional wisdom about Arafat and Palestinian willingness to compromise at Camp David. The Palestinian rejectionism and the "no partner" notion were exposed as personal opinion by several intelligence colleagues, who argued that the prime minister and the country was misled and manipulated by one person.

At the very least, such public disputes break cherished taboos. A successful strategy of the peace camp in any divided society cultivates ties with these potential dissidents on the other side, rather than arrogantly shuns them as incorrigible agents of another world, as frequently happened in the local anti-apartheid struggle. The reassessment within the South African intelligence services started when Afrikaner intellectuals and civil society activists persuaded some state operatives that they exaggerated the ideological intransigence and communist influence in the ANC, that even the few hardline communists were pragmatists interested in negotiations, and that the cherished "total onslaught" theory amounted to a myth, particularly after the collapse of the Soviet Union in 1989.

With a series of wars against neighboring Arab states behind them and ongoing warfare against Palestinian insurgents, the Israeli military holds a different perception of the enemy than their apartheid counterparts did. For the South African generals, the ANC was a remote and elusive opponent; for the Israelis, Arabs are an immediate and visible threat. After General Meiring took over from Kat Liebenberg as chief of the South African Defense Force (SADF) in October 1993, the generals (James Kriel, Joffel van der Westhuizen, and Kat Liebenberg) tried to restart the deadlocked Codesa negotiations by talking to their ANC counterparts from Umkhonto we Sizwe (MK) for the first time. Meiring reminisces condescendingly about the "very friendly" talks:

> We as the military never really fought with them. There was the odd occasion where we bombed a place in Maputo and a base near Lusaka but we never fought them in battle. They were hit and run, they came and placed mines and they were really terrorists at the time in that they instigated terror amongst the black population. . . . so we actually assisted the police in many cases in maintaining law and order, more than anything else. We had a good intelligence situation about them, but there was no occasion when we fought the ANC. It wasn't the same thing as meeting with SWAPO [South West African People's Organization]. With the ANC, we had an open mind. We had the mindset—okay, this is going to happen, so let's go and talk to them. Kat was instigating and we were towing along. It was strange, but it wasn't completely out of this world. . . . They were very easy to get on with, especially Modise. Some were sharp and intelligent others not.[47]

The relatively low level of violence in the South African case, compared with the Middle East, obviously minimized "hard feelings." So did the inevitability of transition, although the military hierarchy also weighed up the coup option. Like the *Wehrmacht* did in Nazi Germany, the South African military bathed in the myth that the police did the dirty work while their hands were clean. Above all, the intense infighting among the military brass and the three intelligence services, as well as the rifts and resentments between the politicians and the generals during the transition period, facilitated the relatively smooth handover of power. It is doubtful that the much better-integrated Israeli military/political hierarchy would ever concede as easily as the apartheid regime did. On the other hand, the Israeli military is more susceptible and dependent on their U.S. sponsors than their apartheid counterparts were.

Violence, Deterrence, and the Psychic Energy of Martyrdom

A vital precondition for the South African negotiations was sharing a perception of stalemate. Both sides realized that they could not defeat each other militarily, save by destroying the country in a drawn-out civil war. In Israel, both antagonists propagate the illusion of victory. In the words of Sharon: "The Palestinians should be hit very hard, because if they don't feel they have been defeated, it will be impossible to return to the negotiating table."[48] This perspective implies that the opponent may only negotiate on terms dictated by the victor.

Palestinians, too, falsely assume that the Israeli retreat from Lebanon can be repeated, because the opponent will not tolerate casualties for long. As the London *Independent* comments: "Palestinian fighters detect a growing despair among ordinary Israelis at the unending carnage. And as they see Sharon's poll rating tumble, they sense that their tactics are working."[49] On the contrary, with each suicide bombing, Sharon's ratings strengthened. Because Palestinians have essentially lost the half-century battle against the Zionist state in their midst, bearing this loss is compensated by phantom victories through martyrdom. Comparative research by the French sociologist Laetitia Bucaille[50] revealed a strange paradox. Palestinian militants viewed themselves as heroes and victors, despite losing the battle. Former MK soldiers, whose cause succeeded, nevertheless all viewed themselves as victims. While sympathetic reporters and filmmakers portrayed the inhabitants of Jenin as "victims of a massacre" by the Israeli army, Palestinians considered this well-meant empathy humiliating and insulting. In their self-perception they were courageous heroes who "fell" as valiant fighters in the epic "Battle of Jenin." How does one explain what appears to be collective masochism? What do we know about the propensity for extreme violence in individuals and groups?

The academic literature on violence ranges over a vast field, stimulated mainly by Holocaust studies and theories of fascism. Stanley Milgram's experiments proved that a disposition for extreme aggression exists in most people, once they are subjected to conformity pressure from an authority they perceive to be legitimate. Hannah Arendt's study of Eichmann highlighted the ordinariness of an insecure bureaucrat, as did Christopher Browning's investigations of special Nazi police battalions. In contrast, Daniel Goldhagen unconvincingly ascribes cruelty and hate to the collective inheritance of anti-Semitism in a national (German) character, as opposed to a fascist predisposition in individuals in every culture. Klaus Theweleit's imaginative focus on young men's fantasies of masculinity and warrior-heroes in the inter-European wars, defending their women from alleged enemy rapists, is suggestive, but empirical evidence shows that women can be as cruel and war obsessed as men. The patriarchal exclusion of women from combat activities and relegation to the private realm, not differential gender dispositions, explains the disproportionate absence of women from war crimes.[51]

The Israeli-Palestinian conflict in particular suggests a shift away from a self-contained individualism to a relational model of violence, which the South African psychologist Don Forster has emphasized in his study of perpetrator motivations exposed by the Truth Commission. In this more sociological conceptualization, organizational dynamics are foregrounded as triggers and filters of violence. The explanation of suicide bombers especially benefits from considering "violence-facilitators" in the relational conditions in which subjectivity is forged and expressed. The lack of empathy by both sides presupposes internalized images of self and of victims that are constructed by organizational interactions. Once caught in an organizational culture, be it an Israeli army unit, a special police force, American troops in Abu Ghraib or an Islamist resistance group, its members feel prone to act according to unique group norms and codes of conduct, rather than individual conscience. Universal morals are largely suspended in these situations.

Don Forster's research unearthed a sense of entitlement for abuse in all perpetrators, because they all blamed the victims for their fate. The cruelty by otherwise moral and decent individuals is rationalized with the excuse that the victims brought the violence upon themselves, because they had started it, just as in the Milgram experiment the subjects "deserved" to be electrically shocked for their slow learning. Any counter-discourse of peace and compromise would therefore have to start with the perpetrator's constructed image of the adversary, the language of mobilization and indoctrination in a militarized culture, and the messages leaders and media communicate to their constituencies. Furthermore, peace education would have to counteract exaggerated and self-ascribed victimization. People who perceive of themselves as victims can justify anything to rectify their status.

Hobbes reasoned that the authority of the state, which citizens bestow on their government, is ultimately grounded in their fear of death. Hobbes' assumed initial human condition of war by everyone against everyone ("bellum omnes contra omnium"; "homo homini lupus est") is prevented by the state's monopoly of force. A strong state disciplines people into compliance with state-enforced laws that guarantee collective security. This deterrence, however, does not work if lawbreakers do not fear death, or other reasons for compliance, such as ideological identification, are absent. Where martyrdom is a reward, suicide bombers are not going to be deterred; on the contrary, they are encouraged to commit the ultimate sacrifice for their cause. Such indoctrination cancels out the normal human fear of death. The state's most powerful weapons are rendered powerless when a community celebrates martyred teenagers as heroes.

Suicide among committed political activists is culture specific. It differs widely in Asia, Europe, South Africa, or the Middle East.[52] During the thirty-year long armed struggle against apartheid, no one ever committed suicide for the political cause, although the security police presented many of their assassinations as suicide cases. By policy, not lack of capacity, no prominent apartheid leader was ever assassinated by the ANC. Apartheid agents, however, actively targeted prominent opposition activists, including white academics at home and abroad (Rick Turner, David Webster, Ruth First, Albie Sachs). The ANC leadership at least wanted to distinguish itself from its PAC/APLA competition in what an operative once called "a civilized struggle" that distinguished between active combatants and innocent civilians, occasional remote-controlled car bombs and landmines notwithstanding. White casualties of the armed struggle constituted a miniscule proportion of the thousands killed before and during the transition. Indeed, whites hardly cared about the black dead. Had there been more Kenilworth Church bombings, which anyway were carried out by an unrepresentative group late in the transition period, it is doubtful that de Klerk would have received the high endorsement in the referendum for negotiations.

Unlike the PAC, the ANC was able to control its radical violent faction to a large extent. A good example was the reigning in of Chris Hani and his close friend Steve Tshwete, the number two and number three in Umkhonto we Sizwe in 1988. They spoke about the need to take the war in South Africa into white areas and turn the country into a wasteland by attacking soft targets. The ANC had always claimed that this contradicted official policy. One account of the infighting states: "Unusual for a man who generally refrained from internal quarrels, [ANC President Oliver] Tambo publicly repudiated the line advanced by Hani and Tshwete . . . saying that the two were speaking in their personal capacities only. In July he fired Tshwete from the position of Umkhonto we Sizwe Political Commissar."[53]

In contrast, as in the 9/11 attacks, Palestinian suicide bombers indiscriminately target civilians. State deterrence is undermined by the increased privatization of violence in so-called failed or weak states. Where warlords or terror networks have replaced effective governments, it is allegiance to *their* laws and expectations that provides collective protection. The proliferation of small arms in private hands enables deadly feuds according to Hobbesian assumption.

Suicide attacks are frequently depicted as retaliatory by the powerless or psychologically disturbed. Yet they are mostly organizationally sponsored and endorsed. Within the honor, bestowed by the collective, specific events trigger the person to offer him or herself. Students of the phenomenon have distinguished a wide variety of motives, far beyond the generally assumed religious prototype. Based on interviews with apprehended bombers, wills left behind, or background information supplied by parents and friends, the reasons usually highlighted range from "personality disorders and psychological damage" to manipulation of vulnerable children, organizational pressure exploiting the longing for recognition, or simple blackmail of collaborators to redeem themselves.[54]

This pathologizing or theologizing of suicide relegates the act to the realm of the irrational. Overlooked are the political reasons that create a culture of martyrdom as well as personal experiences that drive persons to kill themselves. Trying to understand these circumstances does not exonerate the killers or give them the desired publicity, but drains the field that produces the atrocities. The attacks are triggered, and the triggering events frequently result directly from Israeli actions that are out of sight when the atrocity is assessed. Organizational seduction or the quest for status and recognition would rarely be sufficient for rational people to blow themselves up. Misguided as the strategy may be, these politically aware individual warriors have often rationally calculated the impact of their deeds.

From this perspective, the belt is considered "the smart bomb of the poor," equivalent to U.S. missiles. This political focus can also explain the "happy state" or "joyful expressions" that usually describe the state of mind of the more than one hundred shahids before the explosion. Unlike depressive suicidals in the West, Palestinian attackers smile in their last pictures and videos.

Typical would be the trajectory of Hanadi Jaradat, the twenty-seven-year-old apprentice lawyer from Jenin who in October 2003 blew herself up in a Haifa beach restaurant. Her brother had been killed a few months earlier by the Israeli army. The modest Haifa café in an integrated neighborhood was owned by a Christian Arab family and known to be frequented by Jews and Arabs alike. Apart from her, the explosion killed nineteen people, including five children and four Israeli Arabs. It is unclear whether the place had been chosen randomly or was targeted consciously. Given the tense climate of imminent Israeli threats of assassination or deportation of Arafat at the time, the act clearly aided Israeli hardliners, besides enhancing the militant image of Islamic Jihad, which claimed ownership. Any Palestinian strategist must have been aware of the counterproductive impact of the attack. Yet the endorsement of the senseless deed by 75 percent of Palestinians indicates that feelings of retaliation overrode any wider calculation.

The interstate wars of the nineteenth and twentieth centuries, the wars of liberation from colonial rule, the struggle to end racism in South Africa, or the Cold War between communism and capitalism all ended with the collapse of one system and a distinct new order through a truce or negotiated settlement. No similar clear end can be envisaged for the new ethno-ideological strife, because a peace treaty cannot settle mutually exclusive claims for sacred territory or ideological hegemony. For the foreseeable future, a Hobbesian state of nature has reasserted itself and the psychic energy of martyrdom persists. State counterterror provides no lasting solution to the grievances of marginalized, dispossessed peoples.

The Palestinian shift to counterproductive violence instead of Gandhian civil disobedience must be assessed in the context of the failure of nonviolence. Passive resistance and nonviolence requires minimal respect and some empathy for the other side's cause. If that restraint is lacking, civil disobedience falters in the face of overwhelming force. Gush Shalom reports such a situation in the village of Bidou when other protesters had long given up on this:

> We have never seen such brutality. In the morning, thousands of the people of the village went and sat in the path of the bulldozers, where their olive groves are about to be uprooted. Then these huge bulldozers came. Each one was accompanied by 50 soldiers. They attacked the villagers and beat them brutally, driving them into the streets of the village. Inside the village a real battle started. The youngsters of the village threw stones, and the army responded with gas bombs, but very soon moved to using live munitions. They occupied a building in the center of the village and snipers shot at people from its roof.[55]

Such scenes of state-terrorism against unarmed civilians protecting their property and livelihood are no longer rare aberrations, but increasingly even target Jewish and international sympathizers who join the Palestinians. As the eminent sociologist Leo Kuper has described, a similar South African passive resistance campaign against the pass laws in the 1950s collapsed when the police assaulted the women who took a leading part in the protest.[56] When Israeli tanks fire at unarmed protesters, as happened repeatedly in Gaza, helicopters drop one-ton bombs on crowded apartments or target militants with rockets—regardless of bystanders hit, Israel repeats Sharpeville in 1960 or Amritsar in 1946, when state forces indiscriminately massacred a protest assembly.[57] To the victims, preaching Gandhian nonviolence falls on deaf ears, as Mandela also concluded at the time, when decades of petitioning had failed.

The Israeli government makes negotiation dependent on "no violence" by Palestinians. Similarly, the hardline South African president P. W. Botha made the release of Mandela contingent on his renunciation of armed struggle, a condition the respected political prisoner wisely rejected. A unilateral declaration of truce as a precondition for negotiations by an insurgent movement hands extremists a veto over negotiations. Moderates seeking negotiation are thus undermined by uncompromising militants who can start a new cycle of confrontation at any time. Successful negotiations ultimately threaten the extremist position. In turn, the pressure on official leaders to control violent hardliners increases, and if they accede, they are further delegitimized among enraged sections of their community. This was the dilemma facing Yasser Arafat. "His people, under bombardment are balking at the occupied being asked to provide security for the occupier" observes the *Economist.*[58] Even when the battered PA undertook feeble attempts to control the violence, Israeli actions undermined it several times by targeting prominent leaders. A baffled *Guardian Weekly* correspondent in Ramallah reports that, "The latest Israeli attacks seemed an almost wilful provocation to the militant Palestinian factions just as Mr. Arafat was preparing to risk moving against Hamas for ignoring his orders to stop their attacks."[59]

Militant mobilization by leaders resonates in a population that is daily humiliated at checkpoints or harassed by individuals against their own rules. Palestinians report widely differing behavior of Israeli soldiers. As a conscript army, they reflect the divergent attitudes of the wider society, from humane to brutal. What is being remembered, however, is not the correct, professional behavior, but the extraordinary provocations by individuals, who, like in all armies, act out their predispositions when not constrained and disciplined.

Changing public opinion relies on credible sources. Numerous victims' reports about human rights violations are always suspect as exaggerated. Soldiers' testimonies bear more authenticity and have a greater impact on public consciousness. Yet soldiers, like policemen in Western countries, rarely break an informal code of silence and report abuses by comrades. On the other hand, when the "whole nation is an army," in sociologist's Eyal Ben-Ari's apt formulation, information flows more freely. Still, the blunt description of everyday brutality in the Tel Aviv exhibition "Breaking the Silence" or in Liran Ron Furer's book, *Checkpoint Syndrome,* shocks readers. Documenting the blurring of moral senses in raw adolescent language undermines the carefully nurtured image of the "purity of arms." The testimonies and the growing refuseniks movement also prove that the military socialization into unthinking conformity with slogans such as "One for all, and all for one," does not necessarily succeed. When the insecure nineteen-year-old recruits are observed by the women of Machsom (Checkpoint) Watch, their behavior usually follows the public relations lessons of their instructors. Out of sight, however, incredible actions are also reported.

When Israeli armored vehicles enter a Gaza township in search of militants, they can expect youngsters throwing stones or older unemployed men ineffectually shooting rifles at tanks. In a climate of resistance to occupation, the provocative ritual is played out frequently and with predictable regularity. When, however, the superior force encounters a different scene, frustrated soldiers sometimes create their own adversary. The

Spectator (May 17, 2003) reported such an incident, observed by a foreign correspondent:[60]

> Chris Hedges of the *New York Times* witnessed an IDF unit in Gaza taunting children over loudspeakers, in Arabic, to come out and throw stones: "'Come on, dogs. Come! Son of a whore! Your mother's cunt!' whereupon the soldiers shot them with silencers." Hedges commented that he had seen children shot in several other conflicts, ". . . but I have never before watched soldiers entice children like mice into a trap and murder them for sport."

There seem to be no limits to the invention of novel harassments by bored officials. In South Africa mere skin color demonstrated imagined superiority, while in the Middle East the two adversaries of the same Semitic origin have to demonstrate their power more conspicuously and deviously. Soldiers frequently invoke sexual innuendos. Victoria Buch of The Israeli Committee against House Demolitions observes such a scene:

> We see the boots of the resting Border Policeman sticking out of the window. Noises like gunshots emanate from there, produced by the BP by tapping on a loudspeaker mike "for fun," Khader tells me. Then a Hebrew song is broadcast, loud enough to wake the neighborhood. I am told that the BP repertoire includes in addition imitating the muezzin call for prayers, and ejaculations in Arabic such as "Feyn baba?" ("Where is daddy?")[61]

Cecilie Surasky, a director of the U.S. Jewish Voice for Peace describes her interview with a Palestinian woman from Gaza:

> I ask about the checkpoints. She describes sitting in her car waiting to be allowed to drive through. "The young Israeli soldiers are in sniper posts. You can't see them, but they can see you," she explains. "They signal it's time to go by shooting their guns." She waits a long time until the soldiers say, "OK, now the dogs can go." You think, "Do I want to be called a dog, or do I just want to go?" she tells me. "I don t care, so I start my car and they yell 'No! Not you, I said dogs!' " So she turns her car off, and sometime later they say, "OK, now humans can go!" She starts her car and they look at her and the others and say "No! I said humans." And she turns her car off and waits until finally this other category of Palestinian neither human nor animal is allowed to pass.[62]

A Palestinian NGO reports a typical collective humiliation of the male population of a town after a suicide bomber originated from the location. Rather than acting as deterrent, the provocative actions of unsupervised soldiers clearly feed recruits for more extremism.

At around midnight on Wednesday, April 2, forty Israeli military vehicles entered the Tulkaram refugee camp, imposed a curfew and demanded that all males between the ages of fifteen and forty immediately leave their homes and present themselves to the invading forces. Sameir Omar, a seventeen-year-old from the camp explains what happened next:

> When the soldiers came they threatened to arrest, beat or shoot us if we did not come outside immediately. So, as we were ordered to, thousands of male residents went to the grounds of the UN school. Tulkaram camp is home to about 18,000 people, so as you can imagine there were a lot of us who left our homes. This was at around 6 AM. Once we got there, the soldiers split us into groups, forcing the guys who were between 15–20 years into one corner, separated from the rest. Some of the younger ones were too young to have ID, but the soldiers did not care. They then moved us into one of the school rooms. We were in the room together and the commander started to ask us if we wanted to work for the Israelis, saying he would give us money if we did. When the commander left one of the soldiers made us rip up pictures of martyrs and spit on them—for no reason except that he had the gun. Then he took a Quran and threw it on the floor and demanded that one of the guys stood on it, but he refused so the soldier then tried to force him by pointing his gun at his head. But the commander came back then so the soldier stopped it.[63]

Humiliation is imprinted in memory and propels revenge. Jonathan Lear in citing Avishai Margalit refers to humiliation as "moral emotions." They shape our moral behavior through the way they are remembered. Unlike ethical claims, one cannot claim that subconscious memory is illegitimate.

"A crucial fact about humiliation is that it is hard to remember it without reliving it. . . . The memory of humiliation is the bleeding scar of reliving it. . . . Humiliation, I believe, is not just another experience in our life, like, say, an embarrassment. It is a formative experience. It forms the way we view ourselves as humiliated persons."[64]

Neve Gordon, who once lectured young officers on leadership, summarizes his experience with the elite commanders as "moral slide." When challenged on inhuman behavior, the soldiers argued that they could have acted worse. Israelis frequently gloat in their humanity, given the availability of worse alternatives. "Let me give you one example," says the Israeli director of the Simon Wiesenthal Centre during a visit to South Africa:

"Jenin is a city full of terrorists. Instead of Israel carpet-bombing Jenin, which is exactly what it should have done after of course warning the civilian population, the Israeli soldiers were sent in house-to-house fighting under extremely difficult circumstances in which 23 Israeli soldiers lost their lives."[65]

The problematic means–end rationale—that the security of Israelis recognizes no limits to cruelty—justifies any means to achieve the goal. Gordon concludes:

> In the absence of a universal moral approach—whereby there are things that one simply does not do—one is left with a tribal or relativistic worldview. Here the right to human dignity is contingent on national, ethnic or religious affiliation. Because the IDF has rejected the notion that human beings are created equal, every young commander who follows its codes will inevitably slide down

the slippery moral slope. As the soldiers themselves seemed to understand at the outset of the lecture, universal moral values are what distinguish corrupt from worthy leaders—an axiom that must be applied to the IDF, too.[66]

In the late 1970s, Afrikanerdom underwent a similar debate when Minister Connie Mulder argued: "When it is a question of survival, no rules apply." The conservatives lost this debate, because the minority could not afford to rule over a majority without a semblance of legality. The insistence on rules, equally applicable to blacks and whites, saved the higher costs of direct repression by giving the apartheid system a false legitimacy. Israel is under less structural compunction to preserve the mask of legality, although internationally and in the self-image of its domestic dissenters, the ethnic state benefits from being perceived as a legally constrained entity with even sworn enemies also entitled to due process and recourse to the courts.

The difficult strategic question concerns the assessment of the extent to which "the law" provides protection and space for social forces that would otherwise be squashed outright. In apartheid South Africa, resistance movements always cooperated with the courts, despite their obvious juridical bias. Anti-apartheid movements abroad regularly collected money for expensive self-serving lawyers who sometimes enriched themselves by defending political activists. There are hardly any examples where defendants defied the ritual of appearing respectfully before all-white judges. To which extent such surprising compliance can be induced by Israeli military courts remains to be seen. Marwan Barghouti refused to cooperate with the Israeli judge in his civilian trial in 2004.

Rescuing Negotiations

In the predicament between a shrinking middle ground and strengthened extremists on both sides, several steps are necessary to rescue negotiations. They could be labeled unconditional talks, third-party intervention, credible leadership, and inclusive negotiations. The South African experience in the four realms can be applied to the Middle East.

Unconditional open-ended negotiations should be started even in the absence of any trust between the parties. Enemies, not friends, need to agree on rules of coexistence. Increased trust is the outcome, not a precondition of negotiations. Likewise, cessation of hostilities is the intended result but not a requirement for negotiations. That was also the lesson of the fragile compromise in Northern Ireland between Republicans and Unionists in the absence of IRA disarmament. In South Africa, too, armed struggle, massacres, bombings, and regular shootouts accompanied negotiations, until the very day of the first nonracial elections in April 1994.

Third-party intervention may be useful and necessary to bring the parties to the table. Outside pressure on both sides can assist if the outside party carries weight with both sides, even if it is perceived as relatively partial, as the United States is in the case of Israel. Promises of financial incentives after a settlement or as rewards for interim compromises may also be required. In South Africa, neither side sought direct foreign mediation but the expectations of the country's major trading partners were obvious. In the Middle East, this role as interlocutor clearly falls to the United States and to a lesser extent to the European Union and Arab States. Yet, without a prior U.S. decision to lean on Israel to settle with the Palestinians, no progress is likely, as the Palestinians are unable to achieve it on their own. Michael Ignatieff went so far as to recommend a U.S.-imposed solution.

> The time for endless negotiation between the parties is past: It is time to say that.... the United Nations, with funding from Europe, will establish a transitional administration to help the Palestinian state back on its feet and then prepare the ground for new elections before exiting; and, most of all, the United States must then commit its own troops, and those of willing allies, not to police a ceasefire, but to enforce the solution that provides security for both populations.[67]

Similarly, Tony Judt probably expresses a widespread liberal opinion: "There is only one possible peaceful outcome, everyone involved knows what it entails, and it is going to have to be imposed from the outside, the sooner the better."[68] In reality, however, the U.S. president gave Palestinians the ultimatum to recreate themselves on U.S. terms, before the United States would contemplate a provisional Palestinian state. This dictate preempts democratic elections by predetermining which outcome is acceptable. It shuts down negotiations and allows the militants on both sides to shape the events with more tragedies.

It is deeply ironic that the U.S. State Department in its annual Human Rights Report criticizes Israel for its well-known deficiencies. Given its own poor human rights record after 9/11 with six hundred detainees held indefinitely at Guantanamo, the arbitrary arrests of Muslim suspects, and the suspension of civil liberties, not to mention capital punishment and an extraordinarily high prison population of minorities, the United States lacks the moral authority to monitor detention without trial elsewhere. Moreover, riding roughshod over opponents at home encourages others abroad with the excuse that they merely emulate the superpower in even more trying circumstances. If Israel represents merely an extension of U.S. foreign policy, a human rights critique obscures this symbiotic relationship. It exculpates the real power that could stop the abuses. In the opinion of Israeli journalist Gideon Levy:

> The United States bears direct responsibility for the violations of human rights in this country. If Washington truly wanted to, it could put an end to them, just as it could have long since brought the entire Israeli occupation to an end. Just as it was able to get the separation fence moved, the United States

> could have, if it wished, forced Israel to stop the targeted assassinations and the demolition of homes and the use of the method of administrative detention. A nod from the president of the United States and Jerusalem would immediately change its unrestrained rules of engagement. A signal from the White House, and the IDF would dismantle the checkpoints that are intended to harass the population and the Palestinians would be able to move freely on their roads.[69]

However, that assumed total dependency of a client on a patron who could solve the issue by sheer political will may also be an overly simplistic view. Apart from such unwillingness of outside patrons to impose a settlement, third parties may also be incapable of forcing Israel into a solution that a majority opposes. As Meron Benvenisti pointed out long ago:

"The price of refusing to accede to the Partition Resolution of 1947 at the time was that Israel in the meanwhile has become a vital independent actor with impressive maneuverability in the international arena. If in 1947 (Palestinian) independence was achievable in an international forum, that same independence is now obtainable only from the Israelis, who occupy the land with overwhelming force."[70]

The view of Israel as a "U.S. corporation turned into a state," fully manipulable by external diplomatic activity, ignores the simultaneous autonomy of the client state. Reservations are also warranted toward the U.S.-sponsored spread of democracy in the Arab world as essential to a peaceful resolution of the long-standing Arab-Israeli dispute. The slogan confuses the sequence. Desirable democratic reforms would be more facilitated by decisive U.S. pressure for a settlement of the Palestinian issue rather than waiting for Arab democracy to usher in peace. Given the inflammatory nature of the conflict, genuine plebiscites with the burning Palestinian issues unresolved could well bring to power extremist Islamist forces. Besides, the U.S. formula looks like another delaying tactic, as even Zbigniew Brezezinski, the former national security advisor of Jimmy Carter, pointed out:

> The argument that democracy is the precondition for peace appeared to many to be a rationalization for postponing any effort to resolve the Israeli-Palestinian conflict. Moreover, it ignored the historical reality that democracy can flourish only in an atmosphere of political dignity. As long as the Palestinians live under Israeli control and are humiliated daily, they won't be attracted by the virtues of democracy.[71]

During the likely breakdown of negotiations, popular expectations of gains have to be created by moderate *credible leaders* who undercut their uncompromising competitors. People must perceive an inspiring outcome to look forward to in order to back compromises. In South Africa, such prospects had to rescue an abandoned process on several occasions. After the Boipatong massacre, the Bisho shooting, and the assassination of Chris Hani at Easter 1993, the negotiating leaders stepped back from the brink of civil war by agreeing to new compromises. The new compromises were: sunset clauses for civil servants, compulsory power sharing for five years, entrenching constitutional principles and, above all, agreeing on an election date, even if no agreement on major constitutional principles had been reached. Because the much-desired election date could not be postponed without risking major upheaval, rules of the crucial election and its aftermath also had to be eventually agreed upon. With an election looming, the ongoing violence at least became clearly unjustified, because the gains expected from an election outweighed those expected from further confrontations.

As already discussed, the stature and savvy of South African leaders contributed to their being trusted by a doubtful constituency. Although not great orators, Nelson Mandela, Joe Slovo, and Mac Maharaj had acquired a mystique as impeccable foes of a system under which they had suffered much, whether in prison or in exile. Such widely recognized united leadership is lacking among Palestinians and Israelis alike. Both are relatively fragmented camps with internecine struggles more intense than those within either the National Party or the ANC. On the other hand, repression and crises create new leaders and elevate old ones whose greatest danger is perceived cooptation. Israel rescued Arafat from this fate by beleaguering him in Ramallah. One day it may well be necessary for Israel to negotiate in good faith with Palestinian activists who are jailed as terrorists. Most independence leaders in Africa went this route. More often than realized, activists aim at bombing their way to the negotiating table.

The mutual indemnity agreed upon by the South African opponents recognized this reality. The imaginative amnesty provisions of the Truth and Reconciliation Act did not exculpate both sides from human rights violations, but made it possible (after disclosure) to coexist without mutual retribution despite unforgivable abuses. The Middle East is one of the few ethnic conflicts where neither side is interested in an impartial historical accounting through a Truth and Reconciliation Commission (TRC), to be discussed later, because both are dogmatically convinced of the exclusive legitimacy of their own truth and moral fortitude.

Negotiations must include leaders of all factions willing to participate, rather than "await the outcome of the necessary civil war among Palestinians," as William Safire recommends.[72] Encouraging a civil war among opponents, as some Third Force elements attempted in South Africa and some Israelis contemplate, may weaken an opponent, but the destruction and brutalization caused also affect the victor. After free political activity was allowed in 1990 in South Africa, the intrablack political violence caused fourteen thousand deaths—more than the entire anti-apartheid struggle together. At the same time it destabilized the new order through a heightened and widespread sense of insecurity.

It is vital to include in the negotiations all actors who are capable of upsetting a compromise. The two main South African parties included the smaller actors, such as Buthelezi's Inkatha Party, the Pan African Congress, and the liberal Democratic Party, only nominally in the so-called multilateral negotiations about the new constitution. When "sufficient consensus" was reached between the ANC and the NP in essentially bilateral negotiations, this consensus was imposed on the smaller parties by inviting them to rubberstamp it. As a result, Inkatha opted out of negotiations, threatened to boycott the elections and almost derailed the process before being persuaded to join at the last minute. Likewise, agreements reached by the leadership of the ANC and NP were imposed on their constituencies with little input from the grassroots. Thus, South African democracy was paradoxically born autocratically. This unnatural birth survived because of healthy parental authority. It is doubtful that such controversial compromises could be sustained in the Middle East, unless a final peace agreement is supported by an all-party coalition on both sides.

Academic cynics dismiss all this reasoning with an exclusive focus on power relations. Indeed, Israel's unilateralism can be understood from a purely Machiavellian perspective. Since the state commands all the military and economic power, backed by the United States, the government need not negotiate with powerless Palestinians. It can inject settlers, impose borders, or occupy or disengage from conquered territory almost at will. The logic of negotiations implies concessions. Negotiations reconfigure and mitigate political power. If you command absolute power, why would you want to concede part of it through negotiations? In short, even if there are costs attached to dictating your will, the price is lower than you are likely to pay in genuine negotiations. If one adds the discord that the inevitable concessions cause between softliners and hardliners in a ruling party threatened with the disintegration of a fragile coalition government, retaining the status quo or instigating threats and semi-warfare is a convenient option. If war creates unity, why would any dominant group weaken itself by exposing its manifold internal cleavages through peace-seeking efforts? If perceptions of threat guarantee a leadership additional support, it is tempted to manufacture additional public anxieties.

However, given international relations and the diplomatic climate, every state has to pay lip service to negotiations. Even dictatorial regimes, from Burma to Zimbabwe, pretend that they negotiate with their opponents. Israel escapes this dilemma by arguing that is has no partner to negotiate with while Arafat was alive. Unilateralism rests on the "no partner" myth, despite Geneva accords and solid other evidence. Israel has convinced its public at home and abroad that it has offered maximal concessions in Clinton-sponsored negotiations at Camp David, only to be rejected by an intransigent Palestinian leadership. How and why does an informed public buy into such polarizing policies instead of supporting forces of peacemaking?

5

Visions of Endgame

On the two assumptions that no military solution is possible in the Middle East conflict and that no solution is likely to be imposed, it would be logical that sooner or later the adversaries will have to negotiate seriously again. Four basic positions maintain fluctuating constituency support: Islamic extremist, Jewish extremist, two-state solution, and multicultural common state.

Islamic Extremist Positions

The Islamist extremist camp considers the very existence of a Jewish state on Muslim soil an insult to the faith. It aims to defeat the colonizing intruder and restore pre-Zionist Palestine. Clearly, this position, which has long been discredited among responsible Palestinians themselves, has no chance of success. Nevertheless, it necessitates continued Israeli vigilance and military readiness, which are inimical to peaceful coexistence and mutual trust.

Unlike in South Africa, an international support group reinforces this extremist position. Destroying the Jewish state is part of the declared goal of many Muslim states that sponsor their own anti-Israeli guerrillas (e.g., the Hezbollah in Iran) or train and finance Palestinian suicide activists. In this vein, Iran's influential former president Akbar Hashemi Rafsanjani exhorted crowds in Teheran: "The establishment of Israel is the most hideous occurrence in history. The Islamic world will not tolerate the continued existence of Israel in the region and will vomit it out from its midst."[1] If states that massacre their own minorities, such as Iran, Iraq, or Syria, acquire weapons of mass destruction, the Jewish state is indeed highly vulnerable and World War III could be triggered.

In contrast, after the end of the Cold War, all foreign allies of the ANC urged the movement to compromise and withdrew active military sponsorship. While the support of the Palestinian cause occurs mostly for domestic political reasons or even represents a pretence rather than empathy for the Palestinians (who are resented throughout the Arab world), such hostility toward Israel may well continue even after a Palestinian-Jewish settlement.

The overdue democratization of the Arab world would be not only unlikely to change attitudes toward Israel, but could even increase open hostility. Replacing corrupt autocrats through genuine popular involvement likely would result in Islamists taking over in some states. As long as the Arab population is indoctrinated by clerics in pursuit of "an assault on imperialist world Zionism," the sentiment of the street nullifies pacts of negotiating leaders. Does this predicament make a settlement superfluous? On the contrary, Israel has an additional reason to secure the loyalty of the Palestinian population under its control.

The Israeli peace camp is constantly undermined not by what the Palestinian leadership says, but what Arabs locally and abroad really think. Bernie Susser[2] has commented that for Israeli doves, surveys on Arab attitudes toward Israel make for somber and gloomy reading. When Palestinian factions insist on the right of return of all refugees to their Israeli places of origin, the Jewish character of Israel is indeed threatened. When moderate Palestinians counsel compromise, they are denounced. Others keep silent for fear of marginalizing themselves in Palestinian politics.

The anti-apartheid camp always enjoyed a more robust debate about strategy and goals. While the exiled ANC—and particularly its Stalinist South African Communist Party (SACP) wing—also attempted to impose a correct line on its constituency, the appropriateness of sanctions or the use of violence was always openly challenged by moderate black parties (IFP) or white liberals (PFP) with legitimate opposition credentials. Unlike Palestinian militant attitudes blocking an accommodating leadership, popular sentiment in South Africa, on the whole, tended more toward compromise than the ANC/UDF (United Democratic Front) leadership cared to admit at times. When the crunch of real trade-offs arrived, South African negotiators not only enjoyed relatively uncontested credentials, but they closely echoed popular attitudes. Palestinian leaders face the challenge not only of internal cohesion, but also of educating an embittered constituency in accepting necessary compromises.

Jewish Extremist Positions

Jewish extremists mirror their Islamic counterparts. They come in two versions: those aiming at the ultimate forced "transfer" of Palestinians from the occupied territories, and those creating ghetto-like conditions of colonial domination that motivates many Palestinians to emigrate voluntarily or acquiesce to a second-class status. Some Israeli politicians openly advocate expulsion, another *nakba* (catastrophe), and gain steam with every bloody incident. This renewed expulsion would only be possible in the context of another major war. Therefore, these right-wingers prefer dealing with their extremist counterparts in Hamas and Jihad, whose terrorism legitimizes extremist counterterror. Palestine's representation by fundamentalist extremists diminishes European support and guarantees that the United States will never spring a "surprise" compromise on an unwilling Israeli government. Tanya Reinhart comments: "It is easier to justify even the worst acts of oppression when the enemy is a fanatical Muslim organisation."[3] A step in this direction is the destruction and delegitimizing of the Palestinian Authority. Most of the settler population strongly supports this vision. Already, the Sharon government has targeted the infrastructure of the rudimentary Palestinian state. Even before the April 2002 large scale invasion of the territories, sewage plants, radio towers, and power facilities were bombed; the Central Statistics Bureau ransacked, the runway of the only airport bulldozed, irrigation systems destroyed, and more Palestinian orchards uprooted.

However, the full destruction of Palestinian self-rule and eventual expulsion incurs costs and political risks. As Avishai Ehrlich has pointed out, Israel cannot afford to draw comparisons with the Serbian persecution of Albanians in Kosovo and provoke an international response.[4] Therefore, the Bantustan option of minimizing effective Palestinian statehood to dispersed smaller parts of the West Bank and Gaza, and reversing the Oslo Accord, appeals to influential Israeli planners. The lethal attacks by intifada activists provide the rationale for an ever-tighter containment.

The apartheid government pursued the opposite strategy of subsidizing and building homelands and township administrations so that blacks would administer their own poverty and police themselves. Black activists tried to destroy these "institutions of the oppressed" in order to make the country ungovernable. In its attempt to dismember the social fabric of Palestinian society and atomize the population, Israel's direct domination is more excessive than the more-sophisticated apartheid strategy.

Fragmenting the Palestinian territory into fenced-in enclaves resembles the grand apartheid Bantustan policy of pretending that noncontiguous patches of land could eventually constitute viable independent states. Impoverished and overcrowded under corrupt and unpopular authoritarian rulers, these "homelands" in both cases were—and are—doomed to fail in fulfilling the aspirations of their populations. In addition, when two sets of laws apply to residents of the same territory (as is the case for Israeli settlers and Palestinians), then this differential treatment amounts to apartheid.

However, three important differences must also be taken into account when suggesting the Bantustan analogy. First, unlike the rural areas of South Africa with a majority of illiterate peasants, the Palestinian territories mostly comprise an urbanized, educated, and highly politicized people, whose traditional livelihood is threatened by travel restrictions and land confiscations. Second, the apartheid state poured substantial amounts of money into its nine ethnic homelands. This aimed at beefing up their tottering bureaucracies and underdeveloped infrastructure with the goal of providing the artificial states with a semblance of independence (parliaments, airports, universities, courts, etc.). The subsidies were also meant to attract African work seekers back from the white areas and keep the rural population from further migrating away from their places of low-cost living. The Likud state, on the other hand, largely destroyed and undermined the Palestinian institutions of self-government set up after Oslo. The 140,000 employees of the Palestinian Authority are mainly paid through foreign donations. Instead of aiming at creating sovereign states, as in the apartheid designs, the dominant Likud vision intends to prevent a strong and viable Palestinian state.

Third, and most important, the legitimacy of the semi-independent PA rulers, both among their own population as well as internationally, is much greater. Apart from South Africa, no other government recognized the sovereignty of the Bantustans, while in the Palestine/Israel case, the international community widely supports the establishment of a Palestinian state. The Palestinian presidential elections in March 1996 and January 2005 were considered creditable, while the South African Bantustan rulers (with the exception of Chief Buthelezi who rejected independence) were widely perceived as stooges of Pretoria, who suppressed their opposition in sham elections. Homeland leaders were paid and imposed by the colonial power on a subjugated population, not elected in multi-party contests. Although Hamas too rejected the Oslo Accord as a collaborationist recognition of Israel, and the secular Fatah tried to suppress its Islamist foes by force for a while, they also coexisted and frequently collaborated as mutually dependent factions of a people under occupation. The respected Palestinian pollster Khalil Shikaki estimates that a new Palestinian parliament resulting from an internationally supervised election would be shared by three forces: "The mainstream Fatah nationalists are projected to win up to 40 percent of the seats (compared to the 75 percent they now hold); independent nationalists and moderate Islamists a quarter of the seats; and members of Hamas and Islamic Jihad the rest."[5]

Israel, on the one hand, would have an interest in a legitimate Palestinian Authority that could enforce laws against vigilante violence and freelance militias. On the other hand, it could also be seen benefiting from Palestinian divisions and divide-and-rule policies, just as apartheid South Africa ethnicized its population for this purpose.

The Bantustan analogy applies mainly in a geographical sense insofar as noncontiguous patches of land are labeled a viable state. Michael Ignatieff, describing the view from a helicopter over the West Bank, observed: "I knew I was not looking down at a state or the beginnings of one, but at a Bantustan, one of those pseudo-states created in the dying years of apartheid to keep the African population under control."[6] However, Bantustans were established neither at the end of apartheid nor only for control purposes. From the outset of Afrikaner social engineering, pseudo-independent "homelands" formed the core of apartheid rationalization as the abandonment of colonialism and the advent of African self-determination. As reservoirs of cheap labor and dumping grounds for surplus people, Bantustans saved the social costs of old age, unemployment, and education. Huge amounts of taxes were poured into wasteful rural bureaucracies to give the ethnic states a semblance of viability and respectability.

Israel has pursued the opposite strategy of colonial policing. Instead of strengthening the Palestinian Authority to deliver services and control its population, thereby contributing to the security of the Jewish state, it has deliberately weakened, frustrated, and continually undermined the rudimentary state. As Ignatieff has rightly pointed out, "[The Palestinian Authority] failed because Israel never allowed it to become a state. When authorities cannot become competent states, when they cannot meet the needs of their people, they can only survive by playing to the longing of their populations to counter humiliation by acts of suicidal revenge."[7]

In contrast to the rural, impoverished South African Bantustans, the West Bank is inhabited by an educated, far more urbanized and developed population. With such favorable preconditions for statehood as well as resistance in place, imprisoning a people in several enclaves where they manage their "own affairs" has to fail. Indirect rule failed under better conditions in South Africa. With reluctant clients in the form of Palestinian Authority nationalists and opportunists, policing from the outside by an occupation army and aggressive settlers as close neighbors, encounters much greater problems than apartheid South Africa ever experienced with its remote Transkei or Bophuthatswana ruled by dependent clients. Faced with this treatment, extremist organizations will only gain more support by providing social services as well as suicide bombers, who view their vile methods as the last resort of the weak and desperate. Regarding this "Lebanonization" of Israel, Anthony Lewis has written: "Every assassination, every smashed refugee camp brings new recruits to the Palestinian organizations that target Israelis."[8]

The problem with the current and future disentanglement lies in exacerbating the tensions and violence of an unsustainable status quo. More land seizure by the Israeli Defense Force (IDF) for security zones and fences, more restrictions on Palestinian movements, and, above all, fewer economic opportunities create new frustrations and rage. In addition to physical control, Israel has perfected bureaucratic repression. Withholding building-, residency- and family-reunion permits, seizing identity cards, and imposing exorbitant taxes all serve to penalize an aspiring middle class. Palestinian property in Jerusalem is quietly confiscated without compensation or appeal by settlement expansion and new barriers, though the owners have always lived nearby, but are now across a new artificial boundary. In South Africa, the apartheid state rightly cultivated a conservative "non-white" bourgeoisie as a potential ally. Increased economic integration facilitated the South African settlement. Economic interdependence motivated South African antagonists to compromise. The opposite strategies of disentanglement create more impoverishment for one side, which then has little left to lose. In this climate of hopelessness, likely unpredictable atrocities can derail all rational deals and shift populations to all-out confrontations. Even if most parties want to avoid costly direct reoccupation, there is little time to counter the escalation of conflicts.

Two-State Positions

In theory, two-state advocates constitute the overwhelming majority of Jews and Palestinians, but they disagree about borders, Jerusalem, the return of Palestinian refugees, and settlers behind the Green Line, the post-1967 border that demarcates the internationally recognized Palestinian territory. The official Palestinian position is to insist on the recognition of the right of all refugees to return, but leave its implementation to Israel. With various options for refugees dependent on personal choice, compensation for most or a symbolic return of older people only or relocation to a Palestinian state, is envisaged. Furthermore, 97 percent of the occupied territories are expected to form a viable Palestinian state, compared with the 40 percent of territory under Palestinian Authority control after the mutual recognition in the Oslo Accord of 1993.

In the historic Oslo Accord, a transitional period was agreed upon during which Israel would gradually transfer land in the West Bank and Gaza to the Palestinian Authority until a permanent peace was established in final status negotiations. Barak and Clinton aimed at such a final settlement in the hastily called Camp David and Taba negotiations during the last months of the two leaders' terms of office. The talks failed, even though Barak had informally offered between 93 and 95 percent of occupied land and the Palestinians were prepared to accept the principle of Israeli annexation of some of the West Bank settlements in exchange for an equivalent transfer of Israeli land to the Palestinians. Informed observers blamed all three parties' negotiation strategies for the failure, not just the Palestinian delegation's intransigent, incoherent behavior, as has become conventional wisdom.[9] It is also doubtful that Barak would have received Knesset approval for his plan whose failure is now solely blamed on the Palestinians. If the Palestinians had accepted the "generous" Barak offer, a Palestinian "state" would have consisted of three separate West Bank cantons and the distant Gaza strip, all encircled by Israeli troops without a common border with Jordan or Egypt and totally dependent on Israel for power, water, and jobs. Any Palestinian leader would have faced a revolt by militants in his own ranks for agreeing to such a noncontiguous and nonviable Bantustan. Arafat's reported question to Clinton is therefore understandable: "Do you want to attend my funeral?" And yet with further mutual concessions at Taba, both negotiating teams agreed to the statement: "The sides declare that they have never been closer to reaching an agreement and it is thus our shared belief that the remaining gaps could be bridged with the resumption of negotiations following the Israeli election."[10]

Since Oslo, and contrary to the later Mitchell recommendation to freeze settlements, Israel continued with new settlements beyond allowing only "natural" expansion. The increase of the settler population since Oslo has destroyed the trust-building measures envisaged in the accord and has clearly signaled to the Palestinians that Israel is intent on annexing rather than conceding the remaining 22 percent of Mandate Palestine for a viable state. Almost unnoticed, 400 km of bypass roads were constructed, which sliced up Palestinian land, restricted movements, uprooted traditional agriculture, and caged in Palestinians in such a way that Bophuthatswana looks attractive by comparison. With the ascendancy of Likud, the mutual tit-for-tat reprisals assumed their lethal dynamic, so that a large proportion of Palestinians began to sympathize with suicide attacks. Inasmuch as the liberation movements in South Africa never recognized the nine "homelands" offered, so Palestinians are unlikely to accept a rump-state in the West Bank and Gaza with fenced-in ghettoes of noncontiguous territory.

When Egypt and the PLO finally recognized Israel, it happened out of expediency and necessity, not because it confirmed the moral legitimacy of the Jewish state. Agreeing to Israel's existence was conceding defeat. The continuing war of words at least relieved the painful terms of surrender in the reality of a lost struggle. In the imagination of the vanquished, the victims always remained the moral victors. "Bearing this in mind explains the Palestinian's view that Oslo itself is the historic compromise—an agreement to concede 78% of mandatory Palestine to Israel."[11] Therefore, when Israel was "offering" land, being "generous," or "making concessions," it added insult to injury "in a single stroke both affirming Israel's right and denying the Palestinians'. For the Palestinians, land was not given but given back."[12]

Applying these sensitivities to South Africa, a different assessment of the historic compromise can be found. Unlike Palestinians, blacks could feel as if they were victors. It was the colonized who could now prove generous to the settlers, who accepted them as white Africans, provided they shared their spoils and regarded everybody as equals. In contrast, among Palestinian intellectuals, the Oslo Accord is widely perceived as merely a technical document that postpones the most acute issues. With a "newer jargon for the older occupation," Palestinian academic Andre Mazawi noted, Oslo amounts to "a negotiated colonizing de-colonization."[13] Nobody could argue this for the South African political transition. It put the black majority in charge of the state, although the colonial unequal economic relations remained at the core of the compromise. In the end, South African whites were defeated politically (not militarily), although they were able to negotiate the terms of their defeat. By contrast, there is no prospect that Palestinians could defeat Israel. In this respect, Palestinian negotiators resemble white South Africans rather than blacks.

With the reversal of political power in the offing, white South Africans could no longer dictate the terms but had to deal with an equal partner. There are no equal parties in the Middle East. Unlike the Israeli attitude of supremacy when dealing with the adversary, white South Africans, at least in public, easily slipped into a discourse of deference to the new power holders who continued to struggle with the legacy of racism. Nevertheless, with white economic power intact, a black bourgeoisie in office tied to economic growth and in the private sector vying for personal enrichment,[14] the historic compromise was sealed to mutual satisfaction. This sense of victory—or a win-win situation for both sides—that made the abolition of apartheid such a celebrated event despite the continuing economic inequality, will not necessarily be achieved through the creation of a Palestinian mini-state, unless other Palestinian demands (return of refugees, East Jerusalem, settler presence) are also satisfactorily addressed.

In the South African tradition of trade-offs, there could be a gradual abandonment of illegal settlements in the occupied territories in exchange for the Palestinian abandonment of the right of refugees returning to Israel. Together with foreign financial assistance for both sides, Palestinian refugees could move into Jewish settlements in the West Bank and Gaza while Jewish settlers would receive assistance for reintegration into Israel proper. Jewish settlers willing to reside in a Palestinian state could be granted the same citizenship rights as Palestinians in Israel. The existence of each group's minority in the other state could guarantee as well as encourage improvements for the two "hostage" populations.

In any case, the "demographic threat" to the Jewish majority through the return of Palestinian refugees is vastly exaggerated. According to Khalil Shikaki's Palestinian Center for Policy and Survey Research, only 10 percent would want to return to their former homes in Israel.[15] While the great majority insists on the recognition of the *principle* of return, few are interested in putting their right into action. Half of the 4,500 respondents surveyed by Shikaki would like to live in an independent Palestinian state, while 17 percent preferred to stay in their current homes. The vast majority of refugees were willing to accept monetary compensation in lieu of homes and land lost in 1948. It is also widely accepted that if Israel recognizes the right of return in principle, its implementation could be limited to a negotiated annual quota. Another compromise could consider abolishing the "Law of Return" for Jews, but establishing a right of asylum in Israel for persecuted Jews and Palestinians alike, according to the practice of most Western democracies.

A Multicultural Common State

The fourth vision of a denationalized Western liberal democracy would have to be preceded by a redefinition of individual identity on both sides, for which the nationalist mobilization and collective stereotyping of the other undermines all prospects at present. Even the PLO abandoned this position long ago and for Jewish nationalists it implies the demographic capture and abandonment of a Jewish state. Instead of the apartheid model of partition that "relieves" the Jewish state of its conquered population and implants newcomers in their midst, very few now advocate this option of a common secular, bicultural state, where Jews and Palestinians reside in multicultural harmony. Since 1999, the late Edward Said called for a binational state because "Israeli Jews and Palestinians are irrevocably intertwined."[16] In Said's view, "It is the one idea, a vision based on equality, that will allow people to live and not to exterminate each other." Said, however, distrusted compromises and called the peace process (Oslo) simply "a repacking of the Israeli occupation"[17] and a "gigantic fraud." He assumed "classical colonialism" on the Israeli side, when in fact the agenda of political Zionism aims more at displacement. Said also undermined his case for binationalism by speculating that Israel is "laying up a store of resentment and even hatred that is going to endure for generations," asserting that "at some point the reckoning is going to come."[18] If there will be an inevitable reckoning, why should two people trust each other to coexist in the same state? In short, given the polarization, the binational option remains an idealistic illusion at present. At best, it could gradually evolve after a two-state solution in an interim period.

Collective revenge out of accumulated rage was also predicted at the height of apartheid, but never materialized. Instead, the victims mostly turned the frustrations inward against themselves through self-destructive habits, domestic violence, and black-on-black crime. Yet, emulating the new South Africa of inclusiveness would also be the most economically beneficial option for both sides, in line with progressive global trends to separate *cultural* from *political* identity. Already, one million Palestinians with Israeli citizenship live in Israel proper with a tolerable level of animosity, except that they are by definition second-class citizens in an officially Jewish state. Incorporating their stateless counterparts in the West Bank and Gaza would alter the Jewish numerical majority and entail a significant change in the character of the state. Cultural Judaism would have to be distinguished from political "Israeliness." Nationalists reject this vision outright and, in light of such strong feelings, the idea is indeed unrealistic and utopian. Just as many Palestinians find themselves unwilling to compromise about perceived "basic rights,"[19] most Jewish Israelis are unable to shed the Zionist dogma of an ethnic state. The notion that safety lies in numbers is as fallacious as the assumption that the Jewish character of Israel can only be retained by a numerical majority. This presupposes that all Palestinians will possess the vote, which Sharon asserts will never happen. Above all, the myth of a "demographic threat" assumes that all Palestinians, even if they had the vote, would vote as a monolithic ethnic bloc, which is unlikely to be the case. In the first South African democratic election, the majority of the discriminated-against "Colored" group voted for white parties, despite previous oppression by whites.

In economic terms and following the EU model, another interim solution could be a Benelux-type entity that includes Jordan with its majority Palestinian population in addition to a Palestinian state and Israel. In a tri-national confederation like this, Israel would not have hegemony demographically, but would benefit from being incorporated into the Middle East, while a Palestinian state and Jordan would benefit from Israeli know-how and capital. The Jordanian Hashemite rulers would also enjoy a built-in balance against a potential Palestinian takeover. Given the unequal power relationship, however, such an economic–political union could also be perceived as Israeli imperialism, just as the South African dominance of its surrounding states is resented as "big brother" rule.

In an ethnically neutral Jewish/Arab union, both ethnic groups would still preserve their cultural identity, which would be officially recognized and subsidized as in other multinational states. But politically, the new entity would be neither a Muslim Palestine nor a Jewish Israel. Both victimized people could still worship as they desire, educate their children in separate schools, and have Hebrew and Arabic recognized in an officially bilingual state. If Muslims, Christians, Jews, Hindus, and agnostics can live together harmoniously as equal citizens in South Africa, many South Africans have asked, why should this not be possible in a society where both people have legitimate claims to share the land? However, this dream ignores the history of both peoples in the Holy Land, and even the South African government officially supports a two-state solution.

Political realists forecast that more dead will be counted and battle lines frozen after mutual exhaustion, more professionals on both sides will emigrate, more tourists will stay away, and a fatal image of a region in decline will emerge before either a mutually acceptable separation or some form of binational federalism or confederalism will emerge in the economically intertwined contested small space. Direct expulsion of Palestinians by edict and terror or indirect "transfer" by unlivable circumstances should also not be ruled out. Some have argued that both Israel and its Arab neighbors require a perpetual state of semi-war in order to prevent their internal cleavages from exploding. This is a cynical assessment, although the historical reality would seem to confirm it.

Israel was founded as the sanctuary of persecuted Jews the world over. A state of permanent war, however, means that the sanctuary is constantly threatened. With anti-Semitism on the wane at least in North America, the diaspora ironically is now the safe haven, while Jews in the sanctuary are in jeopardy. The continued occupation of Palestinian territory and the extension of settlements have substantially contributed to this insecurity, although it is not the sole cause of Arab hostility. This is all the more reason for the sanctuary to restore its pre-1967 borders by accommodating its Palestinian neighbors with their own state and resettling most settlers. However, inasmuch as a common, binational state may be a distant dream, so peace through separation also denies political and social realities. Perhaps the emergence of new identities within an enlarged EU may point to the possibility of overcoming the ethno-nationalist enmity, just as Europe has finally transcended its intra-European warfare of the last century.

II

After the Violence

The second part of the book deals with post-conflict reconstruction at the symbolic level of narrowing the divergent historical narratives of the two people.

Regardless of whether Palestinians ultimately achieve viable sovereign statehood or equal citizenship in a single or binational state—or, as currently seems more likely, continued apartheid-style, conflict-ridden coexistence prevails—some reckoning with the crimes of the past on both sides will be on the future agenda. Nonviolent and more stable inter-group relations require institutionalized accounting for past injustices. Negotiated agreements on refugees, settlers, borders, or the status of Jerusalem, as necessary as they are, will not end the deep enmity between two people, even if they live side by side in two separate states.

Could a South African–style truth commission help both societies come to terms with their past? An Israeli-Palestinian truth-seeking effort obviously must draw lessons from similar experiences elsewhere and avoid the mistakes of the celebrated South African model. The next three chapters thus focus on how different societies, South Africa in particular, have dealt with the crimes of their past.

There are no universally valid rules as to how an emerging democracy should deal with the crimes of a previous regime. It seems useful to explore empirically how different democracies have coped with the problem of state-sponsored crimes, how victims are recognized or compensated, how the new order attempts reconciliation between warring factions, and how the repetition of an unsavory past may be prevented. In what follows, we examine the South African experiment critically and comparatively with a focus on how future institutional provisions of post-conflict reconstruction generally can be improved. Although the context is different, we venture some suggestions on how these South African lessons apply to the Israel-Palestinian conflict.

6

Collective Memories: How Democracies Deal with the Crimes of Previous Regimes

The Politics of Memory

Human memory is never an objective fact—a collection of fixed, stored data that can be downloaded or accumulated for later use. What is remembered and how events are recalled depends very much on social conditions. Interests shape individual, as well as collective, memory. Memory, therefore, amounts to a contingent social construction.

The academic study of *collective memory* owes much to the classic work by French historian Maurice Halbwachs who coined the term with the same book title in 1941. Conceived in the Durkheimian tradition, Halbwachs stresses that history is constantly being rewritten. Through examples from the Christian scriptures, Halbwachs demonstrates how selective perceptions—rooted in present interests—have resulted in quite different accounts of the Holy Land. The concerns of the present shape the collective memory of the past. For this early postmodern approach, historical research is not a process of retrieving forgotten or buried facts, but a process of constructing the past as it is impinged upon by the present. Far from an eternal truth of the Gospel, Halbwachs argues, the stories of the Apostles differ substantially or are wholly imaginary in describing places or relating identical events. The American sociologist Lewis Coser, who has translated Halbwachs into English, has aptly summarized his insights with the simple observation that each generation of pilgrims and visitors found in the Holy Land what they wished to find.

Ian Buruma has rightly pointed out: "Memory is not the same as history and memorializing is different from writing history."[1] If the two are lumped together, the distinction between fiction and fact, falsehood and truth, is lost. A history concerned with establishing factual events is to be distinguished from the interpretation of those events. About this interpretative and moral truth, opinions can legitimately differ, particularly in divided societies. Because individual morals, feelings, and interests vary widely in a heterogeneous collectivity, it is problematic to assume a collective psyche. Without a collective persona, there can hardly be a collective memory. Only in a loose, metaphorical sense can we speak of a collective identity, a national character, or a collective memory.

Collective memory constitutes the informal widely accepted perceptions of past events that mirror a people's collective identity. This identity is strongly influenced by the official definitions, rituals, and laws of the state. The memorials that a state erects, the national holidays selected, the museums subsidized, the speeches of politicians that celebrate or mourn the past and define a state's self-perception in laws and public institutions are all contributions to collective memory that changes over time.[2] Divided memories exist when sizable groups within the same state simultaneously attribute different meanings to the same history, just as individual witnesses to crimes or car accidents testify to the same event in surprisingly contradictory terms.

Six forms of grappling with the past can be distinguished and compared in their historical context: (1) amnesia (post-war Germany, Japan, Spain, Russia); (2) trials and justice (Nuremberg, International Criminal Court); (3) lustration, that is, the disqualification of collaborators from public office (GDR, Eastern Europe); (4) negotiated restitution (Germany's reparations to Israel and compensations for forced labor, Canada's and Australia's negotiations about indigenous minorities' land rights); (5) political re-education; and (6) truth commissions (Latin America and South Africa).

Several of these strategies are frequently employed simultaneously or with different emphases over time. Of all cases, two countries are of particular significance: Germany, because of its unique past with Auschwitz as the universal paradigm of barbarism, and South Africa. The South African Truth and Reconciliation Commission (TRC) deserves critical scrutiny for three reasons: It is a novel experiment of restorative justice and nation-building through reconciliation; the TRC is often recommended as an international model for similar conflicts elsewhere, from Cambodia to ex-Yugoslavia; and achievements of the TRC are widely overrated outside South Africa, while largely dismissed inside. Among its flaws and problematic assumptions is the fallacy that "revealing is healing." Legislated reconciliation negates the belief that only victims can forgive. The skewed composition of the TRC and its theological perspectives has affected its credibility. The quest for an official truth and common memory denies pluralist interpretations of history. Above all, the focus on gross human rights violations frees the many beneficiaries of apartheid from responsibility and obliterates the structural violence of racial laws for millions of victims not recognized by the TRC process. Before a detailed discussion of the merits and shortcomings of the South African TRC and how its lessons could be applied to the Middle East, we explore how other societies have dealt with the issues of transitional justice.

Amnesia

In Germany, the post-war period up to the mid-sixties represents a typical example of official amnesia and private denial. Chancellor Adenauer, who himself was an anti-Nazi politician, nevertheless defended his heavily implicated aide, Hans Globke, with the demand in parliament "to stop the sniffing for Nazis!" Instead of dealing honestly with the shame of the past, it was not to be remembered. The future and the rebuilding of the nation should be focused upon. Wallowing in a terrible past was futile, could not be reversed and should be considered a catastrophe, like a natural disaster, rather than the result of political decisions. The Nazi period was portrayed as an accident of German history. "In the middle of the 1950s," writes the historian Norbert Frei, "a collective consciousness had emerged that attributed solely to Hitler and his inner circle all responsibilities for the atrocities of the Third Reich."[3] Germans as a whole were ascribed the role of a politically seduced people whom the war and its consequences had made into victims themselves. To this day, the 8th of May is designated as "the day of liberation" by allied forces, implying that Germans were mainly victims of Nazi rule. Daniel Goldhagen's "willing executioners" had shrunk to a small minority. The active complicity and passive collusion of a silent majority was out of sight and memory. The phrase *hour zero* (Stunde Null) dismissed historical continuity, insisting instead on a newborn society that had no relationship with the previous period.

In the communist German Democratic Republic (GDR), official anti-fascism denied all links with the Nazi past. Since the "dark brown period" had—in this economistic Marxist dogmatism—resulted from a capitalist crisis, the heroic rise of socialism in the anti-fascist struggle had also taken care of all fascist remnants and preconditions.

In the West, the theory of totalitarianism reigned supreme in the ensuing Cold War. The free West proudly distinguished itself from both the brown and red totalitarianism. The sociologist Helmut Dubiel asserts that, "The true scandal of German memorializing was not that the Nazi past was simply ignored, but immersed in the ideological competition between East and West."[4] Both states accused each other of failing to draw the necessary conclusions from history. Each side blamed the other for perpetuating conditions in which freedom was denied.

There are two main explanations for the post-war amnesia. The most widely accepted version holds that the economic and bureaucratic reconstruction required the inclusion of Nazi collaborators, given the scarcity of skills available. German rearmament in the 1950s, for example, would have been impossible without falling back on the expertise of previous officers. Large sectors of the colluding population needed to be integrated into the new democracy and could not have been marginalized.

A second, psychologically based explanation focuses on the subconscious reaction to collective trauma. A fragile collective identity—psychoanalytically speaking, a "weak ego"—had to protect itself against an unbearable truth by repressing and rationalizing it. Adorno pointed to the paradox that the factual collapse of the Nazi world had not been reflected in the psychic disposition of the population. With reference to Freud, Adorno draws the questionable conclusion that this proves the survival of Nazi mentalities: "What is missing when collective identities unravel, according to the theory of 'Mass Psychology and Ego Analysis,' is the phenomenon of panic. Unless one wants to dismiss the insights of the great psychologist, this allows for only one conclusion: that the old identifications and collective narcissism were not destroyed but continue secretly dormant in the unconscious and are therefore particularly powerful."[5]

However, one could speculate equally persuasively that perhaps the Nazi identifications were not as deeply internalized and the consciousness of injustice was more widespread than the suspicions of Adorno allow. Otherwise, the allied democratic re-education would not have run so successfully and smoothly. As critical studies in the tradition of *The Authoritarian Personality* have proven, this character type is more shaped by conformity pressure than by internalized ideological convictions. With the change of power holders, the dominant attitudes of ego-weak characters also change. They replace easily one ideological doctrine with an opposite equally authoritarian master narrative. Therefore it is helpful to criminalize hate speech. While attitudes cannot be legislated, discriminatory behavior at least can be constrained by being outlawed.

It was not until the late 1960s that the children of the war generation revived questions about the past, spurred on by the student revolt against authoritarian traditions and general politicization. Debates about the statute of limitations of prosecutions after widely publicized trials of concentration camp guards under German jurisdiction together with moving personalized films about the Holocaust also evoked new interests. Yet another generation later, the meaning of the past has never been more intensely debated. The public controversy started with the 1986 dispute among academic historians about the comparability and relationship between Stalinist and fascist terror (*Historikerstreit*)[6] and continued with the Goldhagen controversy in 1996,[7] the Walser-Bubis argument in 1998,[8] and the simultaneous controversial exhibition about the collusion of the German army in the war atrocities against the civilian population.[9]

There is probably no other country that currently scrutinizes and redefines its collective memory so thoroughly. An eleven-year-debate about a central Berlin memorial for the victims of Nazism[10] culminated in a sophisticated parliamentary debate in June 1999 with the decision that (1) the Eisenmann memorial should be built as proposed, (2) that it will be dedicated exclusively to European Jews, and (3) that it should also have an information and learning center attached to it. Earnest arguments split all parties, and the overwhelming supporting vote surprised everyone, including the head of the German Jewish Council, the late Ignaz Bubis. He had predicted that the memorial would never be built.[11] The German political class support of the huge labyrinthine Eisenmann monument in central Berlin also revealed a substantial discrepancy in public opinion surveys. These had indicated a split population: 46 percent for and 44 percent against the memorial, with 93 percent of supporters in favor of its dedication to all Nazi victims. Parliament's decision to dedicate it exclusively to European Jews indicated that concern about negative foreign reactions outweighed local opinion.

Behind the German debate about whether the nation should define itself as a "normal" polity stands the question of whether the unified state should also shed the constraints on its "moral sovereignty." Full political sovereignty was restored with resocialization into Western democratic habits. Later in 1989, national unification within European rules and values was the final crowning achievement. A growing number on the political right and center now wishes to shed the moral inhibitions resulting from the Nazi legacy. Until the 1998 involvement of the German army in Bosnia and Kosovo, the country had avoided its responsibility for international human rights enforcement with reference to its unique history sixty years ago.

How should one evaluate this process of profoundly redefining collective memory? Is the decision for the holocaust memorial the progressive acknowledgment of collective moral and political responsibility, although "Germans collectively do not bear criminal and moral guilt"?[12] Is it an official rejection of the earlier Walser warning about the "banality of the good," the instrumentalization of Auschwitz for ulterior purposes? Or is the victory of the seemingly progressive remembrance of shame merely the monstrous tombstone in the final burial of an embarrassing past, just as Walser had advocated to the applause of the establishment in Frankfurt's historic *Paulskirche*?

It would seem that the Berlin memorial, above all, fulfills the function of visibly exculpating the new "Berlin Republic" from the suspicion of past nationalist ambitions. With narcissistic self-congratulations, the debate lays to rest the Nazi legacy by demonstrating that the self-confident unified state has successfully come to terms with its shame—just as the victims wished. "The more unique the German crimes, the greater their own achievement of collective cleansing,"comments the historian Gerd Koenen[13] sarcastically. Hermann Lübbe speaks of *Sündenstolz,* the German pride in their sins. Just as minorities the world over clamor for the "vicarious virtue" of victimization, as Ian Buruma has argued in his intriguing article entitled "The Joys and Perils of Victimhood,"[14] so the German political elite of all parties is now keen to demonstrate the opposite: that it has mastered the much more intricate task of coming to terms with being the worst collective perpetrator in history. This negative uniqueness, the ritual acknowledgment of the Nazi break with civilization (*Zivilisationsbruch*), is now almost paraded as interesting a feature of a new national identity as the positive achievements of an economic miracle after total destruction in 1945. A shameful past as nationalist exhibitionism would be merely the other side of the dubious coin of denial and amnesia.

Helmut Dubiel in his study of parliamentary debates diagnoses a correlation between "the inability of Germans to accept collective responsibility for their history and their underdevelopment of democratic virtues."[15] However, neither was the post-war German amnesia a specific German characteristic, nor does historical denial of collective infamy stand in a necessary relationship with the development of democratic culture. Britain, France, or Holland had buried their colonial crimes until very recently but are considered model democracies nonetheless. The United States still lacks a single national memorial to slavery or to the near genocide of the aboriginal people. Nations memorialize their own suffering but not what they inflict on others. The Washington memorial of the Vietnam War lists all the names of Americans who lost their lives, but not a single Vietnamese name.

In Japan, history textbooks hardly mention the atrocities of the imperial army in Korea and China. The Japanese translation of *The Rape of Nanking,* the title of Iris Chang's English bestseller about the murder of thirty thousand inhabitants, had long been bogged down in arguments about its accuracy.[16] The Tokyo government refuses a clear apology even to Chinese or Korean state visitors, despite the worldwide feminist concern with thousands of so-called "comfort women." Recently, the official designation "capitulation" was renamed the more neutral "end of war." National guilt is widely considered to be absolved by the first atomic bomb dropped on Hiroshima and Nagasaki.

After political transformation, many nations rationalize their guilt with new myths. In Austria, collective memory redefined the popular enthusiasm for Hitler into "forced unification" (*Zwangsanschluss*), thereby re-portraying collusion as victimhood. In France, only the recent trials against collaborators of the Vichy regime have undermined the popular myth that half of the French population had joined the underground resistance against the German occupiers. Spain has for a long time avoided coming to terms with its forty years of Franco dictatorship because it would reopen the wounds of the civil war. Paradoxically, Germany has apologized for Hitler's bombing of Guernica and paid compensation, but not the Madrid parliament. Turkey still cultivates its cherished taboo that the massacre of Armenians during the First World War was a war-related event, but not genocide, which is viewed as an invention of hostile foreign propaganda.

The eighty to one hundred million victims of Stalinism still wait to be rehabilitated and even properly recognized. When Stephane Courtois edited *Livre noir du communisme* (The Black Book of Communism) on the eightieth anniversary of the October revolution, it met with a hostile reception on the Left, similar to the earlier exposure of communist crimes by Arthur Koestler, Alexandre Solshenytzin, Robert Conquest, or Francois Furet.[17] Recognizing that Marxist Leninism had a rational, humanitarian goal while Hitler's biological master narrative was by definition irrational should not preclude comparisons with the racial genocide here and class genocide there. Nor are the fascist crimes relativized or trivialized by comparing them with the terror of Stalinism. Comparing does not mean equating.

This sketch of varied collective responses to past state crimes allows some general conclusions. Grappling with the past is not a necessary precondition for a functioning democracy. As Michael Ignatieff has written: "All nations depend on forgetting: on forging myths of unity and identity that allow a society to forget its founding crimes, its hidden injuries and divisions, its unhealed wounds. It must be true, for nations as it is for individuals, that we can stand only so much truth. But if too much truth is divisive, the question becomes, how much is enough?"[18]

It is commonly assumed that public interest in a shameful past fades away among later generations. They carry no personal guilt, unlike their parents who engaged in denial because they were psychologically incapable of admitting the enormity of their own collusion with state atrocities. Paradoxically, public interest in and recognition of national crimes seems to increase over time. Subsequent generations feel free to accept collective responsibility for the sins of their ancestors although motivations differ in each context and divided memories prevail.

In their eagerness to prevent the gruesome past from haunting the future, well-meaning social engineers are intent on creating "a common history" between hostile groups. In their most extreme form, they repress airing of past hostilities, as Tito did with the enforced slogan "Brotherhood and Unity" in former Yugoslavia. Such totalitarian designs are the surest recipe for renewed conflict. "By repressing the real history of the interethnic carnage between 1941 and 1945, the Titoist regime guaranteed that such carnage would return."[19] Only a pluralist interpretation of history may achieve a shared truth at best or reinforce divided memories at worst. History as an ongoing argument is still preferable to the myth making of official collective memory.

Trials and Justice

Prosecuting perpetrators of gross human rights violations requires a clear demarcation between victors and the vanquished. Where there is a stalemate—as in South Africa or in Chile between democrats and the military—historical compromises and amnesties are negotiated. Prosecutions would most likely provoke new violence and even endanger the survival of the emerging democracy.

Apart from the morality of pursuing justice for its own sake, there are good pragmatic reasons for trials of political criminals. Aryeh Neier, one of the most ardent advocates of punishment, has expressed the most convincing reason: "When the community of nations shies away from responsibility for bringing to justice the authors of crimes against humanity, it subverts the rule of law."[20] If the victimized see no one held accountable, they may seek revenge on their own and continue the cycle of violence. Prosecution of individual perpetrators also counteracts the misleading notion of collective guilt. Individualizing guilt does not smear the name of an entire group. Finally, indictments by the International Criminal Court (ICC) cannot be accused of "victor's justice."

However, there are also clear pitfalls to be avoided. If a sovereign state can head off ICC prosecution by bringing alleged war criminals before its own courts, a fair trial depends very much on the independence and quality of its judiciary. This spectrum can range from biased judges of the old order (as alleged in South Africa) to an internal "victor's justice" where the judiciary has been purged and replaced with partisans of the new regime, as happened in Mugabe's Zimbabwe.

Proper trials also redefine national identity and forge collective memory. This was the case with the Auschwitz trials in Frankfurt in the early 1960s, the belated prosecution of Vichy collaborators in France during the late 1990s, and particularly the Eichmann trial in Israel in 1961/62, highlighted in Hannah Arendt's famous controversial account, *Eichmann in Jerusalem*. Hanna Yablonka concludes a thoughtful reevaluation of this event by pointing to the manufacture of ideological justifications beyond individual retribution: "The turning point was expressed in an effort to define the significance behind the existence of the state . . . in setting up a longterm historical overview that could supply a thematic, ideological and conceptual framework for the nation's common memory, and, in its wake, the national identity."[21]

The ICC would be emasculated if prosecutions could only be launched with the consent of the states involved where the crime occurred or the alleged criminals live. A similar paralysis would ensue if vetoes by Security Council members could indefinitely block prosecution. NATO's unilateral military intervention in Kosovo without UN approval already responded to this predicament. NATO's "military humanitarianism" postulated that gross violations of universal rights within a sovereign state necessitates outside intervention in the same way that aggression against a foreign territory would justify war in self-defense. The NATO action, Jürgen Habermas argued, anticipated a world citizenship that unfortunately does not yet exist as an enforceable order.

If the ICC were to be the first practical indicator of a more effective world order for universal human rights, it would be even more imperative to prevent "core" crimes rather than merely punish violators afterward. It is doubtful whether the threat of indictment is sufficient to restrain future Pinochets or Milosovics. In fact, the opposite might happen. Faced with the prospect of being imprisoned in The Hague, future dictators may cling to power strenuously, resulting in more victims, rather than abdicate or remove themselves into unsafe exile.

A great step toward prevention of crimes against humanity could be establishing a similar international tribunal (or including the task in ICC duties) to which aggrieved minorities could appeal for redress. The world lacks an impartial forum to which oppressed groups can formally turn for action against their government. With the realistic prospect of justifiable relief by an international body, armed resistance and civil war would be effectively discouraged. Should a sovereign state refuse to heed the verdict of the tribunal on the treatment of minorities, a variety of sanctions against the outcast could be meted out. The state's chief representatives could even be indicted themselves for contempt of court. Such a verdict must be different from unenforceable and politically tainted resolutions of the UN General Assembly or Security Council decisions that are regularly nullified through veto rights. While the European Court in Strassbourg already hears complaints concerning unjust treatment by European governments and the International Court of Justice pronounces on inter-state disputes, aggrieved national minorities need to be offered a similar legal alternative to taking up arms.

Lustration

The term *lustration* is frequently meant to describe all actions against former regime affiliates, from violent or lawless purges to formalized procedures, to a mere "ceremonial cleansing" of the old order.[22] In this analysis, lustration is used in a narrower sense to define the regulated screening of collaborators for disqualification from public office. Victors establish categories of guilt and responsibility to which varying sanctions correspond. Typical examples would be de-nazification procedures in post-war Germany and "destasification" after reunification in 1989, which barred members and informers of the secret police (*Stasi*) from future employment in the public service

Attitudes of the general public show remarkable similarities between the two cases, though they occurred fifty-five years apart. Susanne Karstedt in a perceptive comparative analysis of polling data notes an initial strong approval of punishment of the top decision makers and beneficiaries, but a readiness to exempt ordinary party members and recipients of orders in the lower echelons.[23] This reaction reflects and reinforces the notion of a "betrayed people." A small clique can be blamed while the collusion or silence of ordinary people is transformed into their being victims as well. With time, the call for indictment of the leadership fades and a general atmosphere of closure of the past takes hold.

Lustration is only possible in situations where extensive files of the previous regime reliably document collaborators. Disqualification for public office also presupposes the availability of sufficient skilled substitutes. This was the case with the reunification of East and West Germany where the Eastern part was taken under the economic and bureaucratic tutelage of the West. In South Africa, the continued employment of apartheid administrators in the civil service for a while was not only part of the negotiated settlement but also a necessity in the absence of sufficiently trained personnel of the new order.

Such predicaments make it problematic to establish collective guilt, if a society harbors perpetrators without punishing or ostracizing them. Bernhard Schlink has defined "collective guilt" as the degree to which a society was "enmeshed" in past crimes: "Enmeshing doesn't happen merely by committing a crime or encouraging or assisting it. There is also an enmeshing through knowing about the crime, through looking or looking away, through not helping and also through not ostracizing the perpetrators from the solidarity of the community."[24] However, how can a society exclude and marginalize perpetrators when they also need to rely on them for basic services and economic well-being, as happened in the immediate post-war German period and after the end of apartheid? Moreover, when the majority of a community supports the crimes of its government by endorsing it in free elections, as did whites during apartheid or Israelis in voting for Likud, how can this enmeshed majority be ostracized in post-conflict reckoning? Clearly a hierarchy of guilt of those implicated has to be established in order to discern responsibility for past atrocities. This is the topic of the next chapter.

Restitution and Reparations

Even established democracies pay reparations to victims mainly under political pressure but rarely out of moral commitment or guilty conscience. Only more than thirty-five years after the establishment of internment camps for Japanese Canadians and Japanese Americans during World War II did the U.S. and Canadian governments finally pay a meager average amount of $20,000 to the survivors. Reparations amounted only to a symbolic restitution of their expropriated property.

The Chinese Canadian National Council has been lobbying the Canadian government in vain since 1984 for redress of the Chinese "head tax." This racist legislation, enacted July 1, 1923, imposed a special tax on Chinese immigrants only. It was aimed at deterring further Asian immigration, considered to be the "yellow peril" at the time. However, since wealthy Asian immigrants are now courted by the Canadian government and only a few hundred head-tax payers survive, the government can ignore calls for compensation of the $23 million extracted by the head tax. The diverse Canadian Chinese community itself does not like to be reminded of its unwelcome past in the country which many now consider a home of unlimited opportunities in which they no longer need their "grandparents' money."

Another dynamic is at work with regard to the long-standing grievances of native people. Canadian courts have found the main churches and the federal government "jointly liable" for horrific sexual abuses of thousands of aboriginal children. During the 1960s and 1970s they were sent to religious boarding schools as part of a government effort to assimilate native youth. Hundreds of former students have filed individual and class-action lawsuits, seeking damages for their suffering, inflicted mostly by Roman Catholic and Anglican church officials. In the case of land claims and hunting and fishing rights by aboriginal groups in both Australia and Canada powerful moral pressure is exerted. The 3 percent scattered Canadian native population possesses no voting strength, physical power, or the economic clout to force the national government to recognize its historical grievances. Yet despite strong opposition from influential oil, mining, and forest companies, Canadian courts have recognized aboriginal land claims and forced governments to enter into good faith negotiations about the transfer of large tracts of crown land to native jurisdiction. Preferential fishing and hunting rights have long been granted, despite strong local voters' opposition and concern for conservation measures. Australia has even instituted a symbolic national "Sorry Day" to create a collective memory of the country's illegitimate conquest by foreign settlers.

At work here is the moral politics of embarrassment. A state is forced by relatively powerless groups into a clear choice: either forfeit its claims of a model democracy based on the rule of law, or live up to broken treaties and admit historical injustice. Since Canada proudly markets itself as an anti-colonial, multicultural model, it can hardly allow itself to be exposed as practicing open internal colonialism. With the help of legal assistance by sympathetic lawyers, even powerless minorities can exercise power over indifferent governments. The Canadian state even bears the costs of the court challenges against itself and finances research into further claims in the name of historical justice.

The political interest of reintegration into the international community motivated substantial German reparation to Israel and individual Jewish victims at the beginning of the 1950s, despite disapproval of the majority of the electorate. Foreign policy considerations also played a major role in the question of German compensation for an estimated one million out of eight to ten million survivors of forced labor in Nazi Germany. Paradoxically, it was globalization with the fusion of German and foreign conglomerates that made the German side vulnerable to boycotts abroad and adverse court judgments in the United States. Like the Swiss banks and insurance companies who had to account for Nazi gold transfers or dormant Jewish bank accounts, German industry was faced with huge claims by U.S. lawyers of the influential Claims Conference. Ongoing negotiations, coordinated by the Chancellors office, not only concern the amount of reparation to be paid into the Remembrance and Future Fund, but above all, the legal exclusion of future claims, whether individual restitution should be paid to the needy only, whether national wage levels and differential living costs should be taken into account, and whether the compensation should be based on underpaid wages or the suffering of Nazi slave laborers.

Although the German government promised to treat all claimants equally, the strength of their lobby and the status of their government played a decisive role. Sinti and Roma (derogatorily called "gypsies"), unorganized gay groups, and Jehovah's Witnesses who were also persecuted by the Nazis, have so far been shortchanged. Claims of U.S. citizens were given greater weight than those originating from Eastern Europe. Constantin Goschler points out that only the end of the Cold War made these demands possible. "Individual Nazi victims play a minor role in the calculation of East European states in light of their own interests in German support and therefore receive less endorsement from their own government than comparable claims originating from the U.S."[25]

Even in a state with a government of liberation, the liberated victims cannot be sure to receive material reparations. The South African government agonized over the recommendations of the TRC to pay twenty thousand recognized victims a modest amount of R 20,000 (US$ 3,000) for six years. In the end, the ANC agreed to a meager lump sum payment.

Advocates of the TRC praise the involvement of broad sectors of society in providing information. The communal experience of public hearings, of being listened to and officially recognized as victims, is said to be as important for the healing of trauma as the testimony itself. Unfortunately, this broad involvement also raises false expectations. In South Africa, one hears disappointment in many communities that no follow up took place, and particularly that the expected compensation for suffering has not materialized. "We have stimulated hopes and then abandoned the people," explains one commissioner self critically.[26] However, the South African TRC, with limited resources and a limited life span, had not been empowered to fulfill the expectations it raised. It could only make recommendations to government, which was free to accept and, more likely, to fudge even the modest TRC suggestions. ANC leaders now argue that liberation should not be reduced to material benefits.

Speculations that "the palpable insufficiency of reparations could stoke fires of revenge or further victimize the victimized as trivializing their harms or suggesting a payoff for silence"[27] do not apply in South Africa. Because a government of victims is responsible for nonpayment it would be a rejection of their own representatives. Nor is anyone coopted into silence. Those twenty thousand recognized by the TRC as theoretically eligible for compensation are envied by the millions of ordinary victims of apartheid laws who did not fall under the legal category of "gross violation." Their suffering caused by the expropriation of the Group Areas Act, low wages under the discriminatory labor policy, and arrests under the Pass Laws are comparatively trivialized by not being worthy of restitution under the TRC legislation. In short, by focusing solely on the illegal transgressions of illegitimate laws, the TRC legislation ignores the structural, legal violence of a racist system. The TRC concerned itself mainly with a select group of victims instead of beneficiaries.

Re-Education and Memorialization

Memory politics frequently includes conscious measures for re-education, from rewriting history books to exchange programs and the official redefinition of collective identity. At the height of the Kosovo war, Daniel Goldhagen recommended, as the only lasting solution, the occupation of Serbia and the resocialization of the population, as had happened successfully after the war in Germany and Japan. Others emphasize the importance of focusing on the suffering of the adversary rather than on own-group pain in order to achieve empathy and tolerance through a shared history.

Education for multicultural understanding always deserves support but must not be overrated in its impact. Another educational approach promises greater success: strengthening the self-confidence of adolescents to develop their critical consciousness and rules of negotiated conflict resolution.

The lessons of Auschwitz do not lie in repeating empty rituals of remembrance or in inculcating collective guilt. Political education in the next century must go beyond Auschwitz by keeping alive an awareness of and sensibility to future injustice. The lessons of Auschwitz are best preserved by exposing the all-pervasive dispositions for racism and discrimination.

The ashes and corpses of previous victims are best honored by providing the living with insights about the causes of their fate. In Germany that should include all victims of Nazism, not only Jews. To be sure, Jews were the most numerous victims and, in the paranoia of the Nazis, their most dangerous enemy. Only for Jews was a "final solution" designed. Yet it would seem wrong to dedicate the Berlin memorial exclusively to Jews, as the German parliament decided. Promises of similar memorials for other victim groups elsewhere lead to rivalry and establish a hierarchy of suffering. Above all, the false impression is created that the motivation for the murder of Jews was based on their particular behavior. Yet Jews as scapegoats were interchangeable.

Memorialization in the form of an official monument always suggests the Nazi past has been laid to rest once and for all. Some consider such finality an advantage. A truth commission, writes Martha Minow, "fails to create potential closure afforded by criminal trials that end in punishment."[28] However, continued soul searching should be welcomed rather than regretted. Political education is advanced by disputes over interpretations of past events that are easily relegated to oblivion with the closure of an authoritative judgment. The more controversial a memorial in the center of Berlin, the better it is for raising consciousness. It ought to hurt as a thorn in national self-satisfaction rather than please. The central German memorial cannot be, as the glib suggestion of Chancellor Schröder implied, "a place which one likes to visit."

The central memorial need not even be confined to Nazi victims. Fascist mentalities survive among an alienated minority in the form of xenophobia and violence against foreigners, particularly in former East Germany where hardly any foreigners lived before. To highlight this continuity, the memorial could open itself to the future and engrave the names of all foreigners murdered for racist reasons in the post-fascist state.

To be sure, this everyday racism amounts to individual deviance and not the state criminality of the Nazis. It is important to stress this difference, because racism is frequently viewed as always originating from fascist social conditions. The East German skinheads who harass "others" know that they will not be tolerated by the state. They embody a syndrome common to hate crimes in London, Paris, or Washington.

How and under what conditions such universal individual predispositions emerge and are successfully mobilized in a mass movement to genocidal levels could be illuminated with the unique Nazi crimes. In this way, the "normal society" of the "Berlin Republic," because of its abnormal past, could prove to itself and the world that it has effectively learned to mourn *all* victims of discrimination.

Truth Commissions

Truth commissions were first established after the successors of the military dictatorships in various Latin American countries came under pressure to reveal the fate of thousands of alleged dissidents who had disappeared. The celebrated South African TRC differed from its Latin American counterparts by being established as an act of Parliament rather than by presidential decree, holding open hearings instead of in-camera investigations and making an amnesty dependent on full disclosure of perpetrators. The South African TRC sees itself in the tradition of "restorative justice," foregoing punishment in favor of reconciliation. Assuming that "revealing is healing," encounters between forgiving victims and remorseful perpetrators were meant to achieve the ambitious goal as the only alternative to continued strife.

Due to the international stature of the TRC's chair, Desmond Tutu, his hopes and predictions have even entered the academic literature as empirical facts. In this vein, Gesine Schwan in her celebrated *Politik und Schuld* falsely credits the TRC with "having engendered pity, empathy and remorse on the part of perpetrators by being confronted with the unspeakable suffering of victims."[29] That was the intention of the TRC hearings but in reality only occurred in rare cases. Interestingly, two of the worst killers, Eugene de Kock, dubbed "prime evil" by the South Africa media as commander of the special Vlakplaas police unit, and his predecessor Dirk Coetzee, fall into this category of remorseful converts.[30] However, in most other cases, judging from participant observation and recorded confessions, apartheid's assassins tried to save their skins by applying for amnesty or turning state witness without conceding the moral turpitude of their actions.[31] The public shaming of confessing perpetrators presupposes a moral reference group that shares the shame. This is doubtful when exposed killers retreat into ethnic enclaves for whom they committed their crimes and whose dominant attitudes range from understanding to open sympathy.

Typically, perpetrators acknowledged suffering caused or even expressed coded regret but rationalized their deeds in terms of the political climate at the time or their assigned role in the apartheid machinery. Like their political leaders in the National Party (NP), genuine acknowledgment of guilt or acceptance of responsibility was not forthcoming. Few offered private compensation within their means.

Black perpetrators on the other side, most prominently among them, Winnie Madikizele-Mandela, also displayed indifference toward the plight of victims. Despite an embarrassing beckoning for a sign of remorse by the TRC chair, she ultimately complied only half-heartedly and reluctantly. The ANC leadership as a whole has yet to remove from office cadres within its ranks for admitted human rights abuses. The ANC only took collective responsibility for "excesses" in the heat of the struggle. In fact, Mbeki criticized the TRC for its "erroneous determination" that indiscriminate bombings or the taking of civilian hostages constitute human rights violations. The ANC saw the TRC findings as an attempt to "criminalize a significant part of the struggle of our people for liberation." The TRC was accused of elevating the ANC's unfortunate "collateral damage" in pursuit of a just cause to the moral equivalent of the defense of an unjust one. To its lasting credit, the TRC has always insisted that no such moral leveling was intended or indeed possible, but even in the fight for a just cause, Geneva Convention rules of warfare have to be upheld.

The South Africa debate has confirmed Michael Ignatieff's insight from the Yugoslav conflict that it is relatively easy for both sides to acknowledge each other's pain: "Much more difficult—indeed usually impossible—is shared acknowledgment about who bears the lion's share of responsibility. For if aggressors have their own defense against truth, so do victims. People who believe themselves to be victims of aggression have an understandable incapacity to believe that they too have committed atrocities."[32]

While truth commissions can confirm the factual truth of an atrocity, they usually fail to establish a common interpretative truth. This moral truth of who is responsible and why it happened is always heavily contested. Divided memories prevail because truth is tied to institutional and collective identity. Apportioning blame in a moral narrative affects the standing of a political party or the self-respect of a people. Even if something is an obvious truth to any "objective" outsider, it is far from acceptable to an insider. For a member of the in-group, the myth about the unrighteous others or the goodness of their own is not just a tissue of lies that can be unmasked. This identity is a daily reality to be lived by, a lens through which the world is interpreted and a tool to make sense and give meaning to life. As Ignatieff has rightly stressed: "It is unreasonable to expect those who believed they were putting down a terrorist or insurgent threat to disown the idea simply because a truth commission exposes the threat as having been without foundation. People, especially people in uniform, do not easily or readily surrender the premises upon which their lives are based."[33]

Particularly if truth is imposed from outside, it is rejected. Foreigners therefore should refrain from interpreting history for indoctrinated locals, no matter how high their academic standing outside and how good their intentions. It is also wise to guard against internal exiles—people of the same ethnicity but little ideological credibility among their own group such as human rights activists or cosmopolitan minds who are viewed as sympathetic to the enemy. If collective identity is to be successfully redefined, it must be communicated by credible ideologues of the inside. If a few respected inside opinion leaders can be won over to the painful truth, their standing alone ensures susceptibility, or at least stimulates some initial doubts about dearly held positions. The South African TRC neglected to enlist such figures from the Afrikaner intellectual or religious establishment. Unlike the Chilean Commission with four members of the old and four of the new regime, none of the seventeen-member South African TRC belonged to the formerly ruling NP. (The two Afrikaners on the Commission were members of rival parties and were isolated among the rest of the ANC-oriented staff.) This skewed composition of the TRC, comprised of otherwise well-intentioned people with predominantly legal qualifications or theological training, nevertheless compromised the reception of its findings. It almost promises better results to appoint reasonable hardliners from both sides to argue about a shared historical truth in the calm of a committee room than to select presumable non-partisan, "objective," politically low-profile representatives of various stakeholders, as the South African legislation stipulated. Should ethnic fundamentalists achieve some minimal consensus, they can communicate their controversial compromise more effectively than even Nobel-prize winning personalities. In fact, the more the outside world courts leaders or heaps praise on interlocutors in order to strengthen their difficult reconciliation, the more suspect they become among their followers. Bestowing honor should wait until results have been achieved.

The historic South African compromise initially benefited from having a range of credible leaders on both sides. With little internal democracy and authoritarian traditions in both the ANC and NP, followers trusted their leaders blindly. Mandela and Slovo could sell a controversial negotiated settlement to their skeptical constituency on the basis of their hallowed record of suffering and militancy. The conservative, cautious de Klerk was given an overwhelming mandate to negotiate because nobody suspected his team would surrender all political power in exchange for preserving economic privileges.

However, more than sanctions and rising costs of minority rule, it was the very nature of racial domination that distinguished South Africa from Yugoslavia or Israel/Palestine. Mobilized ethnic identity in the Balkans and the Middle East prevents reconciliation while discredited racial identity in South Africa facilitated compromise. Long before negotiations about the abolition of apartheid started, the system had been delegitimized from the outside as well as from the inside. Most Afrikaner intellectuals had defected from the ruling group and championed "reform."

Furthermore, the economic interdependence limited ruthlessness in apartheid South Africa. Terror was not applied indiscriminately against all members of an outgroup, as under fascism or throughout the ethno-nationalist strife of Yugoslavia, but mainly against political activists. The vast majority of "non-whites," though heavily discriminated against, could escape direct attacks on their life by being apolitical and complying with "the law." Apartheid ruled through a supposedly equality-based legal system rather than placing its victims outside the law as rightless persons, as fascism did.

Racial discrimination in such a context does not lend itself to the same group cohesion and collective trauma as ethnic mobilization does. Unlike Nazi ideology, based on imagined national blood bonds of common ancestry, apartheid needed to racialize culturally different whites in order to unify a weak demographic base but ethnicize blacks in order to divide and rule. This artificial and imposed social engineering had to fail because it lacked the freely embraced legitimacy of ethno-nationalism elsewhere. When the Cold War ended, Eastern European leaders turned successfully to previously suppressed nationalism to fill the ideological vacuum. In South Africa, costly segregation could finally be abandoned because the elites of both sides benefited from reluctant cooperation. In short, the discredited racism lacked the appeal of a just cause because even apartheid advocates had come to see blacks as victims while the humiliated colonized eschewed vengeance in the name of nonracialism and reconciliation.

A once-powerful Afrikaner nationalism had become a victim of its own economic success through state patronage. Once a mild African nationalism merely claimed political power and civil service positions without threatening the accumulated wealth and relative cultural autonomy of its historic adversary, Afrikaner nationalism unraveled into heterogeneous interest groups and different identity definitions without a common enemy. Graves of ancestors, territory acquired in ethnic cleansing or conflicts over holy sites, as in other nationalist conflicts, would be the last issues on the minds of black or white South Africans. Instead, a thoroughly Americanized society worries about access to the latest consumer goods and capitalist frills and diversions. The white "haves" are silently thankful that black "would-be haves" now keep a huge mass of black "have nots" reasonably pacified and, if necessary, under authoritarian control. It is this constellation, not a Christian ethic or democratic consensus that enabled a truth commission to go through the ritual of grappling with the past in order to proclaim in vain a reconciled memory for the future.

Conclusions

Collective memory of human rights violations could be separated into two broad categories of cases to which appropriate responses differ: (1) historical injustice and (2) contemporary abuses.

1. *Historical injustice* comprises cases where blameless groups were the victims of state aggression a long time ago. Few direct survivors exist and the claims of their descendants relate to the appropriate recognition rather than to the restoration of the situation before the event. Victims of Nazi atrocities, Japanese imperial expansionism, Stalinism, and colonial conquest and slavery fall into this category. Punishment of guilty perpetrators is no longer possible. Repossession of expropriated property or forced resettlement of people after civil wars or ethnic cleansing would create new strife and injustices or is not feasible because of interim economic development. In these cases, collective responsibility consists more of symbolic restitution than material compensation. Keeping the memory of the injustice alive and mourning the victims through political education about the historical crime best does justice to the collective legacy.
2. *Contemporary abuses* call for both justice through legal recourse as well as developing new institutions that facilitate reconciliation or, perhaps more realistically, peaceful coexistence. Particularly where sizable historical antagonists share the same state (South Africa, Northern Ireland, Rwanda, Latin America), truth commissions together with trials of guilty perpetrators can affirm victims, contribute toward common norms, or even create constitutional patriotism. Where ethno-nationalist groups do not support common nation-building (Balkans, Israel/Palestine) and where mutual atrocities have engendered divided memories, separation in independent or semi-autonomous polities would seem the only feasible solution. Here, international trials for state criminals of recent abuses could also act as a deterrent. An international forum to which aggrieved groups can turn for redress would constitute an alternative to renewed violence.

7

The Politics of Reconciliation and Transitional Justice

Truth Commissions and the Globalization of Justice

Globalization of justice denotes the increasing universal jurisdiction over gross human rights violations. Embarrassed by the passivity during the Holocaust, public opinion in Western democracies responded to the mobilization of shame. Influential global NGOs, like "Amnesty International," "Human Rights Watch," or "Doctors Without Borders" concern themselves primarily with protecting victims while others in conjunction with UN-mandated bodies, such as the two special tribunals on war crimes, target perpetrators across national boundaries. Although some major powers, such as China, Russia, and the United States, still resist the politics of embarrassment in the name of national sovereignty, impunity for serious political crimes may become a phenomenon of the past. NATO even started its first war in Kosovo under the slogan of "military humanitarianism." Tony Blair speaks of "globalized values" to be enforced when a humanitarian disaster cannot be averted by other means. Even U.S. unilateralism increasingly justifies its empire building with a moral imperialism. Liberal and left intellectuals like Christopher Hitchens, Paul Berman, Norman Geras, and, above all, Michael Ignatieff have followed suit by endorsing such "democratizing intervention" by the only superpower with the capacity and willingness to act.[1]

With blueprints for a better future thoroughly discredited after the collapse of communism in the Soviet Union and its satellites, concern with the criminal legacies of past and current human rights abuses have replaced the failed utopias. Oppressed indigenous minorities, long forgotten struggles of ethnic groups for self-determination or compensation for slavery, colonial genocides, or physical and sexual abuses of minorities have now usurped the Marxist working class as an indicator of social progress. The fascination with truth commissions (TCs) fits into this trend of official apologies for past institutional sins—from the British Queen, the U.S. President, and the Pope, to Australia's "Sorry Day." Ritualized confessions of past sins resonate with hoped-for absolutions in a secular era, a religious relic eagerly promoted by a marginalized clergy as collective cleansing and healing without costs.

Truth and reconciliation commissions (TRCs) are crafted to substitute for or complement trials where they fall short or are not feasible after a regime change. Within the political constraints and judicial capacities of democracies in transition, TCs are meant to shed light on past atrocities, recognize and affirm victims, make perpetrators acknowledge their deeds, and settle claims for compensation for historical injustices. More ambitious goals include engineering reconciliation, forgiveness, and healing, often inspired by a theological vision and based on notions of restorative rather than retributive justice.

Among the more than twenty TCs that have operated or are in session worldwide, the South African TRC is considered "the most far-reaching and the most effective of its genre."[2] In the Rotberg and Thompson volume, fifteen distinguished academics in a growing literature on the subject[3] agree: "The South African commission's mandate and procedures will become the starting point of all future Truth Commissions."[4] The South African experiment is celebrated as an "African gift to the world,"[5] but also denounced as a travesty of justice and challenged with injunctions by the old and new rulers alike. Some Afrikaners call the TRC "moral terrorism," while the ANC and President Mbeki complained about the TRC's "criminalizing" the liberation movements.

A South African–style TC has been suggested to reconcile, pacify, and "de-Baathify" Iraq. Stuart Eisenstat recommends a South African TRC in order "to document for future generations the ways in which the Ba'ath Party has committed such vast human rights abuses. . . . By encouraging victims of apartheid to tell their stories, it gave them the opportunity to air their grievances and it educated the public—white and black."[6]

In his typical glorification of the TRC, Eisenstat asserts that this was the reason "that a blood bath of retribution against apartheid-era leaders was avoided."[7] This can hardly be true since the TRC was established years after a settlement had been negotiated.

Interestingly, none of the authors mentioned speculates how a TRC could heal the unresolved Israeli-Palestinian conflict. Much of that literature so far is confined to what Villa-Vicencio and Verwoerd label "internal critique."[8] While calling for "a vigorous, open and critical debate" on the TRC, their volume, paradoxically, excludes "the voices of those who reject the Commission in principle."[9] Likewise, Alex Boraine's[10] incisive and frank insider account does not even mention, let alone refute, academics on the Left, like Mahmood Mamdani,[11] who have inveighed against the narrow mandate of the TRC, or liberal critics, like Anthea Jeffery,[12] who have focused on legal deficiencies. While the incisive academic studies by Hayner, Wilson, and particularly Rigby clearly stand out, the debate is still dominated by theologians and well-meaning human rights activists. They often substitute social reality with morality and lose sight of sore points outside political correctness.

Is the TRC a model for other societies or under what circumstances might it be one? One possibility is that the South African transition took place under such unique circumstances that the model cannot be exported. This conclusion would be wrong because many of the conditions favoring the unique South African compromise can also be found elsewhere: (1) a mutual interest in economic growth, (2) support of accommodation by rational leadership on both sides, (3) a religiously motivated collective predisposition to forgive, and (4) outside third-party pressure to compromise in no-win situations for either side. While some conflicts lack these favorable cultural and political preconditions, other unique circumstances make up for it.

Another possibility remains that even though the South African TRC model is exportable, its shortcomings are so grave as to make its uncritical emulation undesirable. If that were the case, the crucial question is what changes to the mandate, structure, and operation of the TRC would make it more or less "exportable." This analysis focuses on how future TCs can be improved and what lessons, if any, can be drawn from the South African experience.

It goes without saying that TCs should not be imposed. Any country must decide for itself. The proposal for a permanent UN-based commission is therefore a bad idea.[13] The particular history, culture, and political circumstances dictate the feasibility and shape of a TC. Unlike more or less universal rules of due process in proper trials, each national TC so far has deviated from others. Some were staffed and financed entirely by outsiders (El Salvador), others only by insiders (South Africa) or a mixture of both (Sierra-Leone). Most TCs met off camera and published their findings without naming perpetrators (Latin America); others held mostly public hearings, televised to the entire nation as political pedagogy. Some TCs awarded blanket amnesties; others did not include amnesty provisions while the most innovative South African model pioneered guaranteed contingent amnesties, dependent on full disclosure and political motives. However, all TCs have mainly focused on perpetrators and victims and ignored the vast majority between these extremes.

Between Perpetrators and Victims

Citizens of a state that systematically violates human rights or commits war crimes can be crudely categorized into seven groups along a spectrum of guilt, responsibility, complicity, passivity, opposition, and victimization: (1) instigators, (2) perpetrators, (3) collaborators, (4) supporters, (5) bystanders (6) dissenters, and (7) victims. How a truth commission deals with these differentially involved sections, and what impact it has on their identity and political consciousness, provides a guide to the success or failure of the exercise. Nobody can reasonably expect major collective attitude changes shortly after a bitter struggle. Affiliations of the pre-conflict era run deep and public revelations about past atrocities may in fact reinforce bitterness and sentiments of revenge. Fuzzy notions of reconciliation, healing, and forgiveness resonate more with normative sermons than with social reality. Nevertheless, TCs can set the stage and initiate changing discourses about a divisive past, if perhaps only in the next generation.

Instigators

Instigators devise, authorize, and propagate crimes at the state's most senior level of power. These leaders of the apartheid regime—cabinet ministers, generals, media ideologues, Supreme Court judges, and senior civil servants—largely escaped the net of the TRC. The few who testified voluntarily and the even fewer who were called upon or subpoenaed did not acknowledge guilt; they denied that they instigated human rights violations or even knew about those violations. Gross human rights violations happened in the ANC camps as well. Palestinian bombings of Israeli civilians also fall into this category as clear violations of the Geneva Convention, as are state-directed Israeli assassinations. In South Africa, these leaders on both sides of the struggle, who are implicated by their very position, were the main beneficiaries of the historic compromise.

Because the negotiated revolution constituted a pact of elites and a trade-off between leaders of a historic struggle, it can hardly be expected that the same negotiation partners expose themselves on their poor human rights record. They let the foot soldiers carry the can. Moreover, if leaders were to accept blame and acknowledge responsibility, they would delegitimize themselves in an ongoing political competition. Neither would their own constituency support such an admission of moral failure nor would their opponents allow them to carry on unscarred after confessions. Hence, both sides are motivated by structural factors rather than personal deficiencies to downplay past misdeeds. Living with lies and hypocrisy is built into the political contest, short of committing political suicide by being moral and honest.

Any future TC would have to define responsibility for political crimes more clearly and devise mechanisms to hold those top instigators to account. Should a state prevaricate on this duty or be unable to call an implicated leadership to account, the International Criminal Court (ICC) could step in. However, home-grown tribunals or TCs are to be preferred for the sake of political education.

Opting for TCs with amnesty provisions does not deny that trials can shape and redefine the collective memory of a nation, as Mark Osiel has persuasively argued.[14] As previously pointed out, the tribunals of Auschwitz guards in Germany in the mid-1960s, the Eichmann trial in Jerusalem, and the court cases of Vichy collaborators during the 1990s in France, all profoundly altered the national discourse about the past. Quite apart from the impossibility of trials in the stalemate of South Africa, there is an additional moral case for the superiority of a TC, as unequivocally expressed by Richard Goldstone, the first Public Prosecutor of the UN Tribunal on War Crimes in former Yugoslavia: "Insofar as South Africa is concerned, if I had to choose between criminal prosecution and the TRC, I would choose the TRC, which has done far more to reconcile and heal than any criminal prosecution."[15]

Truth commissions, particularly home-grown institutions with minimal outside interference or oversight, often err to the detriment of strict requirements of due process. They rely heavily on hearsay and less on cross-examination of witnesses or independent corroboration of evidence, as Anthea Jeffery has rightfully charged.[16] The balance of probabilities rather than the principle of "beyond all reasonable doubt" underlie findings. This may be tolerable because individuals are not convicted under guaranteed amnesty provisions. However, their reputation can be harmed. If due process is not followed, defendants are destroyed politically and psychologically.

There is no denying that TCs are politically partial institutions insofar as they are biased toward victims. For them alone they provide a sympathetic setting and therapeutic counseling. However, this in-built, almost inevitable, empathy can also be viewed as restoring the previous power imbalance by furnishing victims with their lost dignity. Granting victims the moral advantage in a nonadversarial setting may well result in a different truth. Whether this "narrative truth," as the TRC report called it, is also "superior" to the "forensic truth" of trials is debatable. It is certainly less reliable. But because perpetrators and victims are actively involved in telling their own stories, rather than talking mostly through guarded lawyers, much richer information emerges than that produced in a stifling courtroom. Provided this evidence is viewed in context rather than taken at face value as factual truth, it may well be more suitable for the intended catharsis and reckoning with the past. Both sides get their feelings "off their chests," so to speak. What is problematic is the postmodernist TRC assertion of the equal validity of several different kinds of truth. History cannot be equated with memory, unless the subjectivity of such a memorized "truth" is always recognized.

Perpetrators

Perpetrators—mostly policemen in special units on the government side—carry out the dirty work of political supervisors. In South Africa, the politicians allowed their security professionals a free hand and often did not want to know about their misdeeds so they could plausibly deny it. The torturers are guilty of acts of *commission*; the instigators are equally guilty—or more so—of acts of *omission*. During the TRC hearings, the perpetrators felt singled out and were rightly scornful of the politicians' cowardice. This greatly assisted the TRC investigative task together with the confessions of a few leading defectors (de Kock) who implicated their colleagues. Therefore, even those perpetrators who despised the TRC felt obliged to apply for amnesty. No longer were ranks closed.

Conditional amnesty and indemnity from criminal prosecution as well as civil claims of victims proved to be the most controversial issue of the TRC process. There is no question that the alternative to amnesty would have been civil war in South Africa. The late Justice Ismail Mohammed put the dilemma in stark words in his judgment against the Azanian People's Association (AZAPO): "The human rights criminals are fellow citizens, living alongside everyone else, and they may be very powerful and dangerous. If the army and the police have been the agencies of terror, the soldiers and the cops aren't going to turn overnight into paragons of respect for human rights. Their numbers and their expert management of deadly weapons remain significant facts of life."[17]

Between the demand for blanket amnesty by this group and the possibility of trials, the unique compromise of a qualified amnesty constitutes a model of pragmatic negotiation politics. Without this last minute addendum to the agreed upon interim constitutional principles, the first democratic elections of 1994 would have been in serious jeopardy. In short, the ANC was never in a position to institute trials. The alternative to the TRC would have been a blanket amnesty, with which both sides flirted initially. A hidden blanket amnesty applies de facto already to perpetrators who did not seek amnesty, because the under-resourced justice system lacks the capacity for prosecutions. Conditional amnesty could be compared to plea bargaining. Those judicial fundamentalists who argue for retribution at any cost and as the only way to achieve justice should therefore also reject plea bargaining. Without the lure of amnesty, most perpetrators would not have revealed the buried corpses. Victims would still be left in the dark.

Of the seven thousand formal amnesty applications only about one thousand were successful. However, 80 percent of these seven thousand applications originated from ordinary criminals who did not qualify and were denied a hearing. Of the 1,500 cases of applicants heard, about 70 percent received amnesties. Only individual applications were considered and the TRC, to the chagrin of the ANC, took its own amnesty committee successfully to court for violating this legal stipulation and inexplicably granting collective amnesty to thirty-seven ANC applicants.

TRC supporters have argued that "public shaming" represents punishment. Perpetrators are tried in the court of public opinion. Ostracism however assumes a shared moral universe. Much evidence points to the opposite. Perpetrators are frequently celebrated as heroes in their ethnonationalist enclaves. The Serb and Croat war criminals at The Hague are perceived among their nationalist supporters at home as bravely fighting in the frontline. So are some Afrikaner security policemen who are not shamed within their community.[18]

Future TCs could improve the amnesty process by allowing graded amnesty decisions. The stark option of either granting or refusing amnesty could be changed into a range of conditional amnesties dependent on whether the applicant is willing to apologize and reconcile or make some form of restitution within his means to victims. No remorse was required from applicants in South Africa because remorse can be feigned. Contrition also requires a moral transformation of the perpetrator. While repentance cannot be commanded, victims cannot be expected to forgive if there is no indication of regret. Demonstrated atonement as a precondition of forgiveness and an indicator of rehabilitation can take the form of community service, as has been suggested for the militia in East Timor, or assistance in the rebuilding of huts, as practiced in Rwanda. Child perpetrators in particular benefit from such imposed resocialization.

Where the ideological indoctrination runs deep, perpetrators may admit their misdeeds but "sorry" is unlikely to cross their lips, even when confronted with their victims, as frequently happened during the South African amnesty hearings. A typical example of a stubborn refusal to apologize, let alone show remorse, is provided by the former head of the Orwellian-named Civil Co-operation Bureau (CCB), Pieter Johan (Joe) Verster. The notorious secret police unit had, among other crimes, conspired to kill then UDF leader and later Justice Minister Dullah Omar by lacing his medicine with poison; it had planted a monkey fetus on Bishop Tutu's lawn, and it had exploded a limpet mine at the Athlone Early Learning Centre in 1989. After cross-examination by the lawyer for the victims who were asked to stand up so that Verster could see them, the amnesty applicant replied that he would not be intimidated by a one-sided approach to the actions of the past. "I am not sorry for the things I did to protect the sovereignty of the state." He said he had performed to the best of his ability and was willing to apologize for any mistakes that had been made. "However, I am not prepared to act like a Roman Catholic and sit in a box and make confessions about what I did."[19] In the view of this perpetrator, he had been unfairly singled out while his opponents were not called before the Amnesty Committee to explain *their* deeds during the years of conflict. From this perspective, the antagonists were equal players in a sporting contest. Reconciliation consists of shaking hands and socializing with the opposite team after a hard-fought match: "I would like to talk to the people who did the kind of work that I did and there we could talk about how we fought, in the same way that players become friends again at the end of a rugby match."[20]

The apolitical sport analogy conveniently clouded the political cause of both sides. It equalizes the different moral content of the struggle besides reducing the players to mere unquestioning instruments of a superior coach. When questioned why he had targeted an individual (Omar) who was clearly not involved in the armed struggle, Verster replied his sole duty had been to carry out instructions from higher authorities as to who should be eliminated. "Other people evaluated the targets, our job was to shoot them." Proud amoral robots performed a job in compliance with orders from superiors—so why should they now apologize when they feel pride rather than guilt? Likewise, why should victims be expected to forgive under these conditions?

Collaborators

This category deserves particular attention because *collaborators* normally form the main target of revenge during and after a regime change. In East Germany, the three hundred thousand informal collaborators with the security police are hounded to this day by the Gauck administration and purged from holding public office. After World War II, many local women who had entered into relationships with individual German soldiers in Nazi-occupied territories were publicly humiliated and paraded through the streets with shaven heads. It is estimated that in France and Italy up to eleven thousand collaborators each were executed toward the end of the war, often summarily without judicial proceedings.[21] This ghastly revenge was frequently incited by communists who themselves had been Nazi collaborators during the Hitler-Stalin pact previously.[22] In Poland and Czechoslovakia, large areas were ethnically cleansed of all German inhabitants who were collectively considered Nazi sympathizers and collaborators, regardless of their individual behavior. In apartheid South Africa, to be labeled an *impimpi* in the townships amounted to a death sentence. Several hundred blacks, many innocent scapegoats among them, were "necklaced" by "people's courts."

The pinpointed extra-judicial assassinations of Palestinian militants and the effective "ethnic policing"[23] of the occupied territories would not be possible without a large number of Palestinian informers, estimated by Rigby to number up to fifty thousand.[24] Much of the harassment and collective punishment of Palestinians facilitates the recruitment of informers, who can obtain exemptions, building and travel permits, and other favors by reciprocal acts desired by the Israeli authorities.

Successful recruitment of informers constitutes for Israel a more powerful weapon than any armor or barrier provides. Massive inside surveillance also harms Palestinian civil society. It creates a pernicious culture of suspicion that depoliticizes and silences people. Like in South Africa, any well-intentioned criticism of liberation strategies is immediately denounced as "giving comfort to the enemy" or "playing into the hands of the oppressor." This conformity pressure stifles a necessary debate, creates distrust among activists, and often leads to the unjust persecution or stigmatization of innocents who have no means to defend themselves against the often-deadly label of collaborator.

In addition to *personal* collaboration, there exists *institutional* collaboration. An institutional administration makes choices and the unwitting members are subjects of rewards or penalties. MachsomWatch, an Israeli women's rights organization that monitors military checkpoints, reports that Palestinian students in the Nablus area are differentially harassed according to which university they attend. Only students attending certain institutions are allowed to pass the checkpoints. The situation depends on the extent of cooperation of the university heads with the army. Daphne Banai stated in a webmail dated May 27, 2004:

> For example, the administration of the A-Najah University met with the army representatives. The resulting understanding included prohibition of *all political activity* in the university. The administration of the Al-Quds University branch in Nablus refused to be part of such an understanding, and therefore their students are denied passage at the checkpoints. We have witnessed hundreds of cases of denied passage as a result of this decision.

Rhoda Kanaaneh undertook an intriguing study of some of the roughly five thousand Palestinian volunteers who openly serve in the Israeli military and border police, mostly originating from the Christian, Bedouin, and Druze communities. She argues against viewing these subalterns simply as traitors or, less negatively, as opportunists, but classifies them as marginal agents with multiple and contradictory loyalties at the edges of Palestinian society. Like the black policemen or township administrators in South Africa, they often rationalized their jobs as helping and protecting their community and often did so. At the same time, the mistrust of the "other" by the dominant group led some collaborators to be overzealous in proving their loyalty to their masters' cause.[25] Black policemen had the worst reputation during clashes with anti-apartheid demonstrators. Similarly, Kanaaneh reports: "As rumours circulated that the worst infractions—killing, beating, looting—were committed by Arabs in the Israeli military, their ambivalent positioning in their communities takes clearer forms."[26] Apparently 777 Palestinians were murdered by other Palestinians on suspicion of collaboration between 1987 and 1993—mostly suspected informers but oddly hardly those who had worn uniforms and resigned after warnings by Palestinian militants.[27] In South Africa, similar ANC appeals to black policemen or officials "to make the country ungovernable" were hardly heeded. Given the widespread poverty, the apartheid police service did not encounter problems in recruiting blacks, so that during the latter apartheid years the majority of South African police personnel were black. The apartheid regime proudly displayed those loyal servants from the other side and gradually allowed them promotion in the bureaucratic hierarchy after eliminating embarrassing salary discrimination previously.

Israel too has followed this route of splitting an enemy by rewarding those minority groups willing to cooperate. Only the hardliners in the dominant group resent this indirect rule and blind themselves to the advantages of cooptation. Like the Bantustans, even the official Palestinian Authority was initially bitterly denounced, from Islamist fundamentalist to sophisticated intellectuals like Edward Said, as doing the "masters' bidding." Marwan Bishara, for example, writes:

> For seven long years, the Palestinian National Authority (PNA) did the dirty work for Israel. It collaborated with the Labor and Likud governments to fight Palestinian "terrorism" and any form of resistance to the occupation, in order to maintain calm. . . . The PNA launched a campaign of oppression against Islamist figures and activists, permitted the torture of opposition leaders and journalists, and allowed the humiliation and arrest of political opponents of the Oslo process, including Legislative Council Members.[28]

Yasser Arafat, who is regularly portrayed as the arch terrorist, looks different in the report by Michael Bell, the former Canadian ambassador to the region: "Last week, Avi Dichter, the chief of Israel's Shin Bet security service, telephoned his Palestinian counterpart to thank him for information that had led to the arrest of two prospective suicide bombers. The information had been passed to the Israelis on Mr. Arafat's instructions."[29]

The different motives for collaboration obviously determine guilt. Collaboration with an adversary out of necessity or dependency can be more easily excused than when assistance is offered for financial rewards or out of ideological identification. The apartheid authorities blackmailed many captured guerrillas, so-called *Askaris,* under the threat of death to betray their comrades. No wonder that the treatment of suspected traitors in such a charged climate of recriminations and repression does not follow due process.

Greg Myre reports in the *New York Times* how the vital intelligence Israel seeks is not only solicited with the lure of money, the exploitation of drug addiction, or the embarrassing homosexual exposure in Arab society.[30] Muhamed Hilal, a Tulkarm militant in the Al Aksa Martyrs Brigade, described in a video his recruitment through sexual entrapment before his comrades shot him as a traitor:

> Mr. Hilal said he began working for the Israelis after he went to a military office seeking a travel permit for his mother. When it was rejected, he argued with the Israeli official and was taken to a room where a woman in an Israeli Army uniform greeted him. "She asked me what I thought of the Palestinian uprising," Mr. Hilal said. "I said I had no business with the uprising. She put one hand on my shoulder and one on my leg and started to rub. Then she took off all her clothes. When I saw her naked like that, I had to have sex." Afterward, Mr. Hilal said on a videotape that was distributed by Al Aksa Martyrs Brigades to international news agencies, an Israeli officer showed him 15 photographs of the sexual encounter and demanded that he work with the Israelis or the photos would be distributed in Tulkarm.[31]

Since the Israeli army refuses comment on its recruitment of informers, the story cannot be corroborated and sounds implausible as common practice. The informer may well have invented it for more lenient punishment or was forced to tell it under torture. Regardless of the veracity of the tale, it was widely believed on the street. After Hilal's execution, the video was twice shown to rapt audiences in the town's marketplace as a deterrent.

The Palestinian journalist Sa'id Ghazali has described his Israeli prison experience with collaborators in the 1970s:

> In prison, the most feared word is malshan—collaborator. The Israeli inmates punished police informers from their number mafia-style, slashing their cheeks with a knife. The scar, sometimes a 10cm slit, told everybody the man was an informer. The Palestinian activists killed collaborators. They passed a "revolutionary sentence" after getting a confession from him. Some collaborators died from fear. An activist serving a life sentence acted as executioner. He strangled the collaborator with his hands, or used a piece of cloth or a pillow, or slit his throat with a sharp knife stolen from the kitchen, or used a heavy tub to crush his head. The other prisoners in the room made a noise to divert the attention of the guards from the execution. After the killing, the guards would storm the room, and the executioner would admit he did it. They took him to a solitary confinement cell. After a few months, he would come back with another life sentence.[32]

In some cases, collaborators were commissioned as suicide bombers after being confronted with the choice: "Do you want to be remembered as a traitor or as a martyr?"[33]

A resistance movement discredits itself when it treats its suspected collaborators without due process. Handing over presumed collaborators to a street mob for lynching causes divisions in nationalist movements and is exploited by the propaganda of the adversary as proof of the barbaric alternative order. Unfortunately no person of the stature of Desmond Tutu has emerged in Palestinian society who would bravely step into a lynch mob, rescue suspected collaborators and campaign against the populist executions as Tutu did. Denouncing different resistance strategies as collaboration, as happened with Buthelezi's Inkatha supporters, exacerbated the in-fighting. In South Africa, propagation of necklacing split even the Mandela family when Winnie Mandela advocated the popular punishment but the internal ANC leadership vehemently opposed it. Many years later, the South African TRC downplayed the still open sore and basically avoided dealing with the sensitive topic, although the thousands of blacks killed in internecine violence constituted gross human right violations. In the Israeli-Palestinian conflict one can only hope that the suicide bombings and the Israeli state violence of extra-judicial assassinations with many civilian victims does not share a similar fate of amnesia.

In South Africa, hardly any retribution ever took place against white supporters or National Party office holders. Instead, suspected black collaborators were viciously singled out for defying the ANC strategy of making the country ungovernable. Notwithstanding their own discrimination or real or putative intentions of undermining apartheid from within and improving the life of fellow citizens within constraints, these chiefs, local councilors, black policemen, Bantustan officials, or tricameral members were viewed by the liberation activists as "playing the game of the enemy," and therefore "deserving" to be necklaced or "taken out." When a liberation movement ruthlessly enforces adherence among its constituency by terror, it is hardly conditioned to show liberal tolerance when it assumes power. The harsh treatment of dissidents by the PLO, the Kurdish rebels or the Sri Lankan Tamil Tigers bears out this depressing prospect. It was this murderous struggle among the disenfranchised that the TRC barely addressed, let alone healed.

What accounts for the relative tolerance of the real oppressors and the intolerance toward victimized auxiliaries? Differential degrees of intimidation and sanctions for transgressions in both cases can hardly explain the difference. Black collaborators were seen as having betrayed the cause, because of a conscious choice they had made. White oppressors on the other hand were viewed as being born into defending their privilege with little option or incentive to act otherwise. Therefore, whites were not considered "guilty" in a divided society beyond their membership in an oppressive collective. Theirs was a "natural" behavior while collaboration of blacks amounted to treason.

Similar considerations have influenced attitudes in the ideological conflicts of Europe. With a much more homogeneous moral order about what constitutes appropriate behavior, the betrayal of friends and fellow citizens in a repressive system acquired a much stronger condemnation than the defense of ethnic privilege in a racial order. In both criminal states (communism) and states of criminals (military dictatorships in Latin America), to use Tina Rosenberg's astute distinction, the element of assumed ethnic solidarity and ethnic disloyalty is absent. Hence, short of an interethnic war, crimes of an ethnic nature are easily accepted while betrayal of assumed ethnic loyalty is not.

Supporters

Supporters of the dominant ideology range from party members to voters for the ruling group, to teachers who indoctrinate their pupils into the prevailing state ideology. While they themselves did not torture, they provided the supportive context of human rights violations. A telling example of this category of the "indirect guilty" were the teachers in Rwanda who voluntarily separated their integrated classes of Hutu and Tutsi pupils and thereby set up the minority for easy elimination a few months later in 1994. How do you judge a white population in South Africa that, in its majority, through free democratic elections, repeatedly votes into power a party that pursues repressive policies toward minorities? While nowadays few white South Africans will admit that they ever supported apartheid actively and directly, the results of all white elections since 1948 contradict such denial.

The institutional hearings of the TRC tried to address to what extent major institutions and professional organizations facilitated or opposed apartheid. This imposed soul searching targeted societal pillars, like business organizations, the judiciary, the medical profession, media, and churches, which normally claim an apolitical self-understanding. It can be highly recommended in other post-authoritarian transitions. In South Africa, much controversy has focused on whether the TRC merely tried to understand the institutions or intended to berate them. Regardless of intent, exposing institutional support, acquiescence, or opposition raises the sociological question how an authoritarian system manages to operate beyond the capacity or attributes of its personnel. In these hearings, the institutional identity of business, medical associations, the judiciary, the media, or the churches were laid bare. Many a future PhD dissertation will find the most revealing material on why apartheid was sustained for so long in these records of reluctant self-justification by institutional representatives. It would seem a pity that only a few days were allotted to this potentially profound sociological exercise and that these hearings received minimal attention in the public debate, compared with the horror stories of individual perpetrators. Those quiet *Mitläufer*, as the majority of Hitler's supporters were labeled in the German de-nazification process after 1945, are also implicated and should at least be made aware of their supportive roles.

Litigation in U.S. courts sought by South African victim groups against multinational corporations centered on the legal definition of supporters of repressive regimes. Claimants accused foreign and local companies of "unjust enrichment." In line with the TRC's final report, they argued for reparations based on the extent to which decades of profits were based on systematic violations of human rights. In this view, especially companies that ignored UN sanctions "aided and abetted" apartheid. However, because other anti-apartheid groups, such as the IFP or liberals, rejected controversial sanctions for increasing unemployment and thereby weakened black unity, the legal controversy inevitably developed into a political judgment call.

The ANC government's surprisingly strong opposition against foreign court jurisdiction over the role of supporters and beneficiaries of its predecessor underscored reparations debate's political nature. It also revealed starkly the new class alliance between South African business and a neoconservative government acting together to ward off threats to common interests. In contrast to the ANC in exile advocating sanctions, the ANC in power not only objected on the grounds that its own sovereignty and efforts of national reconciliation were being interfered with from abroad, but also argued that holding corporations accountable for past practices would endanger much-needed foreign investment and increase the "risk profile" of the country. It was also pointed out that most of the accused companies now act as good corporate citizens, a role that could be endangered by imposed reparation payments. Praising the "mature and rational manner" with which Mbeki and his ministers have sought "reconstruction, rather than vengeance," the *Johannesburg Business Day* editorialized unwittingly that after ten years of ANC rule, only vague promises but few deeds had been delivered: "Government is consulting with the business community on how it can contribute, in its own self-interest. This could be achieved by seeking to remedy some of the things black people were deprived of during apartheid, such as skills, leadership opportunities and wealth."[34]

To the chagrin of the ANC and its business allies, the chairperson of the state-appointed TRC, Bishop Tutu, supported the lawsuits with the argument that the democratic South Africa could only benefit from universal ethical investment policies: "Placing corporations on notice that they will in future be held responsible for the effects of their investments in repressive regimes may well create an incentive for them to channel such investments into countries with a better human rights record."[35]

At the very least, the late TRC-inspired debate over supporters and beneficiaries of human rights violations has further sensitized boardrooms to risks and responsibilities in dealing with authoritarian regimes. While the appeal of short-term profit may still prevail in most cases, it does so with increased risks, if only to the public image of a company. One could well imagine that corporations involved with illegal settlements in the occupied territories may face similar challenges in the future.

Bystanders

An effective political pedagogy has still to be devised for what most likely constitutes the majority of the population, namely *bystanders*. Collective and individual bystanding need to be distinguished. A particularly odious label has been attached to bystanding states and international institutions, such as the UN in the Rwandan genocide. These entities, despite their capacity, failed in their duty to intervene when the needs arose (e.g., Rwanda, Cambodia), as Samantha Power has shown in her path-breaking study *A Problem from Hell*[36] and Stanley Cohen illustrates incisively in his *States of Denial*.[37]

A politically passive population often redefines itself as victims after a change of regime. Bystanders claim they were seduced by a powerful manipulative clique and also suffered. Yet the passive tolerance of injustices allowed authoritarian rulers free reign in the first place. While many members of the first four categories are beyond ideological rehabilitation, TCs above all could sensitize and politicize bystanders. This impact requires the public's perception of the commission to be fair and impartial.

Unfortunately, the TRC's approval rate declined during its two and a half years of activity, particularly among whites, but also among Africans. On the question of whether the TRC "will be/is fair to all sides," 35 percent of whites and 68 percent of Africans answered in the affirmative in May 1996. The same response dropped to 13 percent among whites and 61 percent among Africans in November 1998.[38] Among all South Africans, the affirmative response declined from 58 percent to 49 percent. On the question, "Do you think the TRC was a good or a bad thing?" in November 1998 (after the TRC report was submitted and publicized), 35 percent responded with "bad," 31 percent with "neither" or "don't know," and 34 percent with "good."[39] While party political orientations obviously influenced these responses, the skewed composition of the TRC (with no member of the former ruling party) also discredited its creditable report in the eyes of Afrikaners while ANC criticism may have confused African support.

When the minister in charge of the TRC (Omar) was asked why there were no people from the National Party on the commission he replied: "We look for people with a track record in human rights. No one in Germany would expect a former Nazi to be in charge of Holocaust memorials."[40] Reverting to the false Nazi analogy hardly justifies what arguably constitutes the single most important factor in the slow local delegitimization of the TRC. Not only did ANC short-sightedness veto National Party opponents as an essential part of selling a painful truth to a resentful constituency, no attempt was made to include Inkatha or PAC representatives either. From the outset, therefore, the TRC was set up to act as an instrument for discrediting ANC enemies and being amenable to ANC visions and control. The vitriolic disillusionment of the ANC with the TRC at the end can only be explained in light of the initial intent gone sour.

The South African TRC also lacked the academic status normally associated with official historical enquiries. It had neither professional historians nor other academic social scientists among its ranks although it consulted several outside academics. Nonetheless, the private critical comment by a South African historian does not stand alone: "What a good historian does is the very antithesis of what our TRC did. My objection to the TRC was not to point out past crimes and misdeeds but to indict an entire people's history—as Tutu said the entire tree was bad—and then the TRC tried to present their hackneyed version as the hegemonic and only legitimate version."[41]

Widely publicized racial aspersions within the commission also affected its standing. Since the TRC did not operate in a social vacuum, it could be expected that the racial sentiments of the larger society would also be somewhat reflected in the microcosm of a small committee. Nonetheless, it came as surprising shock that seventeen sophisticated individuals—who share a common purpose and a past of joint rejection of a racial order—were so deeply influenced by the racial resentments produced by this system. When even activists who both suffered under an oppressive order compete on racial lines about who suffered most, what prospects are there for color-blind non-racialism? Consider the frank reminiscences of Commissioner Wendy Orr in her book, *From Biko to Basson*:

> I sensed that amongst black members of the TRC, there was a feeling that we (white members) had to atone for our whiteness, that we were irrevocably racist simply because we were white. That if we ever disagreed with or displeased

> black TRC members, it was because we were playing the white supremacists. . . . The racist accusation card was pulled (subtly, but nevertheless identifiably) at every opportunity. . . . To compound the issue, it became apparent that only a black African was black enough, that no-one who was not a black African had suffered enough, endured enough humiliation, felt enough pain.[42]

The human rights credentials of the author are impeccable. In 1985, as a young district surgeon in the Eastern Cape, Orr publicized first how political detainees were routinely tortured and then she gained a restraining order from the courts. The embarrassed government fired her, and Orr moved to a private clinic in Johannesburg. While the racism charges have been downplayed and her generalizations obviously do not apply equally to all her colleagues, she nevertheless expresses a sentiment that other white TRC members are too embarrassed to articulate. Yet the tension can only be eased and the air be cleared by the robust discussion of such experiences on both sides.

Advocates of global justice do not absolve bystanders from the crimes that surround them. Apathy in the face of atrocities makes bystanders accomplices. Just as ordinary criminal law recognizes the duty of a witness to assist a victim of a crime, silence constitutes the guilt of having failed to help prevent a crime. Evaluating bystanders as accomplices depends on circumstances. First of all, they must be aware that a crime has been committed. If an entire community has been indoctrinated to view the defense of the crime of apartheid as a moral obligation how can they be considered guilty in the absence of an appropriate political consciousness? Even the perpetrators and supporters of repression displayed selfless motives in fulfilling their "duty." Therefore, to conceptualize perpetrators as "monsters," as an article by Aryeh Neier, "Bringing Monsters to Justice,"[43] is headed, is as misleading as characterizing bystanders as innocent onlookers. Apart from the fact that apolitical white bystanders of a racial order were also obvious beneficiaries, bystanders raise the question of the extent to which a universal morality can be expected from ordinary citizens in the presence of laws to the contrary. In short, to what extent can heroism be demanded in defying unjust laws? The "righteous gentiles" who were hiding Jews under the threat of death in Nazi Germany are celebrated precisely because they represented rare exceptions to the compliance of the silent majority.

Politicizing and mobilizing apolitical bystanders for a righteous cause presents all progressive social movements with a difficult challenge. Under apartheid where rulers and ruled were so clearly demarcated by official racial classifications, even a majority of the disenfranchised fell into the category of bystanders. It is a myth to assume that most blacks were filled with seething rage waiting to be released in a popular uprising. Similar attitudes of reluctant compliance prevail among the majority of Palestinians, the TV images of mobilized rage notwithstanding. If the response to official discrimination is resigned compliance, how much more "normal" is the moral fence sitting of members of the dominant group?

Forfeiting bystanding for taking sides obviously depends on the severity of sanctions for deviance, the expectations of success, as well as in-group pressure and a variety of other factors. As the risks for peaceful opposition to apartheid were comparatively minimal for blacks but especially more so for whites, apolitical bystanding must be considered moral failure at the least, if not unwitting complicity. As already mentioned, nowadays, one finds few whites that in their self-description were not actively or passively opposed to the old order. This imaginary conversion obviously accelerated the more the collapse of the old order assumed realistic prospects. Oppositional forces may dislodge bystanders above all by projecting a reasonable chance of success. On the other hand, overdoing the propaganda of a "panicking enemy," as happened during the last stages of apartheid, may also seriously underestimate the resilience of the adversary. Fatal miscalculations of the ruthlessness and cunning tactics of an authoritarian state have been matched by the equally disastrous initial overestimation of liberation forces in the South African case. Palestinians must be aware that the power asymmetry could make their fate much worse under certain conditions.

Dissenters

Dissenters take various degrees of risk to undermine and combat a regime without becoming direct victims. Historical heroes in this category comprise Poles or Germans who sheltered Jews, despite the Nazi death threats. Dissenters in South Africa did not face those extreme risks. At the most, Afrikaner public opponents were ostracized or professionally marginalized within their social circles, English Black Sash protesters were harassed, or journalists were threatened. The state assumed black dissent as a given and tolerated this opposition as long as it did not turn violent or aligned itself too closely with the banned exile movements. Ironically, black dissent with the ANC strategy acquired the greatest risks, as previously pointed out.

The TRC achieved little in the way of reconciling these deep intra-black cleavages, as it did not include black anti-ANC commissioners, such as Inkatha or PAC representatives. Neither did the Commission ever conceive of honoring individual opposition within apartheid legality. The small group of righteous anti-apartheid liberals, social democrats, socialists, and religious human rights activists was ignored by the TRC. Yet recognition of exemplary behavior under difficult circumstances could serve as an important role model. Indeed, as an NGO draft for a TC in Bosnia formulates: "While a major focus will be on victims, the commission will also acknowledge those individuals who maintained their immunity and protected neighbours of other ethnic and religious groups from abuses."[44]

The small solidarity demonstrations by Israeli and international peace activists may at first sight be as politically insignificant as the few Black Sash women protesting publicly against apartheid laws for decades. However, in addition to combating the collective stereotyping of an adversary, demonstrations of solidarity also sow doubts about the exclusive moral righteousness with which supporters of the state are indoctrinated. Like the apartheid military, an Israeli conscript army, reflecting a diverse population, is particularly vulnerable to alternative appeals. The harsh treatment of the few hundred "refuseniks" (conscripts and reservists who refuse to serve in the occupied territories, but would defend Israel proper) testifies to how seriously Israeli authorities treat the potential moral erosion.[45]

Most of the Israeli army dissidents are not motivated by philosophical pacifism or other grand theories. The accumulated experience of doing harm to innocent civilians troubled the consciences of many refuseniks and finally led to their painful and brave decision to refuse service in the occupied territories. A typical example would be Major Rami Kaplan who described to Jonathan Steele ("I couldn't believe I was doing this") his feelings about cutting down orchards while guarding a fenced Jewish settlement in Gaza:[46]

> One of the Israeli army's regular duties was cutting down Palestinian orchards, vines and palm trees. There was a tactical explanation. It was not to punish Palestinians, we were told, but to make it harder for people to crawl up to the fence and sneak through. Occasionally, explosives were thrown or rockets were fired by the Palestinians, but mainly they were civilians who wanted to get jobs in Israel. I refused to do these orchard-cutting missions, and my commanding officer accepted it. On one occasion I had to replace him, and I regret it very much. It was so painful to see our tanks and bulldozers going through the orchards. I had to sit on a hillside nearby and watch through binoculars. You could see Palestinians coming out of very poor and miserable houses. A soldier shouted out, "They've got guns," but when I looked through the binoculars I saw they only had bags with straps over their shoulders. It wasn't a rifle strap. They wanted to pick as many oranges as possible before the trees were destroyed. It tore me up. I couldn't believe I was doing this. No one thought of cutting trees on the Israeli side of the fence. If we had, we would have had to pay compensation. No one thought of compensating the Palestinians.

Kaplan found it appalling that decisions on whether to cut the trees to a depth of 200m or 500m—an issue that affected the livelihoods of several families—were routinely made by low-ranking officers. "It was completely arbitrary," he says.

Another group of religious dissidents espoused more ideological reasons. In South Africa, compared with the apolitical or xenophobic preachers of the faith, liberal-minded religious leaders were in a minority in the three Calvinist Afrikaner churches, just as they are in Israel. However, even a small minority or a single powerful voice could force conservative colleagues into an acrimonious moral debate that ultimately led to the erosion of biblical justifications for apartheid. Similarly several hundred "Rabbis for Human Rights" (RHR) invoke the Torah, Martin Luther King, and famous diaspora rabbis (Joshua Heschel) who taught that injustice anywhere is a threat to justice everywhere. They preach that all humanity is created B'tzelem Elohim, equivalent to the African concept of Ubuntu that you can realize your own humanity only by embracing and caring for others.

At his trial for civil disobedience in trying to prevent Palestinian home demolitions Rabbi Arik Ascherman argued:

> That moral inheritance tells us that the policy of home demolitions is immoral. It may be technically legal according to Israeli law narrowly interpreted. However, not everything that is legal is just. The policy is certainly illegal according to international law and tramples on the Torah, which I as a rabbi am sworn to uphold. The Torah commands us to love those different to us, not to have double standards and to have one law for all. I would also argue that, according to Israeli law, the order to demolish a home or protect the demolition is an illegal order over which a black flag flies, making it a civic, Zionist and Jewish duty to oppose by standing in front of bulldozers, having tried over the years to stop the policy by other means. I do not believe in civil disobedience for the sake of civil disobedience and getting my picture in the paper. [47]

If the Calvinist Afrikaner reorientation is any guide, such spiritual assaults from within may over time have an unpredictable impact on the legitimacy of government actions in addition to undermining the Palestinian perception of a monolithic adversary. There is the danger that individual dissent merely teaches moral lessons, that the dissenters castigate moral failures and laud individual moral courage. As noble as these role models are, they remain ineffectual gestures without being embedded in, and backed up by state and societal institutions. On the basis of the German experience with fascism, Bernhard Schlink has rightly pointed to "the complete helplessness of individual morality without institutions that recognize it, to which it can appeal and on which it can rely."[48] Therefore, strengthening the power of independent courts, educational institutions, churches, unions, political parties, and civil society in general achieves more in the long run than does the risky, individual heroic protest, as much as it is to be admired and encouraged.

Victims

Finally, at the other end of the spectrum are located the twenty thousand officially recognized *victims* (or their relatives) of gross human rights violations. The first phase of the TRC process aimed at restoring their dignity and establishing a narrative truth from their viewpoint. This successful exercise, however, ended in great disappointment as far as the recommended reparations are concerned, as previously pointed out. For many years, the ANC has refused to provide the modest recommended six-year annual payments. Finally, in March 2003, the government provided a modest lump sum payment for the recognized victims, but vehemently rejected attempts by victim groups to sue international companies for apartheid crimes and discrimination in U.S. courts, similar to the successful judgments in favor of Nazi victims.

Future TCs should therefore be empowered to make binding monetary judgments similar to court edicts that a democratic government has to heed. Perhaps a reconceptualization away from powerless victims to survivors of state-sponsored crimes would assist in realizing such entitlements. If ideals of restorative justice through TCs are given meaning, the impact on those who suffered most stands in the center of this alternative to retribution.

Victims and perpetrators can be synonymous. The indoctrinated child soldiers who were abducted in Sierra Leone, Uganda, and elsewhere are simultaneously victims and perpetrators. While such sequential changes are hardly disputed in the case of adolescents, the proposition is not generally accepted for mature adults. In their case, it is either argued that severe adult suffering excuses and explains subsequent misdeeds or that victimhood immunizes people against ever inflicting similar pain onto others. Both conventional wisdoms can be disproved. Neither does political prosecution establish perpetual victimhood, nor does own discrimination sensitize a people against the temptation of treating adversaries likewise. In fact, the opposite seems to be true: The worse a people's historical suffering the more callous their response when in power.

At the end of the day and to the TRC's great credit, all political parties criticized and rejected crucial findings of the TRC final report. This reaction confirmed the Commission's independence. The ANC denunciation of the TRC findings as "artificial equation" between a just cause and the atrocities committed by an unjust regime, occurred not because of misunderstandings of the moral issues involved. The TRC had clearly outlined the crucial distinctions as well as the circumstances and different weight of the misdeeds. The ANC could not tolerate that its own behavior was "criminalized" in the name of a higher moral code. According to this universally accepted principle, the noble end of liberation does not justify all means employed to achieve the moral goal. Even in a just struggle the right side can commit crimes for which it must take responsibility. By failing to accept this TRC principle, the ANC began to slide from the moral high ground it had occupied so far. The ANC squandered its moral capital.

Success and Failure of the TRC

The South African TRC can be judged a mixed success with crucial shortcomings in process, product, and impact. Most certainly, interpersonal and inter-group reconciliation remains elusive, unless one argues, as Jakes Gerwel asserts, that the negotiated constitution represents the most appropriate form of reconciliation.[49] In any case, making people respectful of their differences is preferable to a false harmony and an impossible consensus.

For example, advocating "a common history" may enhance nation-building but negates a pluralist interpretation of history. Liberals distrust homogenizing and totalizing narratives, which are as misleading as ethnocentric histories. Schoolbooks regularly portray own groups' historical defeat as a calamity inflicted by foreigners. Own victories are celebrated as a proof of ethnic skill and daring. Centuries of glory receive ample space while periods of decline are glossed over. History is abused to exalt a past and deduce an eternity of hostility. In such a context of distrust and enmity, it is imperative that historians of both sides not rewrite textbooks with the aim of sanitizing them. Insisting on a false consensus of a "story that people can share" often means prettifying turbulent struggles where both sides butchered each other and can invoke legitimate reasons for doing so. A far more promising approach to overcoming hostility is to expose young minds to conflicting interpretations. Nationalistic indoctrination would be replaced with interpretative narratives that eschew history as a morality play between forces of good and evil. If Israeli youngsters were also exposed to the suffering of uprooted Palestinian refugees and their legitimate claims, instead of being taken only on tours of Auschwitz, and if their Palestinian counterparts would be confronted with the true face of fascism and the Shoa instead of having it presented only as enemy propaganda, perhaps they would be less motivated to shoot at each other and more to seek peaceful coexistence. Similarly, Peter Novick has singled out controversy as at the core of historical identity. "But collective memory, when it is consequential, when it is worthy of the name, is characteristically an arena of political contestation in which competing narratives about central symbols in the collective past are disputed and negotiated in the interest of redefining the collective present."[50]

Novick's insightful analysis of the Holocaust in American public life doubts that its memory will continue to be a central feature precisely because its public demoralization has changed into an empty ritual, uncontroversial and apolitical, unrelated to the real concerns and divisions of American society.

In other contexts, however, such increasing remoteness to the crimes of the past does not exist because current conflicts are played out in terms of past legacies. Moreover, historical occurrences have defined collective identity so deeply that people are constantly reminded of "who they are" with reference to the past. This defines collective memory for blacks and whites in South Africa, for African Americans, or Jews and Palestinians in Israel. In these divided societies, noble attempts to overcome past divisions by stressing individualism or a common humanity sound artificial and hypocritical. For example, nonracialism in South Africa cannot mean color-blindness. Color divisions are so embedded in the collective consciousness and, above all, related to historical material privilege, that even the most enlightened minds cannot abolish their inherited "race," no matter how hard they try. Whether they like it or not, future Germans are saddled with the stigma of their ethnicity, their personal innocence notwithstanding. Even the Asian immigrants to the United States, Canada, or Australia are confronted with the history of colonial conquest of their European predecessors because as new citizens they too face the claims of indigenous minorities. How a divided society deals with this "burden of the past," whether it denies responsibility or attempts honestly to grapple with ancestral crimes and legacies, distinguishes reactionary and progressive politics.

An open approach to negotiations in good faith does not mean giving in with a guilty conscience to exaggerated demands of alleged victims. There are limits to restitution. Moral blackmail does not have to be heeded. Previous victims too can become victimizers—corrupt, greedy, and emulators of their own oppressors. Past-victim status does not exempt from criticism. To acknowledge misdeeds on both sides does not morally equalize the two conflict parties or criminalize a just cause, as the ANC asserted. In short, TCs and other institutions of transitional justice can teach how people should live together under conditions of difference and even extreme conflict by adhering to rules of conduct. Such modest goals may be far more realistic than illusionary visions of healing, forgiving, and reconciliation.

If universal jurisdiction over crimes against humanity can deter instigators and perpetrators, make supporters and bystanders aware of their collusion, encourage dissenters and affirm victims, it amounts to historical progress. The Israeli ultra-nationalist camp interprets the Holocaust-inspired "never again" admonition narrowly: never again *to Jews*. Other interpretations advocate universal jurisdiction in a wider sense: never again *to anyone*. Gush Shalom's warning that specific Israeli military officers one day could be held accountable for war crimes hit a particularly sensitive nerve. It was almost equated with treason in Israel. Similarly, the extremists on the Palestinian side who indiscriminately target civilians on the basis of ethnicity must be held accountable. David Hirsch speaks of "cosmopolitan trials" as moral "sparks of light." The globalization of justice, however, remains an ideal as long as major states, particularly the United States, reject the fledgling International Criminal Court (ICC) and even pressure smaller states not to sign on.

A reconciliation commission resonated well with a South African Christian religious culture that is geared to notions of confessions, repentance, and forgiveness, even among the secularized. The Judaic tradition of an "eye for an eye" as well as the Palestinian insistence on communal and clan honor do not easily lend themselves to individualized expiation, contrition, and atonement before a higher authority that grants absolution for past sins. The inability to forgive and concede an opponent's right is exacerbated by the mutual feeling of historical collective victimhood among Jews and Palestinians alike. Restorative justice underlies all truth commissions as the most basic assumption. The idea that perpetrators and victims can be reconciled or "healed" by being exposed to "the truth" falls on deaf ears when there are only victims on your own side and only perpetrators in the other camp.

8

An Israeli-Palestinian Truth Commission?

The unexpected collapse of the 1993 Oslo agreement shows that a formal settlement is not the end but at best the beginning of a peace process. Oslo was South Africa in 1990: the return of exiles, delineated areas of exclusive and joint jurisdiction, with the goal of a final status settlement later. While the first South African democratic elections under an agreed-upon constitution achieved this goal, Israel/Palestine reverted to an ever-escalating civil war. The many reasons for these contrasting developments need not be enumerated here, except to draw one conclusion: Unless a negotiated settlement is underwritten by other efforts to bring two antagonists together, it may not last. Engaging with the past in the form of some truth-seeking effort has come to be widely regarded as a crucial precondition for peaceful coexistence.

Collective reticence "to come to terms with the past"—meaning officially acknowledging own crimes and making amends for it—is understandable in dictatorships. It is more difficult to comprehend in societies that consider themselves Western democracies. Israel joins a handful of such states (Spain and Japan as well as semi-democratic regimes such as Turkey and Russia) that intentionally practice official amnesia. The reasons for this refusal differ in each society. However, in Israel even social scientists dispute well-established historical facts and figures, let alone interpret them with minimal consensus.

Thus Hebrew University senior sociologist Eliezer Ben-Rafael writes that "about 200,000 Jews (not 'more than 400,000') have settled in the territories conquered in 1967." The sociologist further argues that in 1948 as a result of the war by the Arab League against the newly established Jewish state "450,000 Arab inhabitants of Israel's territory left. There was no organized mass expulsion of Arabs."[1] Yet the historian Benny Morris, who now thinks that Ben Gurion should have evicted all Palestinians, concludes: "About 700,000 Arabs . . . fled or were ejected from the areas that became the Jewish state."[2] As if Deir Yassin and similar atrocities never occurred, Ben-Rafael asserts: "In any case what happened on the ground cannot be called 'ethnic cleansing' in the sense of the massacres, rape and destruction that the concept denoted in Yugoslavia."[3] Against such widespread denialism and amoral word splitting, could an Israeli TRC at least set the historical record straight? Is such shared historical consensus a precondition for reconciliation?

While most truth commissions around the world were established after a regime change or as part of a negotiated truce, in the Middle East a truth commission could pave the way toward negotiations. In fact, narrowing the opposing historical narratives of the two hostile groups may be a precondition for a formal settlement. It has often been noted that both sides cultivate contrasting meta-narratives on what the conflict is all about, who the aggressor is, and who acts in self-defense, and why a "generous offer" by one side is rejected by the other as an insult. Unless such meta-questions are clarified, they block each side from dealing with the other.

In general, a fundamental regime change facilitates such reckoning, but the continuation of the same order, as would be the case in Israel, should not be viewed as an obstacle for engaging with the past. It may even be an advantage by removing the temptation for revenge or a witch hunt of former adversaries. A liberal democratic society would live up to its claims by not sweeping uncomfortable events under the carpet. Even in the United States, in June 2004 a first TRC has started in Greensboro, North Carolina, to examine events of November 1979 when members of the Ku Klux Klan fired into a racially mixed gathering of political activists, killing five and wounding ten. The expulsion of 750,000 indigenous Arab inhabitants in 1948 or the suicide attacks on Israeli civilians cry out for moral clarification.

At present, neither side pushes for reconciliation through institutionalized truth seeking in the Middle East. Could a joint Jewish-Palestinian Historical Truth Commission narrow the conflicting claims about historical crimes and rights? Utterly convinced of their own version of truth and their own victimhood, none of the Middle East official parties contemplates such an institution at present. However, the various informal peace agreements recognize historical responsibility, but differ on the acknowledgement of blame. The Geneva Accord is completely silent on the issue, but envisages civil societies "creating forums for exchanging historical narratives and enhancing mutual understanding regarding the past."[4] The Ayalon-Nusseibeh document includes "recognizing the suffering and the plight of Palestinians."[5] Only the Gush Shalom peace plan specifies: "Both parties will establish a 'truth commission' of historians—Israeli, Palestinian and international—that will examine the precise causes that lead to the creation of the problem in all its aspects, and will issue an objective, conclusive report within three years. This report will be incorporated into the schoolbooks of both states."[6]

A South African–style truth and reconciliation commission, if at all feasible, would have to overcome great obstacles. The voices that warn against a divisive opening of past wounds, instead of working for a peaceful future, predominate. The surprising silence of Israeli and Palestinian civil society on accounting for its own abuses has many reasons, not least of which is the mutual internalization of victimhood. Zionist ideology in particular has cultivated the notion that Jews, and only Jews, can be authentic victims. Monopolizing victimhood is not conducive to recognizing own culpability in creating new victims on the other side. Similarly, displaced Palestinians and disenfranchised people under occupation wallow in their own suffering rather than self-critically examining their own moral failure and counterproductive strategies.

In South Africa, the impetus for a transitional justice discourse originated from a civil society long steeped in the English libertarian tradition. It was despised by the ruling Afrikaner group as well as by black nationalists, who remained skeptical about truthfully engaging with their past. They would rather deal and settle with each other directly than through the mediation of universal human rights accountability. Civil libertarians were dismissed as "Boerehaaters"—unpatriotic, naive do-gooders—by white and black nationalists alike.

In Israel, an even sharper rejection of NGO dissidents prevails. They are not English outsiders, as in South Africa, but inside Jewish traitors, even in the eyes of the opposition. At the May 2004 peace rally of 150,000 in Tel Aviv's Rabin Square, a critical General shared the platform, but "unpatriotic" refuseniks were banned from addressing the crowd or showing their banners. Therefore, Israeli civil society mostly confines itself to documenting legal violations or demonstrating solidarity with nonviolent Palestinian protesters, but seldom raises the fundamental issue why an ethnic state is in a permanent war with its subjugated others. The IDF is still glorified as a moral institution across the political spectrum. In this context of patriotic pressure to conform, a truth commission would have to originate from a minority within civil society, and be assisted financially and politically by the international community in the absence of any state support.

A similarly uncritical counternationalism prevails among Palestinians. Therefore, only simultaneous, parallel Israeli and Palestinian Truth Commissions would overcome the moral asymmetry. Each body would have to confront the now-unquestioned guilt and innocence of each side by acknowledging its own abuses. An all-party body of reputable individuals from across the political spectrum on each side, rather than only human rights activists, would have to address the cognitive moral dissonance. Unlike the South Africa Commission, on which no members of major parties (NP, Inkatha, PAC) were represented, an Israeli TC must include credible ideologues of all sections of a deeply divided society, from ultra-orthodox rabbis to leaders of settlers, from isolationist Russian immigrants to resentful Sephardic historians, from right-wing militarists to Peace Now activists, from Jabotinski

Zionists to anti- and post-Zionists. A commission mirroring the Knesset party ratios would be better than a body vulnerable to accusations of unrepresentative bias.

Reconciliation requires an admission of past wrongs. Such an acknowledgment of moral failure even the South African TRC did not achieve with most apartheid instigators. The most they would concede was an apology for unintentional harm or expressions of regret. Apartheid was presented by its chief architects as a well-meaning policy, implemented under unfavorable circumstances, and destined for failure not because of its inhuman assumptions, but human mistakes and insurmountable external circumstances. Abuses were attributed to a few misguided policemen, rather than to systemic policy features.

Before even such an admission can be expected in the Middle East, the mutual demonization has to be addressed. In Israel, that means deconstructing an Orientalism that views the other as culturally deficient or even subhuman. In former Prime Minister Barak's assessment, Palestinians "don't suffer from the problem of telling lies that exists in Judeo-Christian culture. Truth is seen as an irrelevant category. . . . There is no such thing as 'the truth.' " If the other habitually cannot tell the difference between truth and lies, he cannot be trusted to honor any agreement and therefore it is not worth even trying to reach a settlement. Barak's predecessor Menachem Begin called Palestinians "beasts walking on two legs." Yitzak Shamir in 1988 equated Palestinians with locusts, to be "crushed like grasshoppers . . . heads smashed against the boulders and walls."[7] Therefore, the educational task of an Israeli TRC consists foremost in clarifying the human equality of an adversary in the minds of the public when even the political leaders of all stripes engage in collective denigration.

Likewise, on the Palestinian side, a TRC would have to delegitimize a similar popular dehumanization of Jews. Palestinian cleric Sheik Ibrahim Mahdi calls Jews "the brethren of apes and pigs" and another preacher on PA TV, Sheik Isma'il Al-Radhwan, pronounces that "they are doomed to annihilation."[8] Even in distant Canada, a South African born mosque leader, Sheik Younus Kathrada of the Dar al-Madinah Islamic Society in Vancouver, in the sermons on his Web site calls Jews a "treacherous people," while a national Islamic leader declares all Israelis over age eighteen legitimate targets because they serve in the Israeli army.[9] Such incitement not only destroys the trust for negotiated agreements on both sides, but also indicates the wide cognitive disconnect to be bridged. The Palestinian TRC would have to establish a counternarrative that is credible both internally and externally.

The Palestinian TRC would gain great popularity at home and abroad if it also were to investigate, publicize, and rectify rampant corruption among PA officeholders. Ensuring financial transparency and punishment for abuse of public funds would restore eroded public confidence in the political system. While the Israeli regime also has its fair share of corruption scandals, its functioning judicial system can deal with it; this redress is absent in the PA administration. None of the two dozen TRCs worldwide has made corruption its focus of inquiry. Yet depriving impoverished constituencies of public revenue through massive systemic graft amounts to a public crime with even more devastating consequences than commonly understood human rights abuses.

In this process, the Palestinian TRC would move away from mere group vindication to a critical assessment of past mistakes and crimes. As long as the killing of civilians is celebrated, even in a just resistance against displacement and occupation, both people cannot break out of the cycle of fatal revenge. Instead of lamenting the crimes of the other, each TRC would focus first on own crimes. At a minimum, each TRC could achieve, in Michael Ignatieff's famous phrase, the ability to "limit the permissible lies"[10] in each society. Eventually, the exercise could open minds to understanding, though not condoning, motives of the other side. As Andrew Rigby has argued: "When you view the past through a different lens, the basis for a kind of organic solidarity embodying a fundamental respect for difference can be laid."[11]

Fine tuning Thomas Nagel's useful distinction between private knowledge and public acknowledgment, five phases of engaging with the past can be realistically envisaged in Israel/Palestine. Each stage depends on a minimal consensus in the preceding work of two parallel truth commissions.

1. In the first phase, the many popular myths would need to be addressed and confronted with an objective, factual historical truth. In Israel, the focus could start with taken-for-granted utterances, such as "In 1948, the Arabs left voluntarily to return victoriously later"; "the Oslo plot aimed at the destruction of Israel"; "there is no Palestinian partner to negotiate with." The Palestinian TC could focus on similar myths—above all, "A Jewish temple never existed in Jerusalem and the notion was invented by the Zionists." Each TRC could invite submissions of its public, collect testimonies of surviving eyewitnesses and make the search for true historical accounts of conventional wisdoms a popular enterprise.
2. Based on this groundwork, the existing private knowledge among a few academics ("new historians") would have to be deepened, broadened, and made hegemonic. This would be the phase of political education by the commission with the result that denial[12] is transformed into ignorance. Placing memorial plaques in places of erased Palestinian villages, as some peace activists undertake now is one such educational effort, which could be supplemented by video documentaries, televised meetings of the commission, and other efforts of mass education. The museums culture in Israel could be reoriented to include the forgotten and denied nakba of the Palestinians in 1948. A Palestinian national museum (which surprisingly does not exist, even in rudimentary form)—while still focused on displacement, imprisonment, occupation, and nation-building—would also include the history of Jews, anti-Semitism, and particularly the Shoa.

3. From this process results official acknowledgment, when the now widely accepted factual historical knowledge is endorsed by the state and encompassed in history textbooks. Thereby truth becomes part of the collective memory. The collective self-concept of a nation is redefined. While a nationalist government will be loathe to officially acknowledge own injustices, it would be constantly exposed to the truth of the TC and challenged with a "politics of embarrassment" by a critical civil society.
4. Depending on the progress of the two TCs in agreeing on a common story of what was done to whom, by whom, and under what circumstances, the two commissions could now merge into a joint Jewish-Palestinian exercise of reconciling opposing historical narratives. The joint commission would focus on interpretative truth—the meaning each side attaches to events—and could even raise the sensitive questions of guilt and responsibility. Cultivating a common story differs from sharing different stories. While the latter is more likely, it still amounts to progress in bridging the deep divide. The quest for a common story does not deny that interpreting historical events legitimately remains an ongoing argument and no official interpretation should be imposed in a pluralist democracy.
5. The acknowledgment on each side of their abuses leads into the last phase of contemplating what kind of apologies, memorialization, restoration, restitution, and reparation would be appropriate and feasible.

A common Christianity is widely considered a precondition for reconciliation. We disagree. A Christian cultural predisposition undoubtedly facilitated the desired South African forgiveness, dominated by soothing rituals of candle-burning, praying, and the cross-cutting legitimacy of an inoffensive clergy as prominent commissioners. Would the absence of this tradition make an Israeli-Palestinian TC impossible? The newly established Moroccan commission demonstrates the value of the institution without a Judeo/Christian predisposition to atonement. Because the institution would not be concerned with confessions, contrition, and healing—but simply with moral clarification—even conflicting religious zealotry among a minority should not preclude a rational discourse among the secular pragmatic intellectual majority on each side.

The problem arises with opposing religious doctrines and zealotry among a minority in each camp. These groups (ultra-orthodox Jews, religious settlers, Hamas, jihadists) invoke providentially ordained missions as guardians of their faith. When settlers "redeem" the land as a fulfillment of biblical prophecy and Islamic holy warriors inveigh against infidels, they apply a logic of divinely ordained destiny, crusades against evil, and collective redemption that is foreign to secular truth-seeking. Habermas' communicative reasoning presupposes an acceptance of common assumptions of an Enlightenment rationality that are missing among adherents of religious mysticism. Anthony Smith whose life-long study of nationalism highlights the sacred perceptions of ethnic communities, writes: "Myths of ethnic chosenness not only underpin peoples and cultures, they also provide charters and title deeds of sacred homelands."[13] Sanctified land and holy places are not easily given up or even shared in a spirit of historical justice or expedient compromise. Historical factual truth hardly affects the believer if it contradicts doctrine.

To be sure, these are small minorities, pitted against vastly more numerous secular majorities among Jews and Palestinians alike. Yet these fanatic ethno-religious fundamentalists are able to inflame an already-heated conflict and undermine rational compromises by defying state power in the name of superior God-given strictures. It is unwise to ignore or underestimate such committed counterforces. Any Middle East TC therefore would have to include those messianic minorities, coopt them, and buy them off in order to marginalize their destructive potential and bind them into secular rules that at the same time respect and accommodate their mythical beliefs in the private realm.

The Calvinist Afrikaner notion of a covenant with a chosen people was supposed to comprise similar stubborn convictions.[14] Yet, as Hermann Giliomee[15] and Andre du Toit[16] have argued, this alleged religious commitment has been generally exaggerated and was more confined to mobilizing rhetoric. The subsequent negotiated settlement has proven this assessment correct. Yet it is doubtful that a similar easy dissolution of divine ordination can be expected in the Middle East. The settlements in the territories continue to attract bigots and a devoted Hamas gains ground against the secular, but corrupt PA. In general, religious revivalism correlates with heightened anxieties and societal crisis, as even the U.S. example after 9/11 has demonstrated. The longing to belong to a religious community of certainty increases with general insecurity.

The Israeli-Palestinian TCs would also be absolved of the controversial quasijudicial functions of granting amnesty, contingent on forensic investigations. If such an institution is not going to be stillborn and the critical deconstructing of myths and metanarratives has value in itself, then unfortunately two divisive issues have to be explicitly avoided from the outset: first, redress, and second, laying blame.

It would be unwise and counterproductive if the last stage outlined were linked to the first phase of truth seeking. People would fear the consequences (litigation, refugee return, land claims) and escape into denial. To be sure, it is difficult to decouple the inquiry from the consequences, but in the interest of getting the first phases of the peace process off the ground, the redress question has to be left unresolved at this phase. The same applies to the question of historical guilt and blame.

In contrast to most TRCs that have focused on perpetrators through conditional amnesties, their Middle East counterparts would be prudent not to put the spotlight on human rights violators. Because more or less the same people will be in charge in the future two communities, these ruling elites will not take kindly to being shamed on public trial in a polarized conflict, let alone assist in investigating themselves. Putting the question of torturers on the backburner for practical reasons does not mean letting them off. After clarifying the legal responsibilities of army and government leaders in war situations, the Jewish-Palestinian TC could at least function as a deterrent for future abuses for the time being. Merely monitoring and publicizing international human rights violations would already be a valuable service.

The doctrine of "command responsibility" has been widely accepted and applied in international law since the Nuremberg trials of 1945. The two UN special courts for Yugoslavia and Rwanda used the same principle of "effective control" to hold those in charge responsible for abuses, even if they did not order or commit the crimes themselves but could reasonably have prevented them on the basis of their position. Pleading ignorance or blaming underlings has not been accepted as a legitimate defense when the command responsibility required that the superiors should have known about the violations. Highlighting such crimes of omission (rather than commission) may constrain ruthlessness on both sides. While truth commissions around the world have generally affirmed victims after they have been tortured or killed, the Israeli-Palestinian institution would primarily prevent and protect victims. Potential victims would then be transformed into actual survivors.

This analysis suggests eight controversial propositions: (1) While truth commissions are normally established after violence ceases, in the Middle East the process could pave the way toward the end of violence and renewed negotiations by narrowing opposing metanarratives; (2) Even in a two state solution, engaging with the past is needed for lasting peace; (3) Two separate TCs should be established initially and merged only after sufficient progress at a later stage; (4) The two commissions should aim at debunking popular communal myths and denials with factual truths and political education; (5) For practical reasons, the TCs should avoid singling out individual perpetrators (whether for punishment or amnesty) and also refrain from laying collective blame; (6) The absence of South African religious predispositions for reconciliation in the Middle East should not be an obstacle, since Christian notions of confessions, forgiveness, and contrition would not be part of the process; (7) Recommendations regarding material restitution and reparations for past injustices should be considered only at the last stage, but memorialization and symbolic acts of remembrance should form part of the process from the beginning; and (8) With official support for TCs lacking in both communities—which are steeped in notions of own victimization—civil society with international assistance would have to initiate the process.

III

Conclusions

When will a final settlement of the Israeli-Palestinian conflict be achieved? Can the South African negotiated revolution be a model for the Middle East? Is the imperial U.S. administration, bogged down in Iraq, appeasing Arab resentment by pressuring their client state Israel? Is a reformed Palestinian administration capable of reigning in fundamentalist extremists and suicide bombers? Will the neighboring Muslim states, particularly Syria, Iran, and Saudi Arabia, under U.S. pressure, normalize relations with Israel and recognize the moral legitimacy of the Jewish state? Will Israel, in a trade-off, withdraw to its pre-1967 borders, evacuate most of its settlers on conquered Palestinian land, and accept Jerusalem as a joint capital of a Jewish and Palestinian state? Any assessment opting for a "yes" to all these questions must face a disappointing reality. However, let's first recap the main arguments about the Israel–South Africa comparison set out in the preceding chapters.

Solutions Revisited and Lessons Drawn

Differences and Similarities between South Africa and Israel/Palestine

Many left-liberal activists advocate similar anti-apartheid strategies (divestment, boycott) against "Apartheid Israel" and assume that strong pressure would produce similar outcomes. Such idealistic optimism may foster illusions. The underlying assumption that the South Africa model of conflict resolution readily lends itself to export ignores unique historical circumstances. It may actually retard imaginative new solutions by clinging to visions or processes of negotiation that may not work in another context. Above all, in South Africa an entire regime had to be changed while in Israel the occupation and the status of the territories is the main contentious issue. Therefore, a more nuanced understanding of differences and similarities may enhance new approaches. Furthermore, just as the apartheid-equals-fascism slogan distorted political strategies in favor of illusionary military solutions, so the Israel-equals-apartheid slogan serves more propagandistic than analytical functions. The simplistic comparison unintentionally assists Zionist propaganda that can easily point to the substantial differences between the two disparate situations while ignoring the useful lessons from South Africa's negotiated settlement.

Six crucial realms stand out for comparison in both contexts: economic interdependence, religious divisions, third-party intervention, leadership, political culture, and violence.

1. Economic Interdependence. Economic interdependence and the emergence of a politicized union movement since the mid-1970s socialized South Africa in negotiation politics and trade-offs. The Israeli economy depends minimally on Palestinian labor and two economies exist more or less side by side. Israel uses closure as collective punishment. Palestinians are deprived of industrial action (strikes, consumer boycotts) that was heavily used by black South Africans to combat apartheid.

2. Religion. Religion in South Africa served as a common bond to assail and delegitimize apartheid, while Judaism and Islam compete for sovereignty in Jerusalem. Religiously motivated settlers and ultra-orthodox believers may not be as easily marginalized as Afrikaner extremists merely interested in territorial autonomy.

3. Third-Party Intervention. Both the ANC and the NP eschewed third-party intervention in their negotiations. An Israeli-Palestinian settlement depends heavily on U.S. policy that strongly supports Israel. Sanctions (divestment and trade boycotts) are generally overrated in triggering South African change. Only loan refusals and, to a lesser extent, moral ostracism impacted significantly on the apartheid government. Such action against Israel by the West is inconceivable at present. Unlike Afrikaners, Israelis enjoy a supportive diaspora. White South Africa finally negotiated when the rising costs of apartheid outweighed the benefits. In Israel, the costs of occupation and conflict are largely compensated from outside.

4. Leadership. The South African negotiations were facilitated by a cohesive and credible leadership mechanism, with a widely endorsed open mandate available to both sides. Leaders could sell a controversial compromise to a skeptical constituency. Both the Israeli and Palestinian leadership is fragmented, with militant outbidding a frequent tool of populist mobilization. The apartheid Westminster electoral system rewarded majority parties, in contrast to the minority influence in the proportional representation in Israel.

5. Political Culture. Much more personal interaction in a vertical-status hierarchy shaped South African race relations, compared with the more horizontal social distance between Jews and Palestinians. Paternalism characterized Afrikaner attitudes. Moral erosion of the apartheid stance among the ruling elite in South Africa contrasts with moral myopia in Israel, a few hundred military objectors notwithstanding. Both sides in the Middle East display a collective sense of victimhood. Apartheid clearly privileged beneficiaries and disenfranchised a majority in a pariah state that lacked the legitimacy of Israel outside the Arab and Muslim world.

6. Violence. During the anti-apartheid armed struggle, suicide was never used as a weapon and martyrdom was never celebrated. Resulting from the huge power imbalance and the imagined Israeli defeat by Hezbollah in Lebanon, the tactics of the second intifada are nevertheless counterproductive: The attacks on civilians unify Israeli public opinion on security and also destroy the social fabric of Palestinian society.

In summary, on most counts, the differences between apartheid South Africa and Israel outweigh the similarities that could facilitate transferable conditions for a negotiated compromise. Above all, opponents in South Africa finally realized that neither side could comprehensively defeat the other, short of the destruction of the country. This perception of stalemate, as a precondition for negotiating in good faith, is missing in the Middle East. Peacemaking resulted in an inclusive democracy in South Africa, while territorial separation of the adversaries in two states is widely hailed as the solution in Israel/Palestine.

Such a different trajectory suggests itself because South Africa, arguably, constitutes merely a multiethnic society with many cross-cutting bonds between the legislated artificial racial groups. In Israel/Palestine, on the other hand, a truly divided society exists. The two Semitic people may look alike and even enjoy the same food. They are however divided by religion, language, and above all, by history and the mythologies that the "burden of history" imprints on the self-concept and collective identity of the two groups. Jews and Palestinians constitute groups competing for meaning, security, and scarce resources in a small space.

Israel/Palestine in the International Context

Pressure on Israel as well as on the Palestinians is widely expected as a result of the Anglo-American invasion of Iraq. If only to ease Arab anti-Americanism, the U.S. administration, under British prodding, is finally expected to solve the unsolvable: A "roadmap" is pushed, containing three phases of reciprocal commitments, culminating in a Palestinian state. The *New York Times* columnist Thomas Friedman has argued that the U.S. strategic interest in establishing a cooperative democratic Iraqi political center will be compromised, if the United States leaves the Palestinian issue unaddressed. "The ability of any Iraqi politician to be openly pro-U.S. will be restricted if the Palestinian conflict burns on and the Bush team is seen as siding only with Ariel Sharon and doing nothing to defuse the situation."[1]

The two-state-solution is widely hailed by moderate insiders and impatient outsiders as the fairest compromise and the only realistic way out of the long-standing dilemma. Yet the international "consensus" on the likelihood and eventual stability after the establishment of two states has also been questioned. The counter-arguments and gloomy evidence can be summarized in five propositions.

1. There will not be much U.S. pressure on Israel to make concessions on settler evacuation, return of refugees, and border restorations. Calculations about U.S. voters' sentiments in presidential elections figure higher than Arab hostility. Despite the "road map," neither U.S. party is willing to alienate influential sections of the American electorate with an even-handed approach on the Palestinian issue. With the Iraqi quagmire dominating the Washington agenda, disengagement from another intractable situation prevails.

While the Bush administration was initially split on how much Israel should be pressured on negotiations, 9/11 and the Iraq war cemented the alliance between the United States and Israel. Bush's antiterrorist mobilization encountered the strongest support among evangelical Republicans. The underestimated U.S. Christian right, numbering forty million in one of the most avowedly religious countries, resembles Islamic fundamentalists in its dogmatism and fervor. As the late Edward Said has written:

> A peculiar alliance between Israel's influential neo-conservative American supporters and the Christian extremists is that the latter support Zionism as a way of bringing all the Jews to the Holy Land to prepare the way for the Messiah's Second Coming; at which point Jews will either have to convert to Christianity or be annihilated. The bloody and rabidly anti-Semitic teleologies are rarely referred to, certainly not by the pro-Israeli Jewish phalanx.[2]

Massive lobbying campaigns by Christian Zionists like Gary Bauer, Pat Robertson, and the Reverend Jerry Falwell warned the U.S. administration that any attempt to be "even-handed" would be "morally reprehensible."[3] In the face of such pressure, the U.S. government subcontracted its policy to a hardline Israeli government. "Unconditional support for Sharon," writes *New York Times* columnist Paul Krugman, "has squandered post-9/11 sympathy and brought relations with the Muslim world to a new low."[4] The convergence of Bush and Sharon, first manifested in their joint rejection of a fumbling Arafat, of course, does not signal a genuine break with previous U.S. policy. Washington always permitted Israel significant latitude and funded its expansionism, regardless of the government in power. However, the open abandonment of the pretence of the United States acting as an "honest broker" and the defiance of international obligations in regard to the Palestinians represents a departure from all previous U.S. policies since the foundation of Israel. The Democratic Party leadership does not differ from its Republican rival on Israel.

Mamdani has called this consensus the "Achilles' heel of American liberalism"[5] that led to a paradoxical situation: "It is easier to criticize the [U.S.] government than it is to criticize Israel." While the assertion that there is "not even a trace of public debate when it comes to Israel" overstates the American blind spot, Mamdani's suggestion remains valid to look for reasons beyond the influence of special interest groups. He stresses the blind American self-image of triumphing settlers over natives in North America. Never having questioned their own colonizing past at home, the American public easily bonds with the myth of Jewish resettlement. Both share a common mindset of a civilizing mission toward natives. Even liberal humanists have long bought into this superiority of a western Judeo-Christian tradition over backward indigenes. For example, the famous American Reform Rabbi and anti-Zionist, Judah Magnes, nonetheless wrote in a letter to Chaim Weizman in 1929: "The Palestine Arabs are unhappily still half savage, and their leaders are almost all small men."[6] This crude Orientalism of an earlier epoch has now metamorphosed into the self-allocated imperial mission to spread democracy among anti-western tyrannies by force (Afghanistan and Iraq) but simultaneously support tyrannical allies (Saudi Arabia and Egypt).

2. Even if there were a serious U.S. push to impose a settlement on a reluctant Israeli government, Israel would and could successfully resist. Though Israel depends heavily on the United States for patronage, it is a fallacy to assume that the United States can dictate its solution to its client. One has to take seriously Israeli government proclamations of a veto right. In a *Haaretz* interview, Sharon insisted that, "I will not make concessions in the future on anything that is related to the security of Israel." He portrayed himself as the protector of "the fate of the Jewish people" by explaining to President Bush "that this is the historic responsibility that I bear for the future.... We will be the ones who in the end decide what is dangerous for Israel."[7] In reluctantly supporting the roadmap (which already had been accepted unconditionally by the PA), Sharon preserves his amiable relationship with the Americans, whose veto is needed when the real bargaining over borders and settlers starts.

3. The stalled Road Map of the Quartet (US, UN, EU, Russia) has to overcome seemingly insurmountable realities on the ground that counteract noble intentions. In their judicious and fair-minded history of the Palestinian people, Baruch Kimmerling and Joel Migdal speak of "politicide." They define the term as "renewed attempts to wipe out [Palestinian] political autonomy."[8] In light of steadfast resistance, however, Israel may have to modify the strategy of "politicide." So far, Israel has not succeeded in installing credible Palestinian collaborators to administer its blueprints in similar ways as Pretoria outsourced its Bantustan administration for a while.

The settler parties and religious nationalists are strongly opposed to Palestinian autonomy and have accused Sharon of treason. Many Likud politicians share this view and oppose even a Palestinian mini-state, reminiscent of the bitter debate between Afrikaner right-wingers and National Party supporters during the 1980s in South Africa. The "Geneva Accord," negotiated by the Oslo architect Yossi Beilin and PA counterparts, and the Nusseibeh-Aylon agreement resemble the early IDASA[9] efforts to work out informal agreements, but at present lack a sizeable constituency and official state support.

4. Among outside supporters, Iran has emerged as a formidable supporter of Palestinian nationalism, particularly Islamist factions. However, both Iran and Syria are under U.S. pressure to stop supporting Hezbollah and the Gaza-based Hamas, whose main financial backer in the past was, paradoxically, U.S.-allied Saudi Arabia. Initially, even Israel supported the Hamas fundamentalists as a counterforce against the secular and nationalist PLO. Even if the reformed PA seriously intended to curb the militancy of the street, it would not be able to do so without the willing cooperation of Hamas and the smaller militias. This cooperation depends on reciprocal

Israeli actions. Several declarations of ceasefires by Hamas were scuttled in the past by Israeli assassinations of targeted leaders. Extremists on both sides goaded each other. Israel claimed in vain that its military measures could successfully deal with an enraged population. Even if roadblocks, fences, and curfews were successful in preventing more suicide bombings, the violence persists, as long as the occupation prevails and the state-sponsored settlers roam freely. Soldiers and armed settlers in the occupied territories were always considered legitimate military targets by the Palestinian resistance, in contrast to civilians in Israel-proper whose killings amount to human rights violations under international law. Although it is not official policy to harm Palestinian civilians, Israel has also killed many more civilians (at a ratio of 3:1) than combatants by using disproportional force to liquidate armed activists who are frequently embedded in the civilian population. Unlike the South African "armed struggle," this has reinforced the notion of a "people's war" on both sides, where the distinction between civilians and combatants is blurred.

Several former Shin Beth leaders and senior military officials expressed reservations about the wisdom of the reckless treatment of civilians. Short-term tactics undermine Israel's long-term strategic interests, argued even the former army chief Moshe Yaalon, who was overruled by his cabinet colleagues. Such elite dissent within the ruling faction rather than the ineffectual protest of the opposition also triggered the change in South Africa. In any case, the South Africa apartheid military always viewed its role as 80 percent political. The South African military campaign to "win the hearts and minds" of the rural African population through development programs constituted the opposite of the Israeli policing and indiscriminate targeting of an entire social fabric.

The author of a book on the IRA, Kevin Toolis, points out that the Provisional IRA twice tried to decapitate the British Cabinet. The British army could have easily assassinated the entire IRA leadership in Ulster. Since this action, according to Toolis, "would not have destroyed violent Irish republicanism or weakened the Provisional IRA," it was instead decided to establish a relationship with the leader Martin McGuiness, which ultimately led to the 1998 Good Friday agreement. The author rightly advises: "If a peace process is serious, each side must accept the other as they find it rather than remold their enemies into a more compliant state by assassination and political diktat."[10]

The security agents of the apartheid regime also targeted ANC supporters, particularly white intellectuals at home and abroad, but acted with restraint toward the top ANC leadership, who responded likewise. Not one apartheid leader was assassinated and most prominent ANC leaders in exile survived the clandestine war against them. Even so-called leading collaborators, such as Buthelezi, were informally protected by the ANC in exile against local militants.

5. Just as most South African homeland leaders were perceived as typical collaborators in the service of anti-liberation forces, so the attempts by PA reformists to pacify a radicalized street are likely to fail, because the PA lacks domestic legitimacy, despite the integrity or noble intentions of some individuals involved. The more the U.S., EU, or Egypt support and welcome such forces, the more they are weakened as perceived stooges of outside powers. Only if the reformed PA were able to deliver on easing high unemployment and travel restrictions, curb settler expansionism, and improve general living conditions, could a moderate Palestinian leadership prevail. Neither Israel nor the United States strengthened the domestic legitimacy of Palestinian pragmatists by releasing prisoners, abolishing check points, opening borders for work seekers or making other concessions in the past. No Palestinian leader can heed the U.S./Israeli demand "to destroy the terrorist infrastructure" without provoking a civil war. Just as the Ian Smith regime in Rhodesia deceived itself by trying to cut a deal with Bishop Muzorewa, or the Vorster/Botha government attempted in vain to have their Bantustan clients exercise legitimate authority, so the Palestinian administration is destined to fail under Israeli/U.S. tutelage. In short, the warmer a Palestinian representative is embraced by the Israeli establishment, the faster his home support melts away.

Only a Mandela solution promises long-term stability. After further polarization and more failed attempts to reach a final status agreement, a "Mandela solution" may emerge. Only an untainted individual with the moral authority to negotiate a controversial compromise on behalf of a fragmented constituency may be able to turn things around. Marwan Barghouti, still in prison, may be one such person. If Israel were wise, it would "groom" its Palestinian Mandela rather than insist on anointing its own negotiating partners."[11]

Zionism, Anti-Zionism, and Post-Zionism Revisited in the Twenty-First Century

The early Zionists and Herzl himself debated whether there should be a state for the Jews or a Jewish state. The two are not identical, and it is debatable which form provides greater security. Could future Jewish security lie in the very dissolution of the Zionist dream? The idea of a secular, single, or binational state has been around for a long time, before the PLO began to champion its own state in the mid-1970s. Even 11 percent of Jews in Israel today, according to the October 2003 Steinmetz "Peace Index," think that "Jews and Palestinians would be able to live together as citizens with equal rights," while the overwhelming majority dreads this vision, just as South African whites once overwhelmingly feared black majority rule.

Particularly the academic diaspora has revived the debate with prominent advocates vehemently arguing for and against the idea of a one-state solution. A serious post-Zionist debate indicates the slow demise of the Zionist consensus, after its original inspiring idealistic quest has long been perverted by religious zealots and short-sighted political Zionists alike. The long hegemony of the two-state solution has been broken, asserts the one side. "Given that the two-state solution promises only more trouble," Virginia Tilley perhaps too confidently concludes, "the one-state solution is the only one that the international community can responsibly now entertain."[12] The North American debate is perhaps best embodied in the sharp exchange between Tony Judt and his many critics, particularly Leon Wieseltier. We add our views on their positions before comparing their arguments with developments on the ground.

Judt is embarrassed by Israel and calls it an "anachronism" in an age of multicultural globalization. For Wieseltier,[13] a binational common state is not a possible alternative *for*, but an alternative *to* Israel. "Judt and his editors," he asserts, "have crossed the line from the criticism of Israel's policy to the criticism of Israel's existence." This is only true if Israel is eternally envisaged as an exclusively Jewish state with a Jewish demographic majority in a self-defined ethnic state.

This dogma rests on Israel as a sanctuary, a safe haven for prosecuted Jews wherever age-old anti-Semitism may rear its ugly head again. The globalized world of the twenty-first century, however, differs from the closed world of the first half of the twentieth century. The anti-Semitic "None is too many" of the 1940s is now remembered as shameful in North America history schoolbooks. Wieseltier himself asserts that many Jews would emigrate from a non-Jewish Israel which implies that they would be accepted somewhere. Given a choice, already more Jewish migrants in search of a homeland ironically prefer to live in the United States than in Israel! During the mass migration of Russian Jews in the 1990s, Israel insisted on non-stop flights and the closure of the Vienna transit camp, because many so-called Russian Jews deserted and longed for the American dreamland rather than the ethnic homeland. In short, two thirds of the world's Jewry live happily outside Israel, despite the Zionists' plea to return to instant Israeli citizenship.

Notwithstanding the totally asymmetric power relations in Israel, Wieseltier asks the question "Who will protect the Jews" in a binational state? It is a legitimate question, given the existence of Islamist extremism. While global anti-Semitism is frequently exaggerated, the potential rise of another Hitler somewhere cannot be ruled out. This is the main justification for the need of a national Jewish sanctuary.

A binational state will not arise without a minimal mutual trust in the possibility of a peaceful coexistence and mutual recognition of the two people. Can the peacemakers and compromisers on both sides marginalize their extremists? Islamist extremism feeds on the occupation and ongoing Zionist expansion. Jewish extremism in turn benefits from Palestinian militancy and particularly the deliberate targeting of civilians. Once the occupation has been dismantled, one major cause for conflict has been removed. The Palestinian moderate middle ground would have been strengthened and the extremists undermined. Yet Wieseltier homogenizes all Palestinians and maligns them with the mocking question: "For what reasons do the Israelis have to depend for security and decency upon the democratic talents of the Palestinians?" In Wieseltier's caricature of the adversary they are all terrorists and their political culture "is now a contest between religious maximalism and terrorism, and secular maximalism and terrorism." A people are labeled "maximalists" who have officially assented in the Oslo Accord to 20 percent of the land between the sea and the Jordan River as their own state. If they are lucky and escape ethnic cleansing, they may eventually control a small percentage of the territory in ghetto-like enclaves, surrounded by walls and settlers. All the while, Wieseltier worries about "the nightmare of ethnic cleansing" by Hamas in the utopia of Greater Palestine, while ignoring the reality of expansionism in Greater Israel.

Wieseltier thinks in binary terms when he contrasts "Greater Israel" with "Greater Palestine" and accuses Judt of wanting to replace a (Jewish) national state with a (Palestinian) national state or "to relieve Palestinian statelessness with Jewish statelessness," which he, not surprisingly, considers "even more vulnerable." This was the model of the Apartheid ideologues who also exhorted their anxious white constituency with the slogan: "Dominate or be dominated!" But a truly binational state would not necessarily be either a Greater Israel or a Greater Palestine. Ideally, one expansionist, ethnic nationalism would not give way to another equally intolerant variety, but to civic nationalism where all the residents have equal rights. Judt is rightly criticized for being naïve and vague on this "constitutional patriotism." Trusting constitutionalism in the Middle East for the security of minorities?

Clearly the end of the occupation and even a "land for peace settlement" does not guarantee instant harmony between two long-feuding nationalisms. Nor should Israelis be expected to place their faith in a UN protection force, which looked away when Bosnian Muslims were slaughtered, as Wieseltier rightly avers. However, there are models for accommodating the anxieties of ethnic minorities in divided societies, ranging from federalist or confederalist arrangements, to consociational power sharing, to ironclad guarantees. For example, in a binational compromise, Jewish Israelis could legitimately retain control over the army and security, while relinquishing ethnic administrative and political monopoly. A sizeable EU and U.S. force could guarantee constitutionalism, at least initially. If a binational Israel were to be admitted to the EU as an economic incentive and reward for peacemaking, there would be additional constraints and penalties for human rights violations. Would Jewish identity be endangered and Hebrew culture swamped in a secularized common state? On the contrary, with Hebrew and Arabic as the two official languages mandatory in integrated or segregated schools according to parental preferences, both cultures would flourish and even the ultra-orthodox could retain their subsidized Yeshivas. The settlers could stay where they are, but land courts would decide about fair compensation. Even the law of return would not have to be repealed, as long as it is extended to Palestinians, with annual immigration quotas for both sides. Indeed, this is a utopia at present when not even a viable two-state solution is in the cards.

Wieseltier argues that Judt should be ashamed of his implicit anti-Semitism, because holding all Jews "responsible for whatever any Jews do" is a typical anti-Semitic stereotype. "But if you explain anti-Semitism as a response to Jews, and racism as a response to blacks, and misogyny as a response to women, then you have not understood it. You have reproduced it." Indeed, whether a minority is despised has little to do with its behavior. *Difference* is not the cause of prejudice, only its vehicle. Yet Judt is right that Israel backfires on Jews everywhere, whether they are supporters or not. Self-definition is only one aspect of identity. Personal disassociation does not erase the other component of identity, which is imposed from outside, whether a person agrees or not with the ascribed label. This is exacerbated by the foundational concept of Zionism that Israel belongs to all Jewish people of the world, not just its own citizens. Therefore, neither whitewashing Israel nor keeping an uneasy silence should be the response to the Middle East conflict by concerned Jews and non-Jews everywhere.

Ignoring the contrary realities on the ground, Wieseltier asserts that "the Jewish state will have betrayed its liberal principles" if the rights of the Arab minority are not "scrupulously respected and vigorously enforced." One has to agree with him that "there is nothing in the ethnic composition of this majority that makes such a betrayal *inevitable*." The current trends, however, make it *highly likely*! Just as in apartheid South Africa, Israeli Arabs are no longer allowed to live with their Palestinian spouses who originate from the West Bank. Attempted property theft in East Jerusalem of Palestinians living nearby on the West Bank under the Absentee Property Law of 1950 resembles the racial expropriation of desirable real estate under South Africa's Group Areas Act.[14] Not only have the rights of Palestinians in the territories been severely restricted, even the life-chances of second-class Palestinian Israelis are threatened when about 40 percent of the Jewish public supports their "transfer." The ongoing creeping annexation of land and resources and the institutional chaos in the territories already achieves "soft expulsion" by creating unbearable living conditions. The two-state solution is in jeopardy when, according to the October 2003 Steinmetz poll, 83 percent support the separation fence, regardless of where it is built. What else than betrayal of liberal principles by the majority should this be called?

One of the more cynical comments by a leading South African apartheid ideologue afterwards was: "We had to try apartheid first in order to know that the system could not work!" Without repeating the crime, Israel can learn from South Africa that locking people into tribal reservations does not secure long-term peace. Nor does forced or induced "transfer" abolish a people's sense of home and quest for return, apart from constituting a worse crime. A governing party without a realistic political vision of peace, wavering between more repression, expropriation, or apartheid, and dominated mainly by military calculations, manifests its moral bankruptcy.

The Two-State versus the Common-State Option

Currently, the very physical possibility of a Palestinian state is being destroyed. Few Palestinians would object to the building of a high security barrier exactly on the 1967 Green Line. The International Court of Justice also conceded that right to Israel, provided the barrier is built on Israeli territory. Just as Americans try to protect themselves in vain with a fence on their own territory against illegal Mexican immigrants, so a great majority of Israelis also support the illusion of an impenetrable protective barrier. Equitable land swaps for Jewish settlements around Jerusalem would also find Palestinian support. However, the colonization continues in the very heart of the potential new state. Tony Judt comments harshly that the electronic fence supporters have "missed the last fifty years of history.... Like the Berlin Wall, it confirms the moral and institutional bankruptcy of the regime it is intended to protect."[15]

Amira Hass has pointed to the powerful myth of Israeli concessions being constantly rejected for no good reason while at the same time a policy of annexation proceeded. The myth of ungrateful Palestinians is reinforced by the deliberate denial of reality in the territories. According to Hass:

> How absurd. During the decade of negotiations, which began in 1991 with the Madrid Conference, the idea of a "Palestinian state" as a solution to the Israeli-Palestinian conflict won ever-increasing numbers of supporters in Israel, and at the very least became a legitimate issue for discussion in the political arena, as it never had been before. But at the same time, the Palestinian lands earmarked for that state shrank, and were carved up and divided.... But like now, back then, most Israelis never went to the territories. Therefore everything that took place was abstract. A bypass road? Land expropriations? Settlement expansion? Uprooted trees? Closure? What's all that compared to talk of Israeli readiness for concessions in some undefined future. Thus the myths became tangible and real—the myth of concessions like the myth of support for a Palestinian state. And those myths continue to feed the nearly unshakable support for the Israeli military policy in the territories.[16]

Uri Avnery[17] has vividly described fifteen phases of the ever-widening circle of colonization and settlement expansion:

> On a hilltop, an "outpost" consisting of one or two mobile homes is set up without government permission. The government declares that it will not tolerate such illegal actions and talks about removing it. The army sends soldiers to defend the outpost, saying that it cannot leave Jews in a hostile region without protection as long as they are there, even illegally. For the same reason, the outpost is connected to the water, electricity and telephone networks. The

> discussion in the cabinet is postponed, and in the meantime the settlement expands. The cabinet decides to accept the accomplished fact and the outpost becomes a legal settlement. The Military Governor expropriates large stretches of cultivated land for the development of the settlement. A bypass road is build to allow for the safe movement of the settlers and soldiers. For this purpose, the army expropriates more stretches of cultivated land from the neighboring Palestinian villages. The road with its "security area" is 60–80 meters wide. Palestinians try to attack the settlement that stands on their land. To prevent attacks on the settlement, an area 400 meters wide around the settlement is declared a "security zone" closed to Palestinians. The olive groves and fields in this area are lost to their owners. This provides the motivation for more attacks. For security reasons, the army uproots all trees that might afford cover for an attack on the settlement or the road leading to it. The army has even invented a new Hebrew word for it, something like "exposuring." The army destroys all buildings from which the settlement or the road could be attacked. For good measure, all buildings from which the settlement can be observed are demolished, too. Anyone who comes near the settlement is shot, on suspicion that he has come to spy or attack.

The more an authentic two-state option is undermined by permanent settlements and security barriers, the more the single-state option may be embraced by Palestinians in the long run. In 2003, a bare majority (52 %) of Palestinians prefer a two-state solution, while there is overwhelming support for "open borders between two states" (82 %), "joint economic ventures" (65 %), and "reconciliation of two peoples."[18] Currently no Palestinian party and only a few intellectuals as well as a few Jewish post-Zionists and anti-Zionists advocate a common state. However, the logic of Zionist expansionism may ultimately destroy the very idea of an exclusive Jewish state. Even sophisticated friends of Israel, such as Thomas Friedman recognize that the two-state option is being discredited as people would simply be caged into apartheid ghettoes. "Rather than create the outlines of a two-state solution, this wall," warns Friedman, "will kill that idea for Palestinians, and drive them, over time, to demand instead a one-state solution—where they and the Jews would have equal rights in one state."[19] The dialectic of uncompromising Zionist exclusivism would have produced its own destruction. Like the long anti-apartheid struggle, this South African solution of equal citizenship would resonate abroad much more than creating another undemocratic, corrupt Arab state. Friedman senses this danger: "If American Jews think it's hard to defend Israel today on college campuses, imagine what it will be like when their kids have to argue against the principle of one man, one vote."

In short, while the Gaza evacuation is debated and resisted, the major fortified Jewish settlements on the West Bank are unlikely ever to be evacuated. The senior advisor to Sharon, Dov Weisglass, has confirmed that "the significance of the disengagement plan is the freezing of the peace process. And when you freeze that process, you prevent the establishment of a Palestinian state."[20] Therefore, some Palestinian intellectuals consider the settlers "the vanguard of a common state." In any case, permanent occupation by settler militias and the Israeli regular army already creates a de facto common entity. In a single Israeli-control system, Palestinian resistance is likely to change from national liberation to a civil rights struggle. In theory, a common state amounts to the economically most rational and politically most democratic solution, since there are no second-class citizens in an official ethnic state or "ethnocracy." It would also solve the refugee problem, when the law of return applies to both Jews and Palestinians equally. Furthermore, settler evacuation would become a non-issue; they could stay where they are and a court would settle claims for compensation, as happened in South Africa for land confiscations under the Group Areas Act.

However, there is no chance of even the Israeli left supporting such a South African solution, as it would be perceived as a threat to the Jewish character of the state. On the political right many fear that even a Palestinian state amounts to a *two-stage* solution. The former Labor Party Speaker of the Knesset, Avraham Burg, has put the dilemma of his idealized "last Zionist generation" into the stark alternative: "Do you want democracy? No problem. Either abandon the greater land of Israel, to the last settlement and outpost, or give full citizenship and voting rights to everyone, including Arabs. The result, of course, will be that those who did not want a Palestinian state alongside us will have one in our midst, via the ballot box."[21] Yossi Alpher, an advisor to Barak, speaks of unilateral disengagement as the only way to "stop the current decline into a South Africa-type situation"[22] and preserving a demographic Jewish state.

A return to the original more humane and secular Zionism, apart from being utopian, does not solve the inherent contradiction of exclusion of non-Jews from the ethnic state. In the European and North American reality of ethnically mixed, multicultural democracies, the very idea of an exclusive ethnic state is considered an "anachronism" by post- Zionists.[23] However, in the Middle Eastern reality of communal hostilities and national identities, the Zionist vision is deeply rooted and more difficult to dislodge than racist supremacist illusions in South Africa. Could the Israeli public ever abandon its Zionist identity and embrace an inclusive civic nationalism of all its inhabitants?

A redefinition of Israel from an ethnic state with a guaranteed Jewish majority to a pluralist, multicultural democracy requires a reciprocal Arab revision of an anti-Zionist identity that frequently flows into anti-Semitic stereotyping of the worst kind. Israel's moral legitimacy has yet to be accepted by its neighbors. As long as crude anti-Semitic stereotypes, such as the Czarist forgeries of the "Protocol of the Elders of Zion" or even Holocaust denial is peddled among Islamists, the South African solution of an inclusive, tolerant common state remains a utopian vision indeed. Yet why should the Shoah and historical suffering of the Jewish people not be part of the Palestinian curriculum? Why should the historical facts of the dispossession of the Palestinians since 1948 not be part of Zionist identity? Why does nobody in Israel/Palestine, apart from a few marginalized post-Zionist historians and writers, demand a truth and reconciliation commission? Can the contradictory historical narratives be reconciled?

Only when people come to grips with their past truthfully, when they no longer feel humiliated, when they can realistically envisage security, recognition, respect, and economic improvements, will they be ready to embrace radical alternatives. Overcoming intolerance depends on diminished threat perceptions and optimistic expectations on both sides in a win-win situation. That is the lesson from the remarkable South African compromise.

While we are skeptical that a viable Palestinian state is in the cards soon, we support the two-state option for different pragmatic reasons than preserving an exclusively Jewish Israel. At the very least, an independent Palestinian state constitutes a strategically necessary interim arrangement. The idea of separation from a security threat may be useful to defeat the sizeable Israeli faction that wants to annex the "promised land" or expel the Palestinians. The "security wall" that gobbles up more Palestinian land at least signifies to the Israeli right that there will be a Palestinian state behind the wall. Ironically, the wall may also protect the Palestinians from right-wing settlers. Even a truncated mini-state preserves Palestinian identity of a people exhausted, demoralized, and utterly at the mercy of their adversary. Above all, given the overwhelming rejection of a common state in Israel and the insistence on its Jewish character, holding out for a single state as the only solution would irresponsibly prolong Palestinian suffering for another generation.

However, the limited sovereignty and fragmentation of the ghettoized Palestinian entity will be a constant source of friction and radicalization. A nominal Palestinian pseudo-state without an economy, except the export of labor, amounts to what could be called the "Lesotho option." Sovereign in name only, the Palestinian entity would lack even the territorial contiguity of Lesotho. Another analogy from North America may also fit. Ian Gilmour has labeled Palestinians "the Native Americans of the contemporary world." Huddled into self-governing enclaves, like America's pacified indigenous inhabitants, Gilmour predicts, "The Palestinians may eventually get something that is called 'a state.' Very possibly, however, it will in reality be a Bantustan or a reservation."[24] In short, the main advantage of the two-state option lies in its potential appeal to an Israeli public that is inclined to back even harsher repression. For the Palestinians, an own state garners international support. It also means survival of an identity as a people in the face of an overwhelming adversary.

In summary: Two states for two feuding people can be an appropriate solution. Neither a common state nor negotiated partition carries moral superiority. Separation understandably has an immediate appeal for people who for good reasons don't trust each other. Just as in Czechoslovakia, peaceful separation is feasible, as long as majorities or governing elites in both camps support just partition. However, a state cannot be imposed on people who do not want it, and Palestinian opinion makers outside the PA and its cronies may turn away from the two-state model. It is now barely supported by a slim majority of the Palestinian public. In the old South African cliché: Time is running out on the two-state option. Could it now be too late for two states which have been endlessly bandied around as an obfuscating fantasy? Could well-meaning advocates of partition deceive themselves if they hope that Jewish settlements would ever be evacuated, bought out, or accommodated by Palestinians confined to noncontiguous enclaves? Huge infrastructural developments on the ground seem irreversible.

However, the Jewish sanctuary need not be lost in a binational state. Most of its opponents falsely assume that Jewish domination would be replaced by Arab domination, once Palestinians constitute a demographic majority in a few decades. This is the "winner-takes-all" outcome of a Westminster voting system, resulting in the perception of "dominate or be dominated." Such a system is indeed unsuitable for plural societies, because legitimate minority interests fall by the wayside. Yet it is often forgotten that there are two types of minority accommodation in ethnically divided societies, which can be dubbed the South African on the one hand and the Canadian or Belgian model on the other side. South African–type individualism or what the PLO used to call a democratic "secular state" would neither satisfy Jewish nor Palestinian clamor for communal recognition and protection. Therefore, post-apartheid South Africa is not necessarily a model for the Middle East.

Post-apartheid South Africa is built on individual rights. It does not recognize African, Afrikaner, Zulu, or Indian sub-nations within the common state. A common "South African-ness" is officially fostered. The previous regime had used imposed ethnicity for divide-and-rule purposes and thereby discredited institutionalized identity politics. Common Christianity of the majority of blacks and whites facilitated a common cultural value system. The South African model of a single state would encounter strong resistance in Israel/Palestine where two distinct and voluntary Jewish and Palestinian identities have developed. How then can the two hostile nationalisms and competing religious communities be accommodated and reconciled in a common state? This unresolved question is likely to dominate the future discussion of Israeli binationalism.

Nobody has yet described how bicommunalism would concretely work in Israel beyond vague and nebulous demands to implement the vision. "It is pointless, now, to guess the material future form of the vision of life together," declares the "Olga Document,"[25] an eloquent poetic plea for a common state by disenchanted Israeli peace activists. Yet without concrete specifics about the alternative, the Olga lament about the "biggest ghetto," and "colonial structure" does not resonate with a security-conscious public.

Who, for example, would ultimately control Israel's nuclear arsenal in a power-sharing deal? The post-colonial record of consociational power sharing remains poor, from Lebanon, Ethiopia, Nigeria, to Rwanda. After the end of the Cold War, many multi-nation states are characterized by violent disintegration, with the Soviet Union or Yugoslavia being only the most obvious cases. However, there are also examples where the ethno-nationalism of subgroups and the trend toward ethnic sovereignty has been successfully reversed through imaginative constitutional compromises.

In the Canadian constitutional model, group rights of various founding nations are entrenched in addition to individual rights of common citizens. Aboriginal rights of "First Nations" as well as special protection for Quebec culture and language maintenance are guaranteed through maximal subsidiarity. Quebec even controls its own immigration. Optimal federalism allows provinces their own taxation laws while equalization payments address the gap between poor and resource-rich provinces. Belgium prospers under similar autonomy for its distinct French and Flemish parts.

In the Middle East, similar communal recognition could be entrenched not only for Jews and Muslims, but for Christians, Druze, ultra-orthodox, and indeed agnostics or "non-ethnics." Self-governing and self-policing communities need not be tied to territory in Carl Friedrich's model of "ethnic federalism" or frozen into eternally fixed power sharing. Between Arend Lijphart's consociationalism and Will Kymlicka's "multicultural citizenship" there are many sophisticated arrangements that could satisfy national subgroups according to local particularities.

The crucial issue in Israel/Palestine, however, will not be cultural maintenance but ironclad guarantees of mutual security and faithful adherence to agreed-upon constitutionalism. Creating a rival Palestinian Islamic state may in the end merely mirror the ethnic exclusivity of the Jewish state, if it ever comes about. At best, two sovereign states constitute an interim "solution" until both people discover their common interests and trust each other sufficiently to coexist in the same small space to their mutual benefit under whatever rules of coexistence they agree on.

South African Lessons for Peacemaking

The South African lessons from the negotiated settlement directly contradict current Israeli policy in several respects. Ten obvious lessons stand out:

1. It is still Israeli government doctrine that the enemy has to be subdued first, before the government will negotiate. In the South Africa stalemate the negotiations took place between undefeated rivals, equal in their inability to defeat the other. In contrast, Likud's policy dictates terms of surrender. Such supremacist talk ensures rejection, because it does not allow the opponent even the face-saving dignity of respect. Peace by ultimatum does not work. The South Africa negotiations started in earnest when a mutual perception of stalemate prevailed, unlike the continuing power asymmetry in the Middle East where each side anticipates victory by wearing the other side down.

Peacemaking requires a mutual basic respect for the adversary. As long as the stronger power persists in humiliating an opponent, sullen quests for revenge result. The weaker party softens its hardline stance not when it experiences defeat, but when it tastes victory. Even if the victory is merely imagined, dramatic attitude shifts toward reconciliation presuppose a perceived reversal of previous humiliation.

One example may suffice. In 1977 President Sadat signed a controversial peace agreement with Israel and visited the hitherto unrecognized "enemy entity." He could do so only because Egypt had convinced itself that by unexpectedly crossing the fortified Suez Canal in the 1973 October War, it had defeated the invincible Israeli army, liberated its territory, and extinguished its previous defeat in 1967. The popular jubilation about the short-lived victory was visible in the elevated mood in the crowded Cairo streets. Many shops depicted the "heroic advance" in handmade posters. Egyptians celebrated their newfound equality, if not their imagined superiority. In short, without recognizing the dignity of an opponent, no outstretched hand can be expected.

Yet the Likud approach to peacemaking asserts the very opposite. When the Israeli Minister of Defense, Shaul Mofaz, visited Israeli troops in Gaza in August 2003, he revealed in one sentence the fallacy of a supremacist strategy. "With our enemies, it seems, no shortcuts are possible. Egypt made peace with Israel only after it was defeated in the Yom Kippur War. That will happen with the Palestinians, too." However, contempt and humiliation breeds more militancy.

2. Israel insists that before negotiations begin, violence must stop first. This condition hands veto power to any individual with a gun or explosives. Nobody is able to enforce such demands. Trust is the *outcome,* not a *precondition* of negotiations. Enemies, not friends, need to negotiate. Negotiations do not depend on a ceasefire, but have to be unconditional. The ANC continued with the "armed struggle" long after negotiations had started, as did the white government's violence to enforce its laws.

3. Negotiators have to be freely chosen by each side. One side cannot dictate to the other who should be their leader. Had the then President de Klerk insisted that he would only talk to the nationalist wing of the ANC and exclude communists (as some had advocated), negotiations would not have started. Likewise, if the Palestinian negotiators are considered unrepresentative stooges, their agreements are unlikely to be acceptable to a radicalized constituency. Free elections can best produce this legitimacy of controversial negotiators. Yet normal elections cannot be conducted under occupation.

4. If controversial compromises are to be accepted by an indoctrinated constituency on both sides, a prudent leadership must educate its following

in political literacy. Yet, giving up dreams and master narratives is painful for activists. The ANC had to shed the socialist dream of capturing the commanding heights of the economy and whites had to give up state power in return for peace. The various informal peace agreements, the Geneva Accord in particular, outline in detail the possible compromise on the three most contentious issues in a two-state solution along the 1967 border: (a) Full Israeli withdrawal from all Palestinian areas and evacuation of most settlers with equitable land swaps for some continuing Jewish settlements behind the Green Line, (b) Israel's recognition of the right of refugee return *in principle*, but limited to a symbolic number in practice, with relocation assistance and compensation for others, and (c) Jerusalem as a joint capital with each state exercising sovereignty over its areas and holy sites.

In such situations, the danger of populist outbidding looms for pragmatic compromisers. This necessitates organization and strengthening of civil society institutions on both sides.[26] Transparency of leadership-deal-making, complementing the top-down process with bottom-up information, is missing on both sides of the Middle Eastern conflict.

5. Israel asserts that Arafat rejected a "generous offer" and there is "no partner to negotiate with." Indeed, the assertion is correct in the sense that the Palestinians did not provide a collaborating partner who would sign on a U.S./Israel–dictated package. Many knowledgeable observers agree that the failure of the Clinton-sponsored Camp David talks were not caused by Arafat's psychological makeup, but by the content of the offer. The Oxford historian Avi Shlaim writes: "Israelis like to demonize Arafat, but no Palestinian leader, however moderate, could accept the offer on package at Camp David."[27] P. W. Botha and F. W. de Klerk and their negotiators also frequently attempted to dictate to the ANC. Rebuffed, they did not adopt unilateralism, but tried out new compromise formulas.

6. Encouraging strife and internal conflict among an opponent backfires. This happened when shadowy "third-force elements" instigated large-scale interblack violence during the first years of the South African transition in order to destabilize and discredit the new order. A brutalized youth and a continuous high crime rate resulted from this disruptive strategy. In a similar vein, some pundits gleefully editorialize: "If Palestinian factions are fighting amongst themselves, they will have less time to conduct terrorist attacks."[28] South Africa's Bantustan policy represented a divide-and-rule policy toward the black South African majority. With the fragmentation of the PA, the emerging autonomous fiefdoms in Gaza and West Bank enclaves also counteract nation-building. However, just as the imposed Bantustans divisions proved unworkable, so the personal rivalries, cronyism, and illegitimacy of Palestinian warlords undermine potential settlements. If Israel aims at a settlement, it has an interest in a cohesive Palestinian partner.

7. The Israeli/Palestinian peace camp can learn a lot from Mandela's conciliatory gestures and the African ubuntu philosophy. It starts with the language of persuasion and condemnation. The apartheid and racism invective, though true in many respects, nevertheless blocks access to the Israeli public mind. The intended shaming and delegitimization fails. It therefore disregards Edward Said's recommendation "to capture the imagination not just of our people, but of our oppressors."[29] Mandela's and the ANC's insistence on the "common humanity" of blacks and whites achieved this unifying vision. Majority Jewish quests for peace and security have not only *not* been captured, but progressively hardened by an inept Fatah leadership and some minority Islamist rhetoric and suicidal martyrdom. Yet even with an unlikely outside intervention by the United States, the support of the Jewish public is a precondition for any lasting peace agreement.

8. If it can be argued that there cannot be peace without justice, the reverse is not necessarily true. Principles of justice and inherent rights of peoples should be upheld even without peace. Initially, Israel and the United States used the dominance of Arafat in Palestinian politics as a convenient pretext not to negotiate. After Arafat's death, Palestinian statehood was made dependent, alternatively, on ending attacks against occupation forces, on instituting democracy and internal reform, or ending incitement in the media and history textbooks. While democratic reforms are always desirable, the universal right of national self-determination cannot hinge on the system of government. Inasmuch as one party should not dictate to its adversary who its representatives should be, so peace cannot be made contingent on how democratically Palestinians behave. If that were the case, Israel should never have signed peace agreements with autocratic Egypt and Jordan, and the South Africa National Party should never have negotiated with a Stalinist Communist Party. As Hanan Ashrawi has argued: "You don't use democracy for justifying the existence of states. You would then have to remove many states."[30] In any case, of all Arab states, the Palestinians have demonstrated the greatest degree of democratic practice. Multi-candidate and violence-free elections ensured a smooth succession to Arafat in January 2005, although less than half of eligible (and three-quarters of registered) voters participated in confirming Mahmood Abbas with 62 percent of votes cast. The more popular candidate Marwan Barghouti remained imprisoned and Hamas boycotted the election, which weakened the new regime. Because demographics outpace the difficult long-term process of democratization, even most secular Zionists now question whether "Must peace wait for Democracy?"[31] To make Palestinian statehood dependent on the end of resistance against occupation or the effective functioning of democratic institutions is particularly ironic since Israel, with U.S. consent, vandalized the institutional infrastructure of the nascent state, from the destruction of police stations, to the bulldozing of the sole airport, to the smashing of computers and records in the PA administration.

9. Efforts must be made to draw the most extreme factions on both sides into the negotiation process. Both in Palestine and South Africa some groups boycotted elections and branded participants in peacemaking as sellouts. This proved less of a problem in South Africa, since the ANC represented the overwhelming majority of the disenfranchised. Smaller radical black and white factions could be ignored or sidelined without jeopardizing the main compromise. This is not the case in the fragmented Palestinian and Israeli politics where extremist sections command more—though not majority—support, if only for the social services they provide or the religious doctrines they espouse. The delegitimization of contested compromises is preempted and the perception of a fair deal increased, if the likely challengers are included or at least voluntary self-exclusion is clearly demonstrated. On the part of the dominant power Israel, that means shedding notions of "no negotiations under duress" or "not giving the enemy the impression that their violence has succeeded." As the veteran South Africa journalist Allister Sparks has wisely commented: "Those who vow never to talk to 'terrorists' are doomed to fight them forever."[32]

10. Preparing an indoctrinated public for a painful transition through a South African–type truth commission remains perhaps the most important lesson. In the aftermath of Arafat's death, a representative survey revealed vast discrepancies in attitudes toward the Palestinian leader: 92 percent of Palestinians in Israel viewed Arafat as a "good leader," while an overwhelming majority of Jewish Israelis judged him to have caused more harm than good.[33] In stark contrast, after the death of Mandela, a consensus will exist among black and white South Africans that he was an outstanding leader and statesman, although blacks and whites can hardly be called "reconciled." While the South Africa Truth and Reconciliation Commission (SATRC) showed many flaws in its design and execution of its task, at least it held out a less divided "truth" about the past. Victims were affirmed and some perpetrators exposed, although beneficiaries were left unchallenged. Denial of past crimes became impossible, although interpretations of causes, guilt, and blame continue to differ.

Peace between Israelis and Palestinians requires a modified SATRC, an introspective investigation into own abuses rather than a lament about own victimhood in each group. Rigby has stressed: "It is vital that people learn to acknowledge the validity of other people's truths."[34] A parallel Israeli and Palestinian Truth Commission (IPTC) could attempt this shared narrative by undermining the sectarian stranglehold on history. The effort would have to originate from a civil society initiative, since neither official authority is likely to support a critical scrutiny of its record. In order to get an IPTC off the ground at all, the initial goal of the IPTCs would have to be modest, neither aiming at ascertaining guilt, punishment, redress, forgiveness, or healing, but merely establishing a common historical record. Opposing metanarratives currently poison relations and negotiations. What Mahmood Mamdani has argued for post-genocide Rwanda applies equally to Israel/Palestine: "It is not possible to think of reconciliation between Hutu and Tutsi in Rwanda without prior conciliation with history."[35] While all other TRCs have focused on post-conflict reconstruction after the violence has ceased or a regime has changed, the unique role of an IPTRC would lay the essential groundwork for bringing this end about in the future. It could bridge the wide gulf of perceptions through a public project of political education for a mutually acceptable compromise. Only when the "cognitive maps" of both publics resemble each other by similar acknowledgments of past traumatic events will the peace accords of elites resonate among their constituencies. A pre-accord TRC would enable the compromise as well as secure its adherence afterwards, unlike the failed Oslo deal.

Yet there should also be no illusions about the widespread hostility toward such introspective soul searching that undermines comforting notions of moral victory in each community. Israeli and Palestinian academics have not exactly clamored for such in-group conscientization. Mottie Tamarkin, historian and director of the Steinmetz Center for Peace Research at Tel Aviv University expresses this reluctance forcefully: "Any attempt to reeducate the Israeli and Palestinian societies to change their disposition towards one another as a means to facilitate the peace process is a non-starter. The most ridiculous idea is that of an Israeli-Palestinian Truth and Reconciliation Commission." Without offering more than the hope that "the passage of time" will result in "the return of both nations to sobriety and normalcy within their respective states," Tamarkin advocates passive bystanding: "Any attempt to heal the wounds through ethnomoral dialogue and collective reeducation while the conflict rages is bound to be counterproductive."[36]

Such advice not to interfere with ongoing confrontations flies in the face of a vast literature on the need to prepare a public for recognizing unpleasant realities. In his magisterial tome about two decades of failed diplomatic efforts at peacemaking in the Middle East, the chief U.S. envoy Dennis Ross singles out as the crucial lesson learned, that "peacemaking can never succeed in an environment dominated by mythologies and untruths."[37] He self-critically deplores that past efforts were mainly construed as top-down processes. Ross recommends "people-to-people programs that break down barriers"[38] and faults both the Palestinian and Israeli leadership for never leveling with its own public about the necessary compromise. An IPTC mainly based on civil society initiatives would be a credible instrument to create this political literacy. Risk-adverse, embattled leaders propagate only their biased versions of truth, if they address the sensitive issues at all.

Future Scenarios

What then is the likely future scenario in light of the South African lessons? While it is foolish to predict an uncertain future, informed speculation on the basis of comprehensive evidence is also to be called for.

Israel is both unwilling and unable to evacuate most settlements on the West Bank. While still a predominantly secular society, the growing messianic nationalists and their local and international supporters of biblical claims increasingly triumph. Let us admit that the settlers have won, argues Daniel Gavron in the persuasive conclusion of his book, *The Other Side of Despair*.[39] Any return to the pre-1967 Green Line, even with equitable land swaps, is unlikely. The Green Line is increasingly obliterated not only symbolically on official Israeli maps, but through the reality of land annexation and ongoing settlement expansion on the West Bank in the shadow of disengagement from Gaza. Dreaming about a *viable sovereign* Palestinian state, that deserves its name, means fostering illusions. In the face of Israeli intransigence more and more Palestinians will eventually revise the mirage of an impotent, discontiguous state behind walls on less than half the Palestinian land that Likud, backed by an Israeli majority, projects as the solution. However, this imposition will just exacerbate the conflict, because no legitimate Palestinian leadership can ever accept it, unless the Green Line is restored and the separation wall deep in Palestinian land is demolished. As David Landau has written: "But the lesson of the Bantustans of South Africa, in the deepest sense, is not just that a people cannot be imprisoned behind a fence, but that it is impossible to halt a demographic trend by geographic arrangements that one side imposes on the other."[40]

Israel will not yield on recognition of Palestinian refugee rights of return, even for modest numbers, which is considered contributing to "demographic suicide." Analysts such as far-sighted Labor Zionist Daniel Gavron therefore advise Israel to prepare for an inevitable common or federal, binational state, unless expulsion ("transfer") or ghetto-apartheid is considered a long-term solution. Gavron suggests entrenching a multicultural constitution with strong minority rights and equal Western immigration laws for both groups, as long as Jews form the numerical majority in Israel/Palestine. Negotiating from a relative position of strength when the long-term demographics work against you was also de Klerk's main rationale for abolishing apartheid in 1990.

At the same time, pressure on the Palestinians and Israelis to settle once and for all on a mutually acceptable two-state solution has increased, mainly because of the U.S. quagmire in Iraq. Palestine and Iraq are now inextricably linked and the Israeli hope that a quick U.S. victory would enhance its scope in the region turned into the opposite. After Arafat's death and Palestinian elections, a new window of opportunity is hailed. Much more money is offered by both Europe and some Arab Western clients to tempt Palestinians into acceptance of these "new realities on the ground" (Bush), provided they give up violent resistance and police themselves effectively in their scattered, walled-in enclaves. By bribing with more foreign aid—with $300 per capita annually already among the highest in the world—the international community may well succeed in enticing more unemployed Palestinian youth away from militancy into regular low-wage jobs, in addition to seducing well-paid functionaries of a pseudo-state. In short, there will be a Palestinian state in one form or another that is now also supported by a majority of Palestinians and Israelis. In a survey by Khalil Shikaki, some 63 percent of the Palestinians and 70 percent of Israelis said they agreed to the statement: "The Palestinian state will be established on all of the West Bank and Gaza, except for the large settlement blocs that will be annexed to Israel though not more than 3 percent. Israel will evacuate the rest of the settlements, and the Palestinians will get in exchange a piece of territory of the same size contiguous to Gaza."[41] Some 35 percent of Palestinians and 16 percent of Israelis said they oppose such a formula.

If and when the Palestinian leadership finally signs on this offer, it will surely face accusations of selling out sacred birthrights and establishing a "Vichy-style quisling regime." Unlike Arafat as "the father of the nation," the untested new leadership has to strive particularly hard for legitimacy and unity among its constituency, if it wishes to avoid a third intifada. That could be achieved through substantial Israeli concessions, which, however, are not in the offing as long as the Israeli public is spooked by notions of Palestinians as subhuman security threats and the well-organized settler nationalists are in a position to sabotage "land for peace" deals. Nor is the U.S. administration likely to lean on Israel, despite Bush's greater independence from the electorate in his final term of office. On the contrary, the "Israelization of U.S. foreign policy" provides a more apt description. Tony Judt has commented: "Israel continues to mock its American patron, building illegal settlements in cynical disregard of the 'road map.' The President of the United States of America has been reduced to a ventriloquist's dummy, pitifully reciting the Israeli cabinet line,"[42] although Israel's policy can hardly afford to turn against vital U.S. interests.

Establishing a Palestinian pseudo-state as a permanent solution paradoxically implies a major shift in the character of colonial administration. After ruining a relatively self-sufficient Palestinian economy, particularly farming, the majority of the population would be employed in Jewish border industries ("industrial zones") and joint ventures with Palestinian entrepreneurs. Historically, Zionism was not primarily interested in labor exploitation, but in expulsion of the indigenous population. Therefore it also eschewed cooptation of a native elite as a tool of domination. In contrast, classical (British and especially French) colonialism always cultivated a small indigenous elite through colonial education, commercial collaboration and mixed marriages, particularly in India. Amos Elon has argued that "Israel's occupation is perhaps the least successful attempt at colonialism that I can think of,"[43] because of such inflammatory direct rule and social distance. In this regard, Israel resembles the apartheid segregation which also had outlawed interracial marriages and stigmatized social contact, but was unable to implement it because of economic interdependence. However, even apartheid South Africa always courted an indigenous collaborating class in the Bantustans and urban administrations for indirect rule. With an eventual Palestinian state in fragmented Bantustans, Israel would finally have to adopt such indirect domination through coopted proxies. Will a Palestinian political class allow itself to be used in such a collaborating role without major concessions? And will a highly politicized population support such an arrangement without turning its ire on its own hapless rulers, as happened in the widespread rejection and boycott of Bantustan officials in South Africa? Without an untainted and trustworthy Palestinian Mandela leading and selling the compromise, its legitimacy on the street will remain doubtful. Without a unifying Mandela, who transcended the tribal and linguistic differences utilized by apartheid domestic colonialism, the more intense ideological rivalries between secular and Islamist nationalists in Palestine will plague the movement.

Any final status deal would therefore have to be tested in a referendum to be legitimate. Just as the ANC relied on a mandate for its elite pact, so the Palestinian leadership would be wise to insist on a UN-supervised referendum among all Palestinians to ratify a controversial final status compromise. The referendum would have to include the UN-registered refugees in other Arab states who comprise the majority of Palestinians. The prior recognition of the need for a referendum also strengthens the bargaining power of the Palestinian negotiators, as minimal concessions would clearly fail the referendum test.

Whether an eventual peace deal is approved by the Palestinian public depends mostly on Israel reviving and revising the failed Camp David/Taba proposals. One should not entirely rule out this optimistic scenario. Widespread acceptance of a leadership accord would turn the PA from an interlocutor on behalf of Israel into a true liberation government. Particularly if Islamists (Hamas) increasingly participate in electoral politics, recognize Israel, and join the secular nationalists in the politics of negotiations instead of violent resistance, Palestinians would present a united, disciplined front, similar to the ANC. Nobody would make the label "sellout" stick. A legitimate negotiated settlement would end the colonial conflict. The relationship between colonizer and colonized would be transformed into one between two native peoples, although the economic dominance of one over the other would persist as in South Africa.

As the South African negotiators had agreed on an unalterable election date long before all the constitutional rules were worked out, so the Palestinian leaders would benefit from a final settlement rather than interim steps with provisional borders, as the Oslo Accord and also the Road Map envisages. Interim measures always favor the stronger party that can create new realities or violate agreements with impunity. In the post-Oslo period Palestinians were rightly blamed for violating the agreement with suicide bombings, while massive simultaneous settlement expansion took place without repercussions. Agreeing to a "provisional state" raises false hopes endlessly and allows the stronger party to finalize its designs in the meantime.

Both sides of course could also continue pursuing scenarios of military victory. "In anti-colonial guerrilla wars, the locals always win," asserts Gwynne Dyer.[44] In the end the foreigners invariably cut their losses and go home and the guerrillas "already are home," argues Dyer. The historical evidence for this valid prediction derives from classical colonialism (the French in Algeria and Vietnam, the British in Kenya, the Portuguese in Mozambique and Angola, or the Dutch in Indonesia). Little patience for long wars with high casualties applies particularly to American military adventurism abroad. However, the confident prediction ignores settler colonialism where the "foreigners" consider themselves "locals" and have no homeland to return to. Ironically, the Palestinian locals face the possibility of further deportation, if they ever were a serious threat in conjunction with other Arab forces. Yet, how can six million intransigent Israelis ever hope to flourish *without peace,* surrounded by three hundred million hostile Arabs and four times as many potentially empathetic Muslims in the rest of the world? The usual stock answer is: With outside assistance as an American base, with U.S. arms manufacturers profiting heavily from supplying both Israel and Arab client regimes. Others add that Israel needs to be in a state of permanent warfare in order to avoid imploding from its internal divisions. Yet U.S. policy on Israel is not written in stone and could change for a variety of reasons. Moreover, U.S. hegemony will not last forever with China emerging as a new superpower and the American designs for Iraq also unraveling.

We emphasize the relative independence of the Jewish state. Sovereign "siege societies," such as apartheid South Africa and Israel strive for self-sufficiency and develop their own substantial weapons industry, unlike the rebellious settlers in Algeria or Rhodesia who were not only under formal administrative authority of their metropole but also dependent on the motherland's military support. Even in the very unlikely event that Israel was seriously threatened, it could wipe out any Arab state by unleashing its nuclear arsenal, which of course motivates other regional powers (Iran) to acquire the same. Under the now fashionable practice of preemptive attacks, would Israel use its atomic weapons in a first strike? Such a Masada-like catastrophe, or the "Samson option" in Israeli parlance, would be the worst-case scenario for the region and the world.[45]

What happens if the rational peace-seekers lose further ground and messianic Jewish ultras pursue the road of escalating confrontation with equally dogmatic Islamist forces, for example by blowing up the Al Aqsa Mosque or implementing ethnic cleansing? Right-wing politicians and rabbis already shifted into the mainstream public discourse what was once the domain of fringe groups only a few years ago. Posters all over

Jerusalem advocate "Transfer"; "It's them or us!"; "Deport the Arab enemy!"; "Kahane was right, Kick out the Arabs!" More than 30 percent of young Israelis consider Yigal Amir, the indoctrinated assassin of compromising Prime Minister Yitzhak Rabin in November 1995, a hero.[46] Dr. Baruch Goldstein, an American émigré in the settlement Kiryat Arba outside Hebron, is still admired among many settlers for gunning down twenty-nine Palestinians while praying in the Ibrahimi Mosque during Ramadan in 1994. The outlawed "Kach and Kahane Lives" Movement flourishes underground and the chief of Shin Beth warns "that extremists had not given up the idea of a strike on the Temple Mount and they had no problem stealing weapons from the IDF."[47] Some rabbis who issue halakhic rulings against obeying state laws legitimize a variety of religious eccentrics to act against the mosques as sources of enemy energies. They also link the failure to establish a tabernacle on the Temple Mount to the disaster of settlement evacuation as the wrath of God.[48] In short, a growing Jewish fundamentalism mirrors its Islamist counterparts and both official sides use their extremist factions for their own advantage without being always able to control and contain their actions.

In a symposium of Middle Eastern experts (Vancouver, October 2004) on possible future scenarios, a wide range of predictions and solutions were advanced. Criminalizing religious zealots in the same decisive way as Western democracies now punish anti-Semitic activities was suggested as an obvious response. However, the Likud-led government comes down harder on weaker left dissent and military noncompliance for fear of alienating much of its own support base.

The most imaginative and utopian proposition relied heavily on the Palestinians to put into action their words about peaceful coexistence with the "Zionist entity" after the end of occupation. This scenario, which harks back to the old secular PLO position without insisting on a common state, warrants elaboration because of its attractive inclusiveness: The PA President invites the settlers to stay with equal rights in the PA-administered state. With Hamas at its side, the PA guarantees absolute security and good neighborliness after IDF withdrawal, provided those Jewish families who opt to stay commit themselves to upholding the laws of their new state. Instead of destroying settlements after evacuation (as envisaged in Gaza), Palestinians are offered the opportunity to buy the houses of those who leave and a concerted effort is made to prove that the new multi-ethnic communities do work well. Extra PA police and even Hamas militants will pride themselves on guarding the showpieces of multiculturalism. With the compensation offered to settlers for their relocation, those who stay will compensate the PA for the initial land confiscation. Foreigners are also invited to buy into the unique experiments of harmonious coexistence. A new international metropolis with attractive tourist/pilgrim facilities would emerge in Ramallah, stretching up to the Old City. An additional new town for returning Palestinian refugees would be built with foreign assistance, including Arab oil revenues. These inclusive zones for intercommunal contact could later include some willing Jewish suburbs on former Palestinian land around Jerusalem. The official offer of multicultural Palestinian communities alone would constitute the greatest image change and PR coup that a powerless Palestinian nationalism can initiate. The promise would be the equivalent of the attractive ANC slogan of nonracialism. Separation walls and fences would become superfluous and there would be no justification for annexing land behind the Green Line. The equal role of the Jewish minority in the Palestinian state would set an example for the treatment of the Palestinian minority in the Jewish state and vice versa.

Alas, this utopia ignores burgeoning oppositional identities. In the current climate of distrust and messianic fervor, the majority of Gaza settlers will undoubtedly leave, unlike most whites in South Africa and most expatriates in British colonies who stayed on after decolonization. Palestinian rocket attacks and resulting security anxieties, unnecessarily generous compensation packages for the Gaza evacuees, and government pressure will see to this exodus. Yet "utopian realists" could argue: Should the multicultural experiment fail and the Palestinian state breaks its word and turn into a Zimbabwe-like anarchy, the minority always has the option to follow suit to the Jewish homeland, just as most unwelcome Jews in the Arab states emigrated to Israel during the 1950s.

Our imaginative scenario planners further asserted that after the end of occupation and the return of the post-1967 land, the vast majority of Palestinians will have few emotional blockages to coexist with Jews or make territorial claims. Eighty-one percent of Palestinians support reconciliation with Israelis, but are split on ending the intifada against occupation.[49] The new Palestinian state will have to pronounce the strict separation of state and religion and entrench a secular, democratic constitution. As long as the ethno-religious communities enjoy wide autonomy, calls for shariah law will not resonate. Those who wish to rely on religious precepts to order their private lives would be free to do so, just as in South Africa state law coexists with customary (tribal) law. Within mainstream Islam, rejectionists form a minority, quite apart from the large number of secularized or nominally religious Arabs and other sizeable religious minorities in Palestine. To be sure, devout Muslims face two challenges: to prove that they can share the same sacred soil with "infidels" and thereby disprove the Jewish exclusivist commandment that "The Nation Shall Dwell Alone" and Jews should never live beside or even be buried with "goyim."

We conclude that an Islamist Palestinian state merely mirroring an increasingly orthodox Jewish state would just prolong the conflict about the shared symbols. In an environmentally fragile small space with scarce water and other essential resources, the two peoples will have to engage with one another, whether in a hostile or friendly fashion. To be sure, they cannot ignore each other. Demonstrating by deeds and transcending mere proclamations that the conflict is not a religious one about mutually exclusive claims will be the hardest but also the most rewarding challenge for pragmatic peacemakers. The progressive alternative in the Middle East, even in a negotiated two-state solution, relies on the demonstration of multicultural cosmopolitanism, beyond the spiritual prisons of Jewish or Islamist exclusivism alike. An ethno-religious ghetto mentality may have seemed natural in the cradle of the three most influential monotheistic religions in Crusader times, but intolerant parochialism defies the common humanity of a globalized world in the twenty-first century.

The U.S. chief Middle East interlocutor Dennis Ross asserts: "Had Nelson Mandela been the Palestinian leader and not Yasir Arafat, I would be writing now how, notwithstanding the limitations of the Oslo process, Israelis and Palestinians had succeeded in reaching an 'end of conflict' agreement."[50] We disagree. As useful as a visionary Mandela in Palestine would have been, we doubt that a single leader, even one of Madiba's stature, could have achieved a solution. The reasons lie in the different nature of the Israeli-Palestinian conflict. In an overused analogy, the South African strife was about an impending marriage contract, the Israeli one concerns the allocation of assets in a drawn-out divorce battle. While we believe that both parties would be better off if they stayed together on equal terms, they share no overarching identity with a common state and identify primarily with their ethnic subgroup. Even in Israel proper, an Israeli nation officially does not exist. Currently Israel recognizes only Jews and Arabs (not Israelis) as parts of an official Jewish state. Imaginary borders between insiders and outsiders are fluid and claims to entitlement ambiguous. All foreign Jews abroad are automatic insiders according to the self-definition of the Jewish state, but all four categories of Palestinians (Israeli citizens, Jerusalem residents, inhabitants of the territories, refugees) are outsiders with different rights, experiences, and aspirations. Differential legal status echoes in different claims to justice and identity.

In contrast, South Africa's disenfranchised "non-whites," while also allocated differential legal status, nonetheless strove to be included with equal civic rights as individual South Africans with a common South African identity. The universal justice discourse served the anti-apartheid struggle well. However, the focus on discrimination applies only to one category of Palestinians, the 20 percent second-class citizens of Israel. As in South Africa, theirs is also a civic rights effort. The colonized and stateless inhabitants of the occupied territories, on the other hand, currently envision justice as self-determination of a separate people in a viable Palestinian state. Theirs is a struggle for freedom from domination and occupation, not inclusion in a common state. For most refugees, recognition of past wrongs and restitution for displacement (*nishul*) is the issue. The strategic logic of the proponents of the simplistic apartheid analogy for Israel/Palestine needs to take cognizance of the differential justice discourse in both contexts.

Compared with the moral, legal, and political complexity of the Middle East conflict, apartheid amorality proved an easy target for analysis and condemnation. Mandela's vision succeeded because it evoked a universal morality. Common ideological and economic bonds existed between the antagonists inside South Africa. An outdated racial hierarchy eventually clashed with economic imperatives when the costs exceeded the benefits of racial minority rule in a global pariah state. In the Israeli case, outside support sustains intransigence. Only when the colonial policies of occupation embarrass and threaten their stronger patrons abroad or can no longer be so easily contained inside (as apartheid racial capitalism did in the Cold War competition) can outside pressure on Israel be expected. This turning of the tables will impact the Israeli public as much as outside perception is affected by visionary local leaders and events. Despite gains in global empathy, Palestinians are still at the mercy of a superior adversary in every respect, which even a Mandela would not have been able to overcome. In this impasse, hope is offered by Israeli progressive moral dissent on the Left as well as opportunistic calculations on the Right that the occupation also harms the occupier. Israel has the capacity to reach a meaningful compromise, but has yet to prove its willingness. The Palestinian mainstream has the willingness, but lacks the capacity, to initiate a fair settlement.

Notes

Preface

1. Cited by Ronald Suresh Roberts in a letter to Nadine Gordimer, "Prize Fighters," *Sunday Times (Johannesburg) Lifestyle Magazine,* March 7, 2004, 12.

2. Ted Honderich, *After the Terror* (Edinburgh: Edinburgh University Press, 2002), 151.

3. Ibid.

4. Ellen Willis, "Is There Still a Jewish Question? Why I'm an Anti–Anti-Zionist," in *Wrestling with Zion. Progressive Jewish-American Responses to the Israeli-Palestinian Conflict,* ed. Tony Kushner and Alisa Solomon, 226 (New York: Grove Press, 2003).

5. Uri Davis, *Apartheid Israel* (London: Zed, 2003), 156. Davis maintains "that the ideological mainstream of the Israeli-Jewish society is predicated upon [this] preposterous claim."

6. Thomas Friedman, "Op-Ed," *New York Times,* October 22, 2003.

7. David Miller, ed., *Tell Me Lies* (London: Pluto, 2004).

8. Mark Chmiel, *Elie Wiesel and the Politics of Moral Leadership* (Philadelphia: Temple University Press, 2001), 97.

9. Edward Said, "New History, Old Ideas,"*AL Ahram Weekly* 378(May 21–27), 1998, reprinted in Ephraim Nimni, ed., *The Challenge of Post-Zionism: Alternatives to Israeli Fundamentalist Politics,* 202 (London: Zed Books, 2003).

10. George Ellis, "Acceptance Speech of the Templeton Prize," *New York Cape Times,* March 18, 2004, 11.

11. Stuart Eisenstat, "Op-Ed," *International Herald Tribune,* July 5–6, 2003.

12. Edward Said, *From Oslo to Iraq* (New York: Pantheon, 2004), 48.

Introduction

1. Hermann Giliomee and Jannie Gagiano, eds., *The Elusive Search for Peace* (Cape Town: Oxford University Press, 1990).

2. See Heribert Adam, "The Politics of Violence in Lebanon," *Middle East Focus* 7, no. 6 (March 1985): 11–25, and "A Visit to Beirut," *Canadian Forum* (May 1985). For the European debate about settler societies in the 1980s, see Heribert Adam, "Ist Israel mit Suedafrika vergleichbar?" *Leviathan* (Berlin) 3 (1988): 299–308, reprinted in *Frankfurter Rundschau,* September 5, 1988. For a summary of

the various conferences, see Heribert Adam, "Israel and South Africa: Conflict Resolution in Ethnic States," *Telos* 82 (Winter 1989–90): 27–46.

3. An accusation leveled against an Anglo-American–sponsored international academic research exercise, in which the chapter on the ANC was especially singled out for a "whitewash of terrorists." See Heribert Adam, "Exile and Resistance: The African National Congress, the South African Communist Party and the Pan African Congress," in *A Future South Africa,* ed. Peter Berger and Bobby Godsell, 95–126 (Cape Town: Human & Rousseau, 1988). Other contributors and South African members of the team were Vincent Maphai, Pieter Le Roux, Jakes Gerwel, Lawrence Schlemmer, Ann Bernstein, and the editors Berger and Godsell—a collection of liberal academics and free-enterprise practitioners par excellence—but hardly "naïve, pink fellow-travelers," as was alleged then.

4. In this analysis, the term *Palestinians* refers to the 3.5 million stateless Arab inhabitants of the West Bank and Gaza and not the 1 million Israeli citizens of Arab origin in Israel who are also Palestinian.

5. Amnon Barzilai, *Haaretz,* March 12, 2002.

6. Jonathan Nitzan and Shimshon Bichler, *The Global Political Economy of Israel* (London: Pluto Press, 2002), 356.

Chapter 1

1. The most ardent and radical advocate of the apartheid analogy since the 1980s is Uri Davis, although virtually all left critics of Israel use the South Africa comparison in one way or another. For Davis' most recent elaborate academic account, see Uri Davis, *Apartheid Israel.* Davis mainly argues idealistically and normatively when detailing legal injustices, rather than sociologically, considering politics as the art of the possible. Instead of analytically discerning what is *likely* to happen, from his anti-Zionist position he outlines what *ought* to occur. For example: "We should remember that the State of Israel will not be transformed into a democratic state when it becomes the state of all its citizens, Arabs and non-Arabs alike—rather, it will become democratic when it is transformed into a state of all its citizens as well as its 'absentees,' the 1948 Palestine refugees" (198).

2. For a detailed critique of Summers' views see Judith Butler, "The Charge of Anti- Semitism: Jews, Israel, and the Risks of Public Critique," in *Wrestling with Zion,* ed. Kushner and Solomon, 249–265.

3. Ian Buruma, "Do Not Treat Israel Like Apartheid South Africa," *The Guardian,* July 23, 2002.

4. Na'eem Jeenah, *Annual Review of Islam in South Africa* 5 (December 2002).

5. Daryl Glaser, "Zionism and Apartheid: A Moral Comparison," *Ethnic and Racial Studies* 26, no. 3 (May 2003): 403–421.

6. Noam Chomsky, "A Wall as a Weapon," *New York Times,* February 23, 2004.

7. Davis, *Apartheid Israel.*

8. Shira Herzog, "Take South Africa's Lead!" *Globe & Mail,* June 24, 2003, A15.

9. Tony Judt, *New York Review of Books,* May 9, 2002, 4.

10. Ehud Olmert, quoted in James Bennett, "Sharon Dismisses Worries of Loss of Jewish Identity," *New York Times,* January 12, 2004.

11. Ehud Barak, "I Did Not Give Away a Thing," *Journal of Palestine Studies* 33, no. 1 (Fall 2003): 84–87.

12. Aluf Benn and Nathan Guttman, "Government Sources: Qureia Can't Take Steps Needed to Renew Talks," *Haaretz*, January 7, 2004.

13. Thomas Mitchell, *Native versus Settler* (Westport, CT: Greenwood, 2000); Maxime Rodinson, *Israel: A Colonial Settler State* (New York: Monad, 1973); Ibrahim Abu-Lughod and Baha Abu-Laban, *Settler Regimes in Africa and the Arab World: The Illusion of Endurance* (Wilmette, IL: Medina University Press, 1974); Stanley Greenberg, *Race and State in Capitalist Development* (New Haven, CT: Yale University Press, 1980). The frequently employed settler-native dichotomy is not unproblematic for an analysis of contemporary divided societies, because it falsely assumes a continuing colonial relationship with the respective differential moral standing. As previously pointed out, there is also no objective criteria by which it can be decided when a newcomer becomes indigenous in the competition for entitlements, based on ancestral arrival in an area. If applied to contemporary immigrant societies, latecomers and recent migrants would be permanently disadvantaged, compared with earlier migrants. Such skepticism does not deny the historical record of colonial settler exploitation and dispossession of indigenous people and the legacy of conquest. The Palestinian definition of a colonial conflict in the Middle East, as opposed to the Jewish nationalist discourse, also obstructs compromises because liberation means departure of the colonial intruder and implicitly denies the right of Jewish "settler" presence in Palestinian "native" territory. In South Africa, only the PAC applied the colonial analogy while the ANC fudged the issue with the theory of "domestic/internal colonialism," in which Europeans belonged to the land, as long as they changed their colonial habits.

14. Donald H. Akenson, *God's People* (Montreal: McGill & Queens' University Press, 1991).

15. James Adams, *The Unnatural Alliance* (London: Quartet Books Ltd., 1984); Benjamin Joseph, *Besieged Bedfellows: Israel and the Land of Apartheid* (New York: Greenwood Press,1988); R. P. Stevens and A. M. Elmessiri, *Israel and South Africa* (New York: New World, 1976).

16. Mahmood Mamdani, "Beyond Settlers and Natives as Political Entities: Overcoming the Political Legacies of Colonialism," *Comparative Study of Society and History* 32 (2001): 651–664.

17. Rick Salutin, "The Uses of an Arafat," *Globe & Mail*, September 19, 2003.

18. Eliezer Ben-Rafael, "Where Stands Israel?" *Ethnic and Racial Studies* 27, no. 2 (March 2004): 310–316.

19. There is a rich polemical and academic literature on the comparison of Israel and South Africa as "settler societies." Comparative accounts range from Donald Akenson's thoughtful *God's People* to the atheoretical and disjointed mere chronology of Thomas Mitchell, *Native versus Settler*. See also, Rodinson, *Israel: A Colonial Settler State?*; Abu-Lughod and Abu-Laban, *Settler Regimes in Africa*; Stevens and Elmessiri, *Israel and South Africa*; and the most scholarly comparison of British-Irish, French-Algerian, and Israeli- Palestinian relations by Ian Lustick, *Unsettled States, Disputed Lands* (Cornell: Cornell University Press, 1993). See also the insightful collection of essays *(The Elusive Search for Peace)* on Northern Ireland, Israel, and South Africa by Giliomee and Gagiano.

20. Donald Akenson, *Journal of Military History* 65 (2001): 571.

21. Shlomo Avineri, *Jerusalem Post*, December 16, 1988.

22. Buruma, *The Guardian*, July 23, 2002.

23. Dena S. Davis, "Why Academic Boycotts Are Wrong," *The Chronicle of Higher Education*, April 18, 2003, and CAUT Bulletin, June 2003.

24. Avishai Ehrlich, personal communication, May 23, 2002.

25. Adam Shatz, "In Search of Hezbollah-II," *The New York Review of Books*, May 13, 2004, 28.

26. Shlomo Avineri, letter, *New York Review of Books*, July 18, 2002, 62.

27. *Al-Quds*, June 21, 2002; Letter, *New York Review of Books*, August 15, 2002, 53.

28. Judt, *New York Review of Books*, May 9, 2002.

29. Buruma, *The Guardian*, July 23, 2002.

30. Philip Krawitz, Letter to the editor, *Sunday Argus*, March 17, 2002, 21.

31. Ibid.

32. According to Ghaith Al-Omari, a Palestinian legal advisor: "This declaration has been of immeasurable benefit to the Palestinian peace camp. It has given us ammunition to counter extremists within our midst who attempt to characterize the Palestinian-Israeli conflict as an eternal one between Muslims and Jews" (cited in Heribert Adam, "Peacemaking in Divided Societies," Occasional Paper 2, Human Science Research Council, Pretoria, 2002, 65).

33. David Makhura, Editorial, *Business Day*, April 10, 2002.

34. Editorial, "Time to Reject Sharon," *Mail & Guardian*, March 26, 2004.

35. Michael Bagraim, Letter, *Mail & Guardian*, April 2, 2004, 38.

36. Milton Shain, "Call to Jews is 'Sinister,'" *Mail & Guardian*, April 2–7, 2004, 39.

37. See the joint statement by Cyril Harris, Warren Goldstein, Charles Wallach, Avrom Krengel, and Michael Bagraim, "Insidious Assault," *Cape Times*, April 2, 2004, 11.

38. Editorial, *Business Day*, April 10, 2002.

39. James L. Gibson and Amanda Gouws, *Overcoming Intolerance in South Africa: Experiments in Democratic Persuasion* (Cambridge: Cambridge University Press, 2003).

40. I. W. Zartman and J. L. Rasmussen, *Peacemaking in International Conflict: Methods and Techniques* (Washington, DC: United States Institute of Peace, 1997); I. W. Zartman and J. Z. Rubin, *Power and Negotiation* (Ann Arbor: University of Michigan Press, 2000); I. W. Zartman, *Preventative Negotiation: Avoiding Conflict Escalation* (Lanham, MD: Rowman & Littlefield, 2001).

41. Joshua Goldstein et al., "Reciprocity, Triangularity and Cooperation in the Middle East," *Journal of Conflict* Resolution 45, no. 5 (October 2001): 594–620.

42. Daniel Lieberfeld, *Talking with the Enemy: Negotiation and Threat Perception in South Africa and Israel/Palestine* (Westport, CT: Praeger, 1999).

43. Robert Rothstein, ed., *After the Peace: Resistance and Reconciliation* (Boulder, CO: Lynne Rienner, 1999).

44. Ibid.

45. Among Habermas' many books, *Die Einbeziehung des Anderen* (Frankfurt: Suhrkamp, 1996) is probably the most illuminating on this topic.

46. Ofer Grosbard, *Israel on the Couch: The Psychology of the Peace Process* (Albany: State University of New York Press, 2003), 1.

47. Patrick Bond, *Elite Transition: From Apartheid to Neoliberalism in South Africa* (London: Pluto Press, 2000); H. Marais, *South Africa: Limits to Change* (London: Zed Books, 2001); Neville Alexander, *An Ordinary Country* (Pietermaritzburg, South Africa: University of Natal Press, 2003); Allister Sparks, *Beyond the Miracle* (Johannesburg: Jonathan Ball, 2003).

48. Hermann Giliomee, *The Afrikaners* (Cape Town: Tafelberg, 2003).

49. James Ron, *Frontiers and Ghettos: State Violence in Israel and Serbia* (Berkeley: University of California Press, 2003), 201.

50. Judt, *New York Review of Books,* May 9, 2002.

51. Patti Waldmeir, *Anatomy of a Miracle* (New York: Norton, 1997).

52. Giliomee, *The Afrikaners.*

53. Ibid.

54. Vaughn Shannon, *Balancing Act: U.S. Foreign Policy and the Arab-Israeli Conflict* (Aldershot, Hants, England; Burlington, VT: Ashgate, 2003).

55. Aruri Naseer, *Dishonest Broker: The U.S. Role in Israel and Palestine* (Cambridge, MA: South End Press, 2003).

56. Robert Malley and Hussein Agha, "Camp David: Tragedy of Errors," *New York Review of Books,* August 9, 2001.

Chapter 2

1. For the views of Magnes see, Arthur A. Goren, ed., *Dissenters in Zion* (Cambridge: Harvard University Press, 1982).

2. Benny Morris, "Survival of the Fittest," Interview with Ari Shavit, *Haaretz Magazine,* January 9, 2004. All of the following quotes of Morris are from this interview and his reply to his critics in the same magazine, January 23, 2004.

3. Cited in Baruch Kimmerling, "Israel's Culture of Martyrdom," *The Nation,* January, 10, 2005, 3.

4. Henry Giroux, *Fugitive Cultures: Race, Violence and Youth* (London: Routledge, 1996), 181.

5. Yossi Sarid, *Haaretz,* January 21, 2004.

6. Ibid.

7. Arieh O'Sullivan and Nina Gilbert, "Boim Blames Arab Genes for Violence," *Jerusalem Post,* February 24, 2004.

8. Neve Gordon, "The Only Democracy in the Middle East?" *Counterpunch,* February 3, 2004.

9. Ibid.

10. *Haaretz,* June 22, 2004.

11. *The Palestinian Chronicle,* December 2003; *Counterpunch,* January 2004.

12. Baruch Kimmerling, *Politicide. Ariel Sharon's War against the Palestinians* (London: Verso, 2003), 5 and 7.

13. Martha Nussbaum. "Patriotism and Cosmopolitanism," in *For Love of Country,* ed. J. Cohen, 2–17 (Boston: Beacon Press 2002).

14. Ibid.

15. Richard Rorty, "The Unpatriotic Academy," *New York Times,* February 13, 1994, E15.

16. Nussbaum, "Patriotism and Cosmopolitanism," 17.

Chapter 3

Acknowledgments: An earlier, shorter version of this chapter, written in collaboration with Kanya Adam, was published in *Encyclopedia of Genocide* (Farmington, MI: Macmillan Press, 2004).

1. Giliomee, *The Afrikaners,* 18.

2. Ibid., 142.

3. P. L. van den Berghe, "Racial Segregation in South Africa: Degrees and Kinds," in *South Africa Socialogical Perspectives*, ed. Heribert Adam (London: Oxford University Press 1969) and van den Berghe, *South Africa: A Study in Conflict* (Middletown: Wesleyan University Press, 1965).

4. Mamdani, "Reconciliation without Justice," *South African Review of Books* 46 (November/December).

5. Kogila Moodley, "African Renaissance and Language Policies in Comparative Perspective," *Politikon* 27, no. 1 (2000): 103–115.

6. Mamphela Ramphele, "Citizenship Challenges for South Africa's Young Democracy," *Daedalus* 130, no. 1 (2001): 7.

7. See Adam Heribert, Frederick van Zyl Slabbert, and Kogila Moodley, *Comrades in Business: Post-Apartheid Politics in South Africa* (Utrecht, The Netherlands: International Books, 1998).

Chapter 4

1. Ronnie Kasrils, "Israel's Wall of Shame," *Sunday Times*, February 22, 2004. Kasrils weakens his arguments with his uncritical support of Arafat at the very time when Palestinians themselves increasingly criticize the PA leadership for corruption and authoritarianism: "Arafat has showed [*sic*] tremendous courage and leadership. I have admiration for him," *Sunday Independent*, February 29, 2004, 5.

2. For a perceptive account of the industrial parks, see Meron Rapoport, "Fenced In All Around," *Le Monde Diplomatique*, June 2004.

3. Pierre Hugo, ed., "Towards Darkness and Death: Racial Demonology in South Africa," in *South African Perspectives*, 237–263 (Cape Town: Die Suid Afrikaan, 1989).

4. Akenson, *God's People*.

5. Malley and Agha, "Camp David," 71.

6. For an excellent history of the contested city see Bernard Wasserstein, *Divided Jerusalem: The Struggle for the Holy City* (New Haven, CT: Yale University Press, 2001). The early Zionists from Theodor Herzl to Israel's first president Chaim Weizmann disliked Jerusalem as a place of religious fanatics and favored a secular "state for Jews" as distinct from a Jewish state. The early Zionists also accepted Jerusalem as an international UN city under the partition plan, which the Arabs rejected.

7. Avishai Margalit, *The New York Review of Books*, September 21, 2000, 6.

8. Neil Silberman, "If I Forget Thee, O Jerusalem: Archaeology, Religious Commemoration and Nationalism in a Disputed City, 1801–2001," *Nations and Nationalism* 7, no. 4 (2001): 487–504.

9. Ibid., 502–503.

10. Pierre van den Berghe, personal correspondence, December 31, 2001.

11. Sammy Smooha, "Ethnic Democracy: Israel as an Archetype," *Israel Studies* 2 (1997): 198–241.

12. Benny Morris, *The New York Review of Books*, June 13, 2002, 42–45.

13. Avishai Ehrlich, "Israel's Religious Right and the Failure of the Peace Process," *Monthly Review* 53 (October 2001): 16–30.

14. Ibid., 26.

15. Uri Avnery, "The Golem Turns on His Creator," Webmail, May 4, 2004.

16. Jeffrey Goldberg, "Among the Settlers," *The New Yorker*, May 31, 2004, 46–69.

17. In the heat of the 2004 presidential election, democratic candidate Senator John Kerry met with a group of Jewish leaders handpicked by the Conference of

Presidents of Major Jewish Organizations. The leaders of the Jewish community put Kerry on notice that the number one Jewish issue was not erosion of the church–state divide, civil rights, or a just peace in the Middle East, but rather support of Israel right or wrong. Almost immediately, Kerry endorsed Bush and Sharon s agreement to accept permanent Jewish settlements on Palestinian land. "I believe that we must stand with Israel, supporting our ally's right to build a security fence and to allow its own Supreme Court—not the International Court of Justice—to address the issue of the route of the fence. The fence has proven its value as an anti-terror measure.... As president, I will never pressure Israel to make concessions that will compromise its security" (John Kerry, in New York Jewish paper, *Forward,* August 26, 2004).

18. There is ample scholarly documentation of the close military ties and political cooperation between Israel and apartheid South Africa, explicitly acknowledged by both South African and Israeli officials. Two books stand out: *The Unnatural Alliance* (1984), by James Adams, a former defense correspondent and senior executive with the *London Sunday Times,* and *Besieged Bedfellows* (1988) by U.S. researcher and later ambassador Benjamin Joseph.

19. Giliomee, *The Afrikaners,* 663.

20. Stanley Cohen, *States of Denial* (Cambridge: Polity, 2001), 146.

21. Sarah Helm, "End the Special Relationship Now," *New Statesman,* 130: 35.

22. Edward Said, 2004; and Peter Novick, 1999.

23. Edward Said, *Sunday Times (Johannesburg),* April 14, 2002. David Horovitz, *Still Life with Bombers* (New York: Knopf, 2004), lodges the opposite complaint about the poor-accented presentation of the Israeli cause in the United States.

24. Said, *Sunday Times.*

25. Jonathan Kay, "Managing the Latest Intifada," *National Post,* December 4, 2002.

26. Paul Kellog, "Further Debate in the Israel Lobby," *Canadian Dimension* 36 (6): 3.

27. Mordecai Briemberg, "Reflections on Permanent War and Palestinian Resistance," *Canadian* Dimension (November/December 2002), 8.

28. Ibid.

29. Ibid.

30. Said, *Sunday Times.*

31. Andre Jacquet, personal conversations, November 25, 2001.

32. Jannie Gagiano, "Ruling Group Cohesion," in *The Elusive Search for Peace,* ed. Hermann Giliomee and Jannie Gagiano, 191–208 (Cape Town: Oxford University Press, 1990).

33. Herzog, "Take South Africa's Lead," A15.

34. Malley and Agha, "Camp David," 71.

35. Amos Elon, "The Deadlocked City," *New York Review of Books* XLVIII, no. 16 (October 18, 2001): 10.

36. Steven Friedman, *Cape Times,* 28 February 2002.

37. Michael Sfard, *The Observer,* 19 May 2002.

38. Waldmeir, *Anatomy of a Miracle,* 30.

39. Elon, "The Deadlocked City," 11.

40. Suzanne Goldenberg, *Globe & Mail,* August 17, 2002, F4.

41. Cohen, *States of Denial.*

42. Ibid., 157.

43. Ibid., 165.

44. Arthur, in *After the Peace,* 96.

45. Ibid.

46. Richard Ben Cramer, *How Israel Lost* (New York: Simon Schuster, 2004), 268.

47. Hilton Hamann, *Days of the Generals* (Cape Town: Zebra Press, 2001), 225–226.

48. Ariel Sharon as quoted in The *Cape Times,* March 5, 2002.

49. *London Independent,* March 6, 2002.

50. Personal communication and paper presented at SFU Conference, "Negotiating Compromises in Divided Societies," Vancouver, October 15–16, 2004.

51. For a perceptive review of the literature on women's direct and more indirect involvement in support for wars, see Laura Stovel, "Behind the Myth of Innocence: Regendering the Violence of War," *Journal of Conflict Studies* (Fall 2003): 142–161.

52. Tamil Tigers use suicide bombers—often less-suspect women—to assassinate political opponents. Tiger activists swallow cyanide capsules before they are about to be captured. Hence, Sri Lankan authorities are unable to torture information out of their captives. Japanese Kamikaze fighters volunteered to cause havoc among the U.S. Pacific fleet. Jailed IRA guerrillas starved themselves to death in order to publicize their cause. Much-debated force feeding only heightened resistance politics.

53. Stephen Ellis and Tsepo Sechaba, "Comrades against Apartheid," in *The ANC and the South African Communist Party in Exile,* 181 (London: James Curry, 1992).

54. For an interesting account in this tradition, based on interviews with relatives and prisoners in Israeli jails, see Barbara Victor, "Army of Roses," in *Inside the World of Palestinian Women Suicide Bombers* (London: Robinson, 2004). Anne Marie Oliver and Paul F. Steinberg, *The Road to Martyrs' Square: A Journey into the World of the Suicide Bomber* (New York: Oxford University Press, 2005), is a similar engrossing documentary narrative.

55. Gush Shalom, international release, February 28, 2004.

56. Leo Kuper, *Passive Resistance* (New Haven, CT: Yale University Press, 1957).

57. As to the justification that the IDF does not intentionally target civilians, consider among much similar evidence of disproportional use of force the statement by the commander of the Samaria Brigade, Colonel Harel Knafo ("A Job Well Done," *Haaretz Magazine,* August 27, 2004): "Every entry into Balata required positioning three to four tanks in a row and massive firing on the camp, whether or not an enemy was identified. Only then did we storm the area." The cliché that Israel has a right to defend itself implicitly defines all resistance to occupation as aggression and also obscures the question of *how* they defend themselves. For abuse of civilians, see also the evidence collected by decommissioned soldiers in the 2004 Tel Aviv exhibition, "Breaking the Silence."

58. *Economist,* December 8, 2001.

59. *Guardian Weekly,* June 27, 2002.

60. *The Spectator* quoting Chris Hedges of the *New York Times.*

61. Webmail, August 25, 2003.

62. Cecilie Surasky, Webmail, February 19, 2004.

63. Omar Samer.

64. Avishai Margalit, *The New York Review of Books,* September 21, 2000, 6.

65. Efraim Zuroff, interviewed by Paddy Harper, "Hunting Nazis, Dreaming of Carpet-Bombing," *The Sunday Independent,* March 21, 2004, 4.

66. Neve Gordon, "Israel's Sippery Moral Slope," *In These Times,* January 31, 2003.
67. Michael Ignatieff, *National Post,* April 23, 2002.
68. Tony Judt, *New York Review of Books,* July 18, 2002, 64.
69. Gideon Levy, *Haaretz,* April 27, 2003.
70. Meron Benvenisti, "The Peace Process and Intercommunal Strife," in *The Elusive Search for Peace,* ed. Hermann Giliomee and Jannie Gagiano, 117–131 (Cape Town: Oxford University Press).
71. Zbigniew Brezezinzki.
72. *New York Times,* December 3, 2001, A23.

Chapter 5

1. *National Post,* December 28, 2001.
2. Bernie Susser, personal communication, February 14, 2002.
3. Tanya Reinhart, *Tikkun* 17, no. 2 (March/April 2002).
4. Ehrlich, "Israel's Religious Right."
5. Khalil Shikaki, "Stop Hamas with a Vote," Op-ed, *New York Times,* March 26, 2004.
6. Michael Ignatieff, *National Post,* April 23, 2002.
7. Ibid.
8. Anthony Lewis, *The New York Review of Books,* April 25, 2002, 4.
9. Malley and Agha, "Camp David." For an insightful analysis of the issues and dynamics of the failed negotiations see also the long interview of former Israeli Foreign Minister and Negotiator Shlomo Ben-Ami by Ari Shavit and the critique of Ben-Ami by Uri Avnery in *Journal of Palestine Studies* XXXI, no. 2 (Winter 2002): 152–164.
10. Shavit and Avnery, *Journal of Palestine Studies,* 152–164. See also Dennis Ross, *The Missing Peace* (New York: Farrar, Straus, and Giroux, 2004).
11. Malley and Agha, "Camp David," 70.
12. Ibid.
13. Andre Mazawi, personal correspondence, January 16, 2002.
14. Heribert Adam, Frederick van Zyl Slabbert, and Kogila Moodley, *Comrades in Business: Post-Apartheid Politics in South Africa* (Utrecht, The Netherlands: International Books, 1997).
15. *Haaretz,* July 13, 2003.
16. Edward Said, *Culture and Resistance: Conversations with Edward W. Said,* ed.David Barsamian and Edward Said, 5 (Cambridge, MA: South End Press, 2003).
17. Ibid., 33.
18. Ibid., 149.
19. For example, in a typical maximalist stance, The National Society for the Defense of the Internally Displaced in Israel condemned Sari Nusseibeh for suggesting that negotiated compromises on the right of return should be considered. "We, the displaced in our homeland, reaffirm the right of return of all refugees and displaced wherever they are now, each person to his village or town. We reject all substitutes, including compensation, re-settlement and exchange of territory or populations" (Adam, *Peacemaking in Divided Societies,* 67).

Chapter 6

Acknowledgments: This analysis is based on involvement in the early conceptualization of the South African Truth and Reconciliation Commission (TRC) during several international conferences and frequent discussions with TRC Deputy Chair Alex Boraine and other commissioners, and participant observation of the commission's work. An earlier shorter version of the chapter's section on Germany was the opening address at a symposium on the Walser-Bubis debate at the Max Weber College at the University of Erfurt, and was subsequently published in the *Frankfurter Allgemeine Zeitung,* 24 July 1999. All translations of German quotes are by the authors. An English version was published as "Divided Memories: Confronting the Crimes of Previous Regimes," *Telos* 118, Winter 2000, 87–108.

1. Ian Buruma, "The Joys and Perils of Victimhood," *The New York Review of Books,* April 8, 1999, 9.

2. James Young, in *The Art of Memory: Holocaust Memorials in History* (New York: Prestel, 1994), 19, has emphasized that the very debate about where and by whom memorials are constructed is an essential part of remembering, in that the sites themselves "recall the past according to a variety of myths, ideals and political needs." Beyond the explanation of past events with the aim of educating succeeding generations, memorialization always utilizes group-specific imagery with a multitude of political and religious signals that bind predisposed observers into the unique collective.

3. Norbert Frei, *Vergangenheitspolitik. Die Anfänge der Bundesrepublik und die NS-Vergangenheit* (Munich: Beck, 1996), 405.

4. Helmut Dubiel, *Niemand ist frei von der Geschichte* (Munich: Hanser, 1999), 405.

5. Cited in Jicama Perels, "Die Zerstoerung von Erinnerung als Herrschaftstechnik. Adornos Analysen zur Blockierung der Aufarbeitung der NS-Vergangenheit," *Leviathan* 18 (1988): 58.

6. Hans-Ulrich Wehler, *Entsorgung der deutschen Vergangenheit* (Munich: Beck, 1988).

7. Wolfgang Wippermann, *Wessen Schuld? Vom Historikerstreit zur Goldhagen- Kontroverse* (Berlin: Elefanten Press, 1997).

8. Gert Wiegel and Johannes Klotz, eds., *Geistige Brandstiftung? Die Walser-Bubis Debatte* (Cologne: Papy Rossa, 1999); Joachim Rohloff, *Ich bin das Volk. Martin Walser, Auschwitz and die Berliner Republik* (Hamburg: KVV Konkret, 1999).

9. Hans-Günther Thiele, ed. *Die Wehrmachtsausstellung: Dokumentation einer Kontroverse.* Bremen, Germany: Temmen, 1998; Hamburger Institut für Sozialforschung, *Eine Ausstellung und ihre Folgen* (Hamburg: IfS, 1999).

10. Peter Reichel, *Politik mit der Erinnerung. Gedächtnisorte im Streit um die nationalsozialistische Vergangenheit* (Frankfurt: Fischer, 1999); Michael S. Cullen, ed., *Das Holocaust-Mahnmal Dokumentation einer Debatte* (Zurich: Penta, 1999); Michael Jeismann, ed., *Mahnmal Mitte* (Cologne: Du Mont, 1999).

11. Ignaz Bubis, interview, *konkret,* February 1999.

12. Aryeh Neier, *War Crimes: Brutality, Genocide, Terror and the Struggle for Justice* (New York: Random Books, 1998), 228.

13. Gerd Koenen, "Der verstörende Unterschied. Warum Stalinismus und Nazismus doch nicht über einen Kamm zu scheren sind." In *Horst Möller (Hrsg.):*

Der rote Holocaust und die Deutschen. Die Debatte um das "Schwarzbuch des Kommunismus" (Munich-Zürich, 1999), 98.

14. Buruma, "Joys and Perils of Victimhood."

15. Dubiel, *Niemand ist frei von der Geschichte,* 288.

16. Iris Chang, *The Rape of Nanking: The Forgotten Holocaust of World War II* (New York: Basic Books, 1997).

17. Stephane Courtois et al., eds., *The Black Book of Communism* (Cambridge, MA: Harvard University Press, 1997). See also Horst Möller, ed. *Der rote Holocaust und die Deutschen. Die Debatte um das 'Schwarzbuch des Kommunismus'* (Munich: Piper, 1999).

18. Michael Ignatieff, *The Warrior's Honour: Ethnic War and the Modern Conscience* (Toronto: Penguin Books, 1998), 170.

19. Ibid., 185.

20. Neier, *War Crimes: Brutality, Genocide, Terror and the Struggle for Justice,* 213.

21. Hanna Yablonka, *The State of Israel versus Adolf Eichmann* (New York: Schocken Books, 2004), 254.

22. Susanne Karstedt, "Coming to Terms with the Past in Germany after 1945 and 1989: Public Judgments on Procedures and Justice," *Law and Policy* 20, no. 1 (January 1998): 15–56.

23. Ibid.

24. Bernhard Schlink, "The Presence of the Past," Unpublished lecture in Cape Town, Fall 2003.

25. Constantin Goschler, "Offene Fragen der Wiedergutmachung," *Leviathan* 18 (1998): 49.

26. Personal conversation, February 7, 1999.

27. Martha Minow, *Between Vengeance and Forgiveness* (Boston: Beacon Press, 1998), 132.

28. Ibid., 127.

29. Gesine Schwan, *Politik und Schuld* (Frankfurt: Fischer, 1997), 245.

30. Eugene de Kock, *A Long Night's Damage: Working for the Apartheid State* (Saxonwold, England: Contra Press, 1998). The conversion of de Kock has been analyzed and forgiveness based on remorse celebrated in the perceptive account by South African psychologist, Pumla Gobodo-Madikizela, in *A Human Being Died That Night* (New York: Houghton Mifflin, 2003).

31. Jacques Pauw, *Into the Heart of Darkness: Confessions of Apartheid Assassins* (Johannesburg: Jonathan Ball, 1997).

32. Ignatieff, *Warrior's Honour,* 176.

33. Ibid., 173.

Chapter 7

1. Michael Ignatieff, *Empire Lite: Nation-Building in Bosnia, Kosovo and Afghanistan* (Toronto: Penguin, 2003).

2. Robert Rotberg and Dennis Thompson, eds., *Truth versus Justice: The Morality of Truth Commissions* (Princeton: Princeton University Press, 2000), 19.

3. Charles Villa-Vicencio and Wilhelm Verwoerd, eds., *Looking Back, Reaching Forward: Reflections on the Truth and Reconciliation Commission of South Africa* (Cape Town: UCT Press; London: Zed Press, 2000); Alex Boraine, *A Country Unmasked:*

Inside South Africa's Truth and Reconciliation Commission (Cape Town: Oxford University Press, 2000); Priscilla Hayner, *Unspeakable Truths: Confronting State Terror and Atrocity* (London: Routledge, 2000); Antjee Krog, *Country of My Skull* (Johannesburg: Random House, 1998); David Dyzenhaus, *Truth, Reconciliation and the Apartheid Legal Order* (Cape Town: Juta, 1998); Minow, *Between Vengeance and Forgiveness*; Ruth Teitel, *Transitional Justice* (New York: Oxford University Press, 2000); Richard Wilson, *The Politics of Truth and Reconciliation in South Africa: Legitimizing the Post-Apartheid State* (Cambridge: Cambridge University Press, 2001); Andrew Rigby, *Justice and Reconciliation after the Violence* (Boulder, CO: Lynne Rienner, 2001).

4. Rotberg and Thompson, *Truth versus Justice,* 20.

5. Ibid., 92.

6. Stuart Eisenstat, "Reconciliation, Not Just Reconstruction," *International Herald Tribune,* July 5–6, 2003.

7. Ibid.

8. Villa-Vicencio and Verwoerd, *Looking Back, Reaching Forward,* xiv.

9. Ibid.

10. Boraine, *A Country Unmasked.*

11. Mamdani, "Reconciliation without Justice."

12. Anthea Jeffery, *The Truth about Truth Commissions* (Johannesburg: Institute of Race Relations, 1999).

13. Michael Scharf, "The Letter of the Law: The Scope of the International Legal Obligation to Prosecute Human Rights Crimes." *Law and Contemporary Problems* 59, no. 4 (1998): 41–61.

14. Mark J. Osiel, *Obeying Orders: Atrocity, Military Discipline and the Law of War* (New Brunswick, NJ: Transaction Publishers, 1999).

15. Boraine, *A Country Unmasked,* 398.

16. Jeffery, *The Truth about Truth Commissions.*

17. Quoted in Rotberg and Thompson, *Truth versus Justice,* 159.

18. Pauw, *Into the Heart of Darkness.*

19. "Ex-CCB Chief Refuses to Apologize for Blast," *Cape Times,* March 16, 2000.

20. Ibid.

21. Paul Gottfried, "On the Politics of Memory: Reply to Adam," *Telos* 118 (2000): 116.

22. Eic Conan and Henry Rousso, *Vichy: Un passé qui non passé pas* (Paris: Fayard 1994).

23. Ron, *Frontieres and Ghettos.*

24. Rigby, *Justice and Reconciliation after the Violence.*

25. Rhoda Kanaaneh, "Embattled Identities: Palestinian Soldiers in the Israeli Military," *Journal of Palestinian Studies* 127, XXXII, no. 3 (2003): 5–20.

26. Ibid., 19.

27. B'Tselem, "Collaborators in the Occupied Territories," Jerusalem, 1994, p. 9 (Webmail).

28. Marwan Bishara, *Palestine/Israel: Peace or Apartheid?* (London: Zed Books, 2001), 12.

29. Michael Bell, "Prometheus Unbound," *Globe & Mail,* January 5, 2004, A9.

30. Greg Myre, "Coerced or Not, Palestinians Who Assist Israel Face Death," *New York Times,* November 29, 2003.

31. Ibid.

32. Sa'id Ghazali, Webmail, October 23, 2003.
33. See Chapter 4 for more information on this paradox inherent in the violence.
34. Johannesburg *Business Day,* February 3, 2004.
35. Bishop Desmond Tutu, *The Sunday Independent,* February 1, 2004.
36. Samantha Power, *A Problem from Hell* (New York: Basic Books, 2002).
37. Cohen, *States of Denial.*
38. Market Research Africa/AC Nielsen, E0624 and E1422, 1996 and 1998.
39. Ibid.; and HSRC, 1998.
40. Cited in Erna Paris, *Long Shadows: Truth, Lies and History* (Toronto: Random House, 2000), 274.
41. Personal interview, March 2, 2001.
42. Wendy Orr, 2000 quoted in *Southern Africa Report,* August 4, 2000, 4.
43. Aryeh Neier, "Bringing Monsters to Justice," *New York Review of Books,* March 3, 2001.
44. Boraine, *A Country Unmasked,* 397.
45. Peretz Kidron, ed, *Refusenik,* with a foreword by Susan Sontag (London: Zed, 2004); comprises the voices of conscientious objectors since the 1970s.
46. Jonathan Steele, *The Guardian,* October 22, 2002.
47. Webmail, March 20, 2003.
48. Bernhard Schlink, "The Presence of the Past," Unpublished lecture, Cape Town, Fall 2003.
49. Jakes Gerwel, in Villa-Vicencio and Verwoerd, eds., *Looking Back,* 277–286.
50. Peter Novick, *The Holocaust in American Life* (New York: Houghton Mifflin, 1999), 279.

Chapter 8

Acknowledgment: This chapter has benefited from discussions with Ron Dudai, an Israeli fellow at the Transitional Justice Program in Cape Town, who wrote an imaginative paper on the same subject.

1. Ben-Rafael "Where Stands Israel?" 310–316.
2. Benny Morris, *Righteous Victims* (New York: Vintage, 2001), 252.
3. Ben-Rafael, "Where Stands Israel?" 310–316.
4. www.mideastweb.org/general1.htm
5. www.circlepoint.org/ncongoing0600.html
6. http://www.gush-shalom.org/Docs/Truth_Eng.pdf
7. All quotes cited in Cramer, *How Israel Lost,* 236.
8. MEMRI, 9/12/2004, Clip 258.
9. *Vancouver SUN,* October 23, 2004.
10. Ignatieff, *Warrior's Honour.*
11. Rigby, *Justice and Reconciliation after the Violence,* 190–191.
12. Cohen, *States of Denial.*
13. Anthony D. Smith, *Nations and Nationalism in a Global Era* (Cambridge: Polity Press, 1996), 450.
14. Akenson, *God's People.*
15. Giliomee, *The Afrikaners.*
16. Andre du Toit, "Puritans in Africa?" *Comparative Studies in Society and History* 27, no. 2 (1985).

Conclusions

1. Thomas Friedman, "Regime Change, Part 2," *New York Times,* April 23, 2003. Parts of this chapter were delivered as the The Leon and Thea Koerner Foundation Lecture in the Liberal Arts, Fletcher Challenge Theatre, SFU Harbour Centre, Vancouver, October 23, 2003.

2. Edward Said, Webmail, March 2003.

3. Craig Nelson, "Christian Zionists," *Atlanta Journal-Constitution,* December 25, 2003.

4. *New York Times,* October 21, 2003.

5. Mamdani, *Good Muslim, Bad Muslim* (New York: Pantheon, 2004), 240–241.

6. Cited in *Wrestling with Zion,* ed. Kushner and Solomon, 18.

7. *Haaretz,* April 24, 2003.

8. Baruch Kimmerling and Joel Migdal, *The Palestinian People: A History* (Cambridge, MA: Harvard University Press, 2003). Compared with the Oslo Accord, the Road Map is a progressive document inasmuch as it spells out a clear end of a three-phase process: an independent, sovereign Palestinian state. For the first time, an Israeli government has formally endorsed the creation of a Palestinian state. However, the plan only mentions "provisional borders" of this state. It is silent on what to do with settlers who refuse to depart. The Road Map lacks enforcement mechanisms. It operates on the basis of violation of trust instead of binding international law. Because decisions of the Quartet are made by consensus, it gives the United States (and indirectly, Israel) veto power.

9. IDASA (Institute for Democratic Alternatives), founded by F. Van Zyl Slabbert and Alex Boraine was the main catalyst for the many 1980s contacts between the exiled ANC and liberal whites. IDASA later metamorphosed into a watchdog organization, monitoring progress in the new democracy.

10. Kevin Toolis, "You Can't Make a Deal with the Dead," *The Guardian,* Sept. 10, 2003.

11. Ron, *Frontieres and Ghettos,* 201.

12. Virginia Tilley, *London Review of Books* 25, no. 21 (November 6, 2003).

13. This and the following are cited from Leon Wieseltier, "Israel, Palestine, and the Return of the Bi-national Fantasy," *New Republic,* October 27, 2003.

14. See Meron Rapaport, "Land Lords," *Haaretz,* January 20, 2005.

15. Tony Judt, "Israel: The Alternative," *New York Review of Books,* October 23, 2003, 10.

16. Amira Hass, "The Myth of the State and the Reality of Annexation," *Haaretz,* February 12, 2003.

17. Uri Avnery, Webmail, January 11, 2003.

18. JMCC and PSR Public Opinion Polls, 2003; quoted in Alan Dowty and Michelle Gawerc, "The Intifada: Revealing the Chasm," *Meria* 5, no. 3.

19. Thomas Friedman "One Wall, One Man, One Vote," *New York Times,* Sept. 14, 2003.

20. Interview with Ari Shavit in *Haaretz Magazine,* October 8, 2004.

21. Avraham Burg, "The End of Zionism," *The Guardian,* September 15, 2003.

22. See www.bitterlemons.org., October 18, 2004.

23. See, for example, the informative collection of articles in *The Challenge of Post-Zionism,* ed. Ephraim Nimni.

24. Ian Gilmour, "Road to Nowhere?" *The Guardian Weekly*, June 19–25, 2003, 21.

25. The Givat Olga Document: Sincere Anguish over Israel's Policies of Repression and Discrimination (http://ga3.org/jvfp/jpn_home.html#2).

26. Herzog, "Take South Africa's Lead," A15.

27. "The Lost Steps," *The Nation*, August 30/September 6, 2004, 31–38.

28. *National Post* editorial, July 22, 2004, A15.

29. Edward Said, *From Oslo to Iraq* (New York: Pantheon, 2004), 51.

30. Interview with Ruthie Blum, *Jerusalem Post*, December 15, 2004.

31. So the title of an essay by Leon Wieseltier, *The New York Times Magazine*, January 9, 2005, 15–16.

32. *Cape Times*, November 30, 2004.

33. E. Yaar and T. Hermann, "Post-mortem: Arafat's Collective Image among the Palestinian and Israeli Publics," *Steinmetz Center Peace Index*, December 22, 2004.

34. Rigby, *Justice and Reconciliation after the Violence*, 190.

35. Mamdani, *When Victims Become Killers* (Princeton, Princeton University Press, 2001), 267.

36. "Conflict Resolution in South Africa and Israel/Palestine," Paper presented at the SFU International Conference "Negotiating Compromises in Divided Societies," Vancouver, October 15–16, 2004.

37. Dennis Ross, *The Missing Peace*, 773.

38. Ibid., 770.

39. Daniel Gavron, *The Other Side of Despair: Jews and Arabs in the Promised Land* (Lanham, MD: Rowman & Littlefield, 2003). See also Peter Hirschberg's interview with Gavron in *Haaretz Magazine*, December 10, 2003.

40. *Haaretz*, January 16, 2004.

41. Reported in *Haaretz*, January 18, 2005.

42. Judt, "Israel: The Alternative."

43. Interview with Ari Shavit, *Haaretz*, December 23, 2004.

44. Gwynne Dyer, *Future: Tense. The Coming World Order* (Toronto: McClelland and Stewart, 2004), 25.

45. For a brutally frank description of Israel's military options see the writings of Martin van Crefeld, *Defending Israel* (New York: St. Martin's Press, 2004), who argues that a Palestinian state would not effect the loss of "strategic depth," given Israel's increased superiority in all fields. The author also hopes "that Arab Israelis can be dispatched there in case they continue to cause trouble" (180).

46. Cited in Michel Warschawski, *Toward an Open Tomb* (New York: Monthly Review Press, 2004), 81, 34.

47. Avi Dichter, *Haaretz*, January 4, 2005.

48. For an excellent description of the many strands of harmless and dangerous Jewish mysticism, see Nadav Shragai, "A Mounting Sense of Urgency," *Haaretz Friday Magazine*, December 31, 2004.

49. Palestinian Center for Policy and Survey Research, cited in Wieseltier, *The New York Times Magazine*, 2005.

50. Ross, *The Missing Peace*, 726.

Works Cited

Abu-Lughod, Ibrahim, and Baha Abu-Laban. 1974. *Settler Regimes in Africa and the Arab World: The Illusion of Endurance.* Wilmette, IL: The Medina University Press.

Adam, Heribert. 1989–90. "Israel and South Africa: Conflict Resolution in Ethnic States." *Telos* 82:27–46.

———. 1998. "Widersprüche der Befreiung: Wahrheit, Gerechtigkeit und Versöhnung in Südafrika." *Leviathan* 18:350–370.

———. 1999. "The Presence of the Past: South Africa's Truth Commission as a Model?" In *Religion and Politics in South Africa,* ed. Abdulkader Tayob and Wolfram Weisse, 140–158. Münster/New York: Waxmann.

———. 2000. "Divided Memories: Confronting the Crimes of Previous Regimes." *Telos* 118:87–91.

———. 2002. *Peace-Making in Divided Societies. The Israel-South Africa Analogy.* Pretoria: Human Sciences Research Council.

———. 2003. "Visions of the Future during Political Transitions: Comparing Afrikaner and Israeli Attitudes." *Social Text* (New York) 75 (Summer): 95–110.

Adam, Heribert, and Kogila Moodley. 1993. *The Opening of the Apartheid Mind.* Berkeley: University of California Press.

———. 2002. "Political Travel through the Holy Land." *Global Review of Ethnopolitics* 11 (2): 67–74. Reprinted in 2003 in *Outlook* 41 (3): 18–20, 43, and (4): 21, 41–42. In German, also in 2003: in *Der Ueberblick* 39 (1): 60–68.

Adam, Heribert, Frederick van Zyl Slabbert, and Kogila Moodley. 1998. *Comrades in Business: Post-Apartheid Politics in South Africa.* Utrecht, The Netherlands: International Books.

Adams, James. 1984. *The Unnatural Alliance.* London: Quartet Books Ltd.

Akenson, Donald H. 1991. *God's People.* Montreal: McGill & Queens' University Press.

Alexander, Neville. 2003. *An Ordinary Country.* Pietermaritzburg, South Africa: University of Natal Press.

Amadiumi, Ifi, and Abdullahi An-Naim, eds. 2000. *The Politics of Memory: Truth, Healing, and Social Justice.* London: Zed Books.

Arthur, Paul. 1996. In *After the Peace: Resistance and Reconciliation,* ed. Robert Rothstein. Boulder: Lynne Rienner, 1999.

Barak, Ehud. 2003. "I Did Not Give Away a Thing." *Journal of Palestine Studies* 33 (1): 84–87.

Benvenisti, Meron. 1990. "The Peace Process and Intercommunal Strife." In *The Elusive Search for Peace,* ed. Hermann Giliomee and Jannie Gagiano, 117–131. Cape Town: Oxford University Press.

Bergmann, Werner. 1998. "Kommunikationslatenz und Vergangenheitsbewältigung." *Leviathan* 18:393–408.

Bishara, Marwan. 2001. *Palestine/Israel: Peace or Apartheid?* London: Zed Books.

Bond, Patrick. 2000. *Elite Transition: From Apartheid to Neoliberalism in South Africa.* London Pluto Press.

Boraine, Alex. 2000. *A Country Unmasked: Inside South Africa's Truth and Reconciliation Commission.* Cape Town: Oxford University Press.

Borneman, John. 1997. *Settling Accounts: Violence, Justice, and Accountability in Post-socialist Europe.* Princeton NJ: Princeton University Press.

Buruma, Ian. 1994. *The Wages of Guilt.* New York: Farrow, Straus, and Giroux.

———. 1999. "The Joys and Perils of Victimhood." *The New York Review of Books,* April 8, 4–9.

Cohen, Stanley. 2001. *States of Denial.* Cambridge: Polity.

Conan, Eric, and Henry Rousso. 1994. *Vichy: Un passé qui non passé pas.* Paris: Fayard.

Connerton, Paul. 1989. *How Societies Remember.* Cambridge: Cambridge University Press.

Cox, Murray, ed. 1999. *Remorse and Reparation.* London: Jessica Kingsley Publication.

Cullen, Michael S., ed. 1999. *Das Holocaust-Mahnmal Dokumentation einer Debatte.* Zürich: Penta.

Davis, Uri. 2003. *Apartheid Israel.* London: Zed 1987.

de Kock, Eugene. 1998. *A Long Night's Damage: Working for the Apartheid State.* Saxonwold, England: Contra Press.

Drinan, Robert F. 2001. *The Mobilization of Shame.* New Haven: Yale University Press.

du Toit, André. 1985. "Puritans in Africa?" *Comparative Studies in Society and History* 27 (2).

———. 2001. "Perpetrator Findings as Artificial Even-handedness?" Unpublished manuscript, 98 pp.

Dubiel, Helmut. 1999. *Niemand ist frei von der Geschichte.* Munich: Hanser.

Dyer, Gwynne. 2004. *Future Tense: The Coming World Order.* Toronto: McClelland and Stewart.

Dyzenhaus, David. 1998. *Truth, Reconciliation and the Apartheid Legal Order.* Cape Town: Juta.

Ehrlich, Avishai. 2001. "Israel's Religious Right and the Failure of the Peace Process." *Monthly Review* 53 (October): 16–30.

Ellis, Stephen, and Tsepo Sechaba. 1992. *Comrades against Apartheid. The ANC and the South African Communist Party in Exile.* London: James Curry.

Elon, Amos. 2001. "The Deadlocked City." *New York Review of Books* 48 (16): 6–12.

Frei, Norbert. 1996. *Vergangenheitspolitik: Die Anfänge der Bundesrepublik und die NS-Vergangenheit.* Munich: Beck.

Gagiano, J. 1990. "Ruling Group Cohesion." In *The Elusive Search for Peace,* ed. H. Giliomee and J. Gagiano, 191–203. Cape Town: Oxford University Press.

Gavron, Daniel. 2003. *The Other Side of Despair.* Lanham, MD: Rowman & Littlefield.

Gibson, James L., and Amanda Gouws. 2003. *Overcoming Intolerance in South Africa: Experiments in Democratic Persuasion.* Cambridge: Cambridge University Press.

Giliomee, Hermann. 2003. *The Afrikaners.* Cape Town: Tafelberg.

Giliomee, Hermann, and Jannie Gagiano, eds. 1990. *The Elusive Search for Peace.* Cape Town: Oxford University Press.

Giroux, Henry. 1996. *Fugitive Cultures: Race, Violence and Youth.* London: Routledge.

Glaser, Daryl. 2003. "Zionism and Apartheid: A Moral Comparison." *Ethnic and Racial Studies* 26 (3): 403–421.

Goldstein, Joshua S. et al. 2001. "Reciprocity, Triangularity and Cooperation in the Middle East." *Journal of Conflict Resolution* 45 (5): 594–620.

Goschler, Constantin. 1998. "Offene Fragen der Wiedergutmachung," *Leviathan* 18:38–52.

Gottfried, Paul. 2000. "On the Politics of Memory: Reply to Adam." *Telos* 118:115–118.

Greenberg, Stanley. 1980. *Race and State in Capitalist Development* New Haven, CT: Yale University Press.

Grosbard, Ofer. 2003. *Israel on the Couch: The Psychology of the Peace Process.* Albany: State University of New York Press.

Habermas, Juergen. 1996. *Die Einbeziehung des Anderen.* Frankfurt: Suhrkamp.

Hamann, Hilton. 2001. *Days of the Generals.* Cape Town: Zebra Press.

Hamburger Institut für Sozialforschung, ed. 1999. *Eine Ausstellung und ihre Folgen.* Hamburg: IfS.

Hayner, Priscilla. 2000. *Unspeakable Truths: Confronting State Terror and Atrocity.* London: Routledge.

Helm, Sarah. 2001. "End the Special Relationship Now." *New Statesman* 130 (January): 35.

Hirsh, David. 2003. *Laws against Genocide: Cosmopolitan Trials.* London: Glasshouse Press.

Hugo, Pierre. 1989. "Towards Darkness and Death: Racial Demonology in South Africa." In *South African Perspectives,* ed. Hugo Pierre, 237–263. Cape Town: Die Suid Afrikaan.

Ignatieff, Michael. 1998. *The Warrior's Honour: Ethnic War and the Modern Conscience.* Toronto: Penguin Books.

———. 2003. *Empire Lite: Nation-Building in Bosnia, Kosovo and Afghanistan.* Toronto: Penguin.

James, Wilmot, and Linda van der Vivjer, eds. 2000. *After the TRC: Reflections on Truth and Reconciliation.* Cape Town: David Philip.

Jeffery, Anthea. 1999. *The Truth about Truth Commissions.* Johannesburg: Institute of Race Relations.

Jeismann, Michael, ed. 1999. *Mahnmahl Mitte.* Cologne: Du Mont.

Joseph, Benjamin. 1988. *Besieged Bedfellows: Israel and the Land of Apartheid.* New York: Greenwood Press.

Judt, Tony. 2002. "The Road to Nowhere." *New York Review of Books.* May 9, 4.

———. 2003. "Israel: The Alternative." *New York Review of Books,* October 23.

Kanaaneh, Rhoda. 2003. "Embattled Identities: Palestinian Soldiers in the Israeli Military." *Journal of Palestine Studies* 127 (32): 3, 5–20.

Karstedt, Susanne. 1998. "Coming to Terms with the Past in Germany after 1945 and 1989: Public Judgments on Procedures and Justice." *Law & Policy* 20 (1): 15–56.

Kimmerling, Baruch. 2003. *Politicide: Ariel Sharon's Wars against the Palestinians.* New York: VERSO.

Kimmerling, Baruch, and Joel S. Migdal. 2003. *The Palestinian People: A History.* Cambridge, MA: Harvard University Press.

Knox, Colin, and Padrica Quirk. 2001. *Peace Building in Northern Ireland, Israel and South Africa: Transition, Transformation, Reconciliation.* New York: St. Martin's Press.

König, Helmut, Michael Kohlstruck, and Andreas Wöll, eds. 1998. "Vergangenheitsbewältigung am Ende des zwanzigsten Jahrhunderts." *Leviathan* 18.

Krog, Antjee. 1998. *Country of My Skull.* Johannesburg: Random House.

Kuper, Leo. 1957. *Passive Resistance in South Africa.* New Haven, CT: Yale University Press.

Kushner, Tony, and Alisa Solomon, eds. 2003. *Wrestling with Zion: Progressive Jewish-American Responses to the Israeli-Palestinian Conflict.* New York: Grove Press.

Lieberfeld, Daniel. 1999. *Talking with the Enemy: Negotiation and Threat Perception in South Africa and Israel/Palestine.* Westport: Praeger.

Lustick, Ian. 1993. *Unsettled States, Disputed Lands.* Cornell: Cornell University Press, 1993.

Malley, Robert, and Hussein Agha. 2001. "Camp David: Tragedy of Errors." *New York Review of Books,* August 9. Reprinted in *Journal of Palestine Studies* 31 (Autumn 2001): 62–85.

Mamdani, Mahmood. 1997. "Reconciliation without Justice." *South African Review of Books* 46 (November/December).

———. 2001. "Beyond Settlers and Natives as Political Entities: Overcoming the Political Legacies of Colonialism." *Comparative Study of Society and History* 32:651–664.

———. 2001. *When Victims Become Killers.* Princeton, NJ: Princeton University Press.

———. 2004. *Good Muslim, Bad Muslim.* New York: Pantheon.

Marais, H. 2001. *South Africa: Limits to Change.* London: Zed Books.

Mattes, Robert. 2002. "Democracy without the People?" *Journal of Democracy* 13 (1).

Miller, David, ed. 2004. *Tell Me Lies.* London: Pluto.

Minow, Martha. 1998. *Between Vengeance and Forgiveness.* Boston: Beacon Press.

Mitchell, Thomas G. 2000. *Native versus Settler.* Westport, CT: Greenwood.

Möller, Horst, ed. 1999. *Der rote Holocaust und die Deutschen: Die Debatte um das 'Schwarzbuch des Kommunismus.'* Munich: Piper.

Moodley, Kogila. 2000. "African Renaissance and Language Policies in Comparative Perspective." *Politikon* 27 (1): 103–115.

Morris, Benny. 2001. *Righteous Victims.* New York: Vintage.

Naseer, Aruri. 2003. *Dishonest Broker: The U.S. Role in Israel and Palestine.* Cambridge, MA: South End Press.

Neier, Aryeh. 1998. *War Crimes: Brutality, Genocide, Terror and the Struggle for Justice.* New York: Random Books.

Nimni, Ephraim, ed. 2003. *The Challenge of Post-Zionism: Alternatives to Israeli Fundamentalist Politics.* London: Zed Books.

Nitzan, Jonathan, and Shimshon Bichler. 2002. *The Global Political Economy of Israel.* London: Pluto Press.

Novick, Peter. 1999. *The Holocaust in American Life.* New York: Houghton Mifflin.

Nussbaum, Martha. 2002. "Patriotism and Cosmopolitanism." In *For Love of Country,* ed. J. Cohen, 2–17. Boston: Beacon Press.

Orr, Wendy. 2000. *From Biko to Basson: Wendy Orr's Search for the Soul of South Africa as a Commissioner of the TRC.* Johannesburg: Contra Press.

Osiel, Mark J. 1999. *Obeying Orders: Atrocity, Military Discipline and the Law of War.* New Brunswick, NJ: Transaction Publishers.

Paris, Erna. 2000. *Long Shadows: Truth, Lies and History.* Toronto: Random House.

Pauw, Jacques. 1997. *Into the Heart of Darkness: Confessions of Apartheid Assassins.* Johannesburg: Jonathan Ball.

Perels, Joachim. 1998. "Die Zerstörung von Erinnerung als Herrschaftstechnik. Adornos Analysen zur Blockierung der Aufarbeitung der NS-Vergangenheit." *Leviathan* 18: 53–58.

Power, Samantha. 2002. *A Problem from Hell: America and the Age of Genocide.* New York: Basic Books.

Ramphele, Mamphela. 2001. "Citizenship Challenges for South Africa's Young Democracy." *Daedalus* 130 (1): 1–17.

Reichel, Peter. 1999. *Politik mit der Erinnerung: Gedächtnisorte im Streit um die nationalsozialistische Vergangenheit.* Frankfurt: Fischer.

Rigby, Andrew. 2001. *Justice and Reconciliation: After the Violence.* Boulder, CO: Lynne Rienner.

Rodinson, Maxime. 1973. *Israel: A Colonial Settler State?* New York: Monad.

Rohloff, Joachim. 1999. *Ich bin das Volk: Martin Walser, Auschwitz and die Berliner Republik.* Hamburg: KVV Konkret.

Ron, James. 2003. *Frontiers and Ghettos: State Violence in Israel and Serbia.* Berkeley: UCP.

Ross, Dennis. 2004. *The Missing Peace.* New York: Farrar, Straus, and Giroux.

Rotberg, Robert, and Dennis Thompson, eds. 2000. *Truth versus Justice: The Morality of Truth Commissions.* Princeton, NJ: Princeton University Press.

Rothstein, Robert, ed. 1999. *After the Peace: Resistance and Reconciliation.* Boulder, CO: Lynne Rienner.

Said, Edward. 2004. *From Oslo to Iraq.* New York: Pantheon.

Scharf, Michael. 1998. "The Letter of the Law: The Scope of the International Legal Obligation to Prosecute Human Rights Crimes." *Law and Contemporary Problems* 59 (4): 41–61.

Schwan, Gesine. 1997. *Politik und Schuld.* Frankfurt: Fischer.

Shannon, Vaughn P. 2003. *Balancing Act: U.S. Foreign Policy and the Arab-Israeli Conflict.* Aldershot, Hants, England and Burlington, VT: Ashgate.

Silberman, Neil Asher. 2001. "If I Forget Thee, O Jerusalem: Archaeology, Religious Commemoration and Nationalism in a Disputed City, 1801–2001." *Nations and Nationalism* 7 (4): 487–504.

Smith, Anthony D. 1996. *Nations and Nationalism in a Global Era.* Cambridge: Polity Press.

Smooha, Sammy. 1989. *Arabs and Jews in Israel.* Boulder, CO: Westview Press.

———. 1997. "Ethnic Democracy: Israel as an Archetype." *Israel Studies* 2: 198–241.

Sparks, Allister. 2003. *Beyond the Miracle.* Johannesburg: Jonathan Ball.

Stevens, R. P., and A. M. Elmessiri. 1976. *Israel and South Africa.* New York: New World.

Taruchis, Nicholas. 1991. *Mea Culpa: A Sociology of Apology and Reconciliation.* Stanford: Stanford University Press.

Teitel, Ruti G. 2000. *Transitional Justice.* New York: Oxford University Press.

Thiele, Hans-Günther, ed. 1998. *Die Wehrmachtsausstellung: Dokumentation einer Kontroverse.* Bremen, Germany: Temmen.

van Crefeld, Martin. 2004. *Defending Israel.* New York: St. Martin's Press.

Villa-Vicencio, Charles, and Wilhelm Verwoerd, eds. 2000. *Looking Back, Reaching Forward: Reflections on the Truth and Reconciliation Commission of South Africa.* Cape Town: UCT Press; London: Zed Press.

Waldmeir, Patti. 1997. *Anatomy of a Miracle.* New York: Norton.

Warschawski, Michel. 2004. *Toward an Open Tomb.* New York: Monthly Review Press.

Wasserstein, Bernard. 2001. *Divided Jerusalem: The Struggle for the Holy City.* New Haven, CT: Yale University Press.

———. 2003. *Israelis and Palestinians.* New Haven, CT: Yale University Press.

Wehler, Hans-Ulrich. 1988. *Entsorgung der deutschen Vwergangenheit.* Munich: Beck.

Wiegel, Gert, and Johannes Klotz, eds. 1999. *Geistige Brandstiftung? Die Walser- Bubis Debatte.* Cologne: Papy Rossa.

Will, Donald S. 2000. "Non-Racialism versus Nationalism: Contrasting Solutions to Conflict in South Africa and Israel/Palestine." *Peace and Change* 25 (2): 255–264.

Wilson, Richard A. 2001. *The Politics of Truth and Reconciliation in South Africa: Legitimizing the Post-Apartheid State.* Cambridge: Cambridge University Press.

Wippermann, Wolfgang. 1997. *Wessen Schuld? Vom Historikerstreit zur Goldhagen-Kontroverse.* Berlin: Elefanten Press.

Wistrich, Robert S. 2003. "Muslim Anti-Semitism: A Clear and Present Danger." *American Jewish Committee Publication,* March 19.

Yiftachtel, Oren. 1998. "Democracy or Ethnocracy: Territory and Settler Politics in Israel/Palestine." *Middle East Report* 28 (2): 8–13.

Younis, M. 1995. "Class, Resources and Resistance: A Comparative Study of National Liberation Movements in South Africa and Palestine, 1910–1993." PhD. diss., University of California, Berkeley.

Zartman, I. W. 2001. *Preventative Negotiation: Avoiding Conflict Escalation.* Lanham, MD: Rowman & Littlefield Publishers.

Zartman, I. W., and J. L. Rasmussen. 1997. *Peacemaking in International Conflict: Methods and Techniques.* Washington, DC: United States Institute of Peace.

Zartman, I. W., and J. Z. Rubin. 2000. *Power and Negotiation.* Ann Arbor: University of Michigan Press.

Index

Heribert Adam is a political sociologist at Simon Fraser University in Vancouver and also teaches at the University of Cape Town. He has published extensively on comparative ethnic conflicts and peacemaking, particularly socio-political developments in South Africa. He was awarded the 1998 Konrad Adenauer Prize of the Alexander von Humboldt Foundation and elected Fellow of the Royal Society of Canada.

Kogila Moodley is a sociologist at the University of British Columbia and was the first holder of the David Lam Chair. Raised in the Indian community of apartheid South Africa, her research is focused on critical multiculturalism, anti-racism education, and citizenship. She has served as President of the International Sociological Association's Research Committee on Ethnic, Minority and Race Relations (1998–2002).

Adam and Moodley live in Vancouver and Cape Town.